BUILDING ON BASICS

A Thematic Approach to Reading Comprehension

Joan Baker-González

Eileen K. Blau

Longman

Building on Basics:
A Thematic Approach to Reading Comprehension

© 1999 by Addison Wesley Longman, Inc.
All rights reserved.
No part of this publication may be reproduced,
stored in a retrieval system, or transmitted
in any form or by any means, electronic, mechanical,
photocopying, recording, or otherwise,
without the prior permission of the publisher.

Pearson Education, 10 Bank Street, White Plains, NY 10606

Editorial director: Allen Ascher
Director of design and production: Rhea Banker
Senior acquisitions editor: Louisa Hellegers
Development editor: Debbie Sistino
Managing editor: Linda Moser
Production manager: Marie McNamara
Associate production editor: Robert Ruvo
Photo research: Diana Nott
Cover design: Elizabeth Carlson
Senior manufacturing manager: Patrice Fraccio
Manufacturing supervisor: Edie Pullman
Text design: Betty Mintz
Text composition: UG Division of GGS
Text art: Tom Sperling, Moffitt Cecil, Teco Rodrigues
Text credits: see page 235
Photo credits: p. xi, © Michael Dwyer, Stock, Boston; p. 1, © photographer, Stock,
    Boston; p. 2, Courtesy of America's Promise; p. 15, Reprinted with permission of
    King Features Syndicate; p. 35, © photographer, Stock, Boston; p. 75, Photo of
    Albert Einstein courtesy of the Archives, California Institute of Technology; p. 75,
    Photo of Maria Callas courtesy of EMI Classics; p. 75, Photo of Buckminster Fuller
    reprinted with permission of the Buckminster Fuller Institute; p. 75, Photo of Kofi
    Annan courtesy of the United Nations / DPI; p. 75, Photo of Martina Navratilova by
    Gus Bower / Compliments of IMG; p. 115, courtesy of the Ellis Island Immigration
    Museum; p. 153, © Frederick Boden, Stock, Boston, Inc.; p. 195, UPI / CORBIS-
    BETTMANN; p. 195, Courtesy of Apple Marketing Tool Kit and FCI
    Communications

Library of Congress Cataloging-in-Publication Data
Baker-González, Joan.
    Building on basics : a thematic approach to reading comprehension /
Joan Baker-González, Eileen K. Blau.
        p.   cm.
    ISBN 0-201-34052-6 (alk. paper)
    1. English language—Textbooks for foreign speakers.   2. Reading comprehension—
Problems, exercises, etc.
3. Readers.   I. Blau, Eileen K.   II. Title.
PE1128.B274   1998
428.2′4—dc21   98-34159
                                                                CIP

6 7 8 9 10 -VH -09 08 07 06 05

Contents

Teacher's Introduction

Building on Basics, like the higher-level *Building Understanding*, is a thematic or topical reader for young adult and adult ESL students. Whereas *Building Understanding* is designed for students at the intermediate to advanced level, *Building on Basics* is designed for intermediate students who need more support in order to be able to read authentic texts. The nonfiction selections in the book range in length from approximately 300 to 1,000 words, and the short story selections from 450 to 1,800 words. A few selections have been adapted slightly to make them more accessible to ESL students.

Each of the six units consists of five closely related readings on a topic of personal or world interest. The benefit of reading several selections on the same topic is this: previous readings provide background knowledge and vocabulary for later readings, making it easier to read about that topic. With increased knowledge of a topic, students have more to talk, think, and write about as they acquire the language and improve their reading ability.

Description of the Text

The book begins with a **Student's Introduction**, which is designed to help students handle new vocabulary. It is an integral part of *Building on Basics*, and your students will benefit from using it.

ESL students tend to think their biggest problem with reading in English is understanding vocabulary. Although it is not the only thing students need to work on to develop reading abilities, it is very important. It is, moreover, an essential foundation for comprehending completely authentic texts.

The Student's Introduction is designed to:

- show students that they do not need to consult a dictionary as soon as they encounter a new word;

- familiarize students with the types of exercises used throughout the book; and

- illustrate the way to handle new vocabulary (the first paragraph of the first reading selection of Unit One is used as an example).

Each of the six units consists of five authentic texts, including:

- three nonfiction selections (magazine or newspaper articles and excerpts from nonfiction books, including autobiography and oral history);

- a short story; and

- a poem or the lyrics to a song.

To benefit from a thematic reader, students must read several selections on a single topic. When making choices about what to include in a reading program, you should think in terms of whole units rather than individual reading selections. Omitting a single selection or a selection and a poem, for example, would leave enough material for students to benefit from related readings; but choosing a single reading from a unit would not. Also, remember when choosing selections that the nonfiction selections build background knowledge that facilitates the comprehension and enjoyment of the literature selections.

Unit Organization

The **Introductory Page** is a useful part of the unit. The title, focus questions, picture, and quote can all be used to activate students' background knowledge of the topic of the unit, as well as to make predictions about its content. Use the focus questions to create purposes for reading, but do not expect students to have more than partial answers to the questions until they have completed the unit.

A three-part **Before Reading** section precedes each reading selection. (1) **Discussion** introduces the topic and activates students' background knowledge. Sometimes this part introduces vocabulary that is essential for comprehension of the selection, and this vocabulary may be included in the Vocabulary Review exercise. (2) **Previewing** is something that good readers generally do before reading nonfiction material. It gives students an idea of what to expect and, consequently, a better chance to understand. Though readers do not usually preview short stories, teachers do introduce them; the previewing exercises for stories suggest a way to do that. There is no previewing for poems or songs. (3) Students will read each selection twice; **Focus for the First Reading** is a set of questions that they should be able to answer after finishing the first reading of a given selection. These questions are text-bound and require a basic comprehension of the whole text; they cannot be answered simply by reading the beginning of the selection. These questions are restated in slightly different format in Comprehension Check, First Reading.

Note that Unit Four includes a world map (page 117) that can be referred to when introducing a selection that mentions or relates to other parts of the world, for example, Jamaica, China, Armenia, or Vietnam.

In an effort to help students while they are reading, certain vocabulary items have been **glossed**. These are culture-bound vocabulary items, technical vocabulary, or important words or expressions that are not easily inferred. In some cases the glosses are in the form of a small picture.

The **after-reading exercises** appear in the following order: Comprehension Check, First Reading; Comprehension Check, Second Reading; Vocabulary; Sharing Your Thoughts; Text Analysis; and Writing Task. You don't have to follow this order strictly. Suggestions for slight variations in order of use follow the descriptions below.

The **Comprehension Check** for the first reading involves a variety of formats, but all require students to answer the Focus for the First Reading questions. The Comprehension Check for the second reading requires more thorough understanding but still focuses on the text and

its meaning as opposed to students' opinions of it. Formats include true/false, multiple choice, matching, listing, filling in charts, sorting, and the more traditional *wh-* questions (*who? what? where? when?*).

Students should always be required to support their answers with evidence from the text. There are good reasons for doing this:

- Having students explain how they arrived at an answer or a conclusion can help us see where their comprehension is weak, enabling us to guide them back onto the right track if necessary.

- Sometimes students see things in the text that we may have overlooked.

- Sometimes we don't notice ambiguities that students do notice. What appears to be an "incorrect" answer might actually be supported by evidence from the text.

Thus, the primary purpose of all comprehension exercises is not to test students' comprehension but, rather, to help them learn how to comprehend authentic texts on their own.

Vocabulary exercises follow Selections One through Four of each unit. The primary purpose of vocabulary work in this book is to help students derive meaning from the text in ways that efficient readers normally do without turning first to the dictionary. Of course, the exercises also help students expand their vocabulary. After all, vocabulary acquisition is a gradual process that requires multiple exposure to words and expressions; the first step is to notice authentic uses in context.

The first exercise, and occasionally the second, is *Vocabulary Building*, in which words and expressions are presented in the exact context in which they are used in the selection. A second exercise, which occurs only with nonfiction selections, helps students use the steps described in the Student's Introduction: recognizing and skipping non-essential vocabulary; noticing and learning multi-word expressions as single units; locating definitions in the text; using prefixes, suffixes, and the parts of compound words to figure out their meaning; inferring meaning from context; and practicing dictionary use. Throughout the book, each step is associated with a different icon.

The last vocabulary exercise, *Vocabulary Review*, is a cloze exercise that draws mainly on vocabulary in the previous exercises but may also include important glossed items and words introduced in the Before Reading section. This exercise gives additional exposure to some of the words (an important factor in vocabulary acquisition) and also provides a summary of the selection. Another way that you can foster vocabulary acquisition is to list vocabulary items on the chalkboard and encourage students to use them in answering Comprehension Check or Sharing Your Thoughts questions.

Sharing Your Thoughts offers a choice of discussion questions and interactive activities. These range from (1) those that relate closely to the text to (2) broader, related issues. They provide a forum for thinking and discussing that depends on adequate knowledge of a topic.

Text Analysis exercises help readers derive meaning from a selection at a variety of levels. Some require looking at overall organization of texts common in North American writing. Others involve analysis of sentences in order to discover their meaning, and still others focus on minor writing conventions such as how definitions are marked in a text. The purpose of this section is to help students notice elements that can aid their reading comprehension and serve as a model for their own writing.

Writing Task exercises close the sequence of activities for each selection. Writing about reading enhances reading comprehension and language development, clarifying and sometimes causing changes in students' ideas about the reading. There are always two choices in this section. To help students prepare a comprehensible and coherent written product, be sure that:

- they do not simply answer one question after another where guide questions are provided; they should use them *as a guide* to write a series of integrated sentences; and
- they do not presume that the reader of their writing has read the selections to which they refer; for example, students should use names, not pronouns, when first referring to a person mentioned in a reading.

Flexibility in Ordering Exercises

Varying the order of exercises for a selection might be advantageous for your students. For example, it might be beneficial to do Vocabulary Building and the second, more skill-oriented exercise (when there is one) between the first and second readings. In this way students can benefit from a stronger awareness of vocabulary and sensitivity to context during their second reading. The Vocabulary Review, however, could be done later because it serves the dual purpose of reviewing vocabulary and summarizing the selection itself.

It may also be helpful to do a Text Analysis exercise before the second reading when the exercise provides an overview of how the entire selection is organized, because an awareness of text organization can aid comprehension.

Decisions about ordering of exercises are best made by you, the teacher, the person who knows most about the students' needs.

A Final Look provides closure after reading five selections on a given topic. It has two parts—a *Discussion* section and a *Unit Project*. The Discussion section includes a choice of questions. The first one involves returning to the unit opening page to reconsider the photo, quote, and focus questions and to note any changes in students' knowledge and points of view as a result of working through all the unit readings. There is also a suggestion for a Unit Project related to the unit topic; each project ends with a writing task. In both the Discussion and Unit Project there is further opportunity to guide students to reuse the vocabulary they have been learning in the unit. In addition, you might want to recycle vocabulary in creative and enjoyable ways such as games and puzzles.

There is an Answer Key on pages 239–251. It includes answers to the vocabulary and other objective exercises. It is on perforated pages which you can remove at the beginning of the term if you think it's best that your students not have access to it. Some teachers believe that their students will misuse the Answer Key and consequently not benefit from doing the exercises. Other teachers like to use exercises as quizzes and therefore do not want their students to have access to the Answer Key. The decision on how to use this feature is up to you.

Acknowledgments

We would like to thank the following colleagues, friends, and family members who have generously supported us in the process of developing this book: Mark Bergel, Evan González, Anthony Hunt, José Irizarry, Robert Smith, and Barbara Strodt. In addition, we gratefully acknowledge the help of staff at Addison Wesley Longman who have helped us along the way. We give special thanks to Debbie Sistino, our development editor, who took on this project midstream and saw it through to the end, and to Robert Ruvo, who oversaw the production process. We also wish to thank the writers whose work constitutes the core of this book.

Building Vocabulary

A powerful agent is the right word.
—Mark Twain
from "Essay on William Dean Howells"

FOCUS

➤ How should you handle new vocabulary as
you read?

Before Reading

Discussion

Talk with your classmates. What's the biggest difference between reading in your first language and reading in English?

Previewing

Previewing is getting some idea of what a reading is about before you actually read it. One thing you can do is read the title. Many long pieces of writing are divided into sections. Headings, or subtitles, indicate the topics of these sections and subsections. Looking at headings before you read can help you get an idea of what the reading is about. Headings are often in darker print, called *boldface*.

Read the title and section headings of the reading below. Answer these questions.

1. What are each of the three sections of this reading about?

2. What aspect of reading will this selection help you with?

Focus for Reading

Read this question before you read the selection. You should be able to answer it after you finish the first reading.

What are the five steps in handling unknown vocabulary?

BUILDING VOCABULARY

As intermediate students of English, you already know a lot of English words, but you need to know even more to be able to read the types of things that native English speakers read. Although building vocabulary is not the only important step in becoming a good reader, it is a very important one. Of course, you can always use a dictionary to build your vocabulary. But you can also **increase** your vocabulary by using what you already know and what is in the text *before* you look at a dictionary. *Building on Basics* will teach you many other things about becoming a better reader, but this introduction focuses on building vocabulary.

FIVE STEPS FOR HANDLING UNKNOWN VOCABULARY

The following five steps can help you handle unknown vocabulary.

Step 1: Locate the problem.
Decide what you do not understand. Is it a single word, a multi-word expression (for example: *Look out!* There's a car coming!), or a whole idea? If the problem is a single word, does it look or sound like a word in your first language? If so, it may have the same meaning, and then there is no problem.

If your native language doesn't help you understand the word or expression, then you can follow Steps 2, 3, or 4. If the problem is a whole idea, it could be that you do not have the cultural or technical knowledge that is necessary for understanding. In that case, follow Step 5.

Step 2: Identify essential and non-essential vocabulary.
Efficient readers know that some words in the text are more important than others, that is, they don't need to understand every single word in order to understand the meaning. Read the sentence without the word or expression you don't understand. Can you understand the sentence without it? If you can, the word or expression is non-essential, or not important, and you can continue reading.

Step 3: Look for a definition in the text.
If the word or expression is important, look for a definition in the text itself. Sometimes definitions are given between commas right after the word. For example, look at the word *non-essential* in the last sentence in Step 2 above. The definition, *not important*, is given right after the word. The words *or* and *that is* also point to a definition that comes after the word. For example: Headings, *or subtitles*, indicate the topics of these sections and subsections. (See Previewing, page xii)

Step 4: Use the information in the text.

A. Look to See if You Know Parts of the Word
If there is no definition, look for other information right in the text that can help you. Sometimes the word itself has parts that you already know. For example, *cookbook* is made from two words that you already know, so you can probably figure out what it means. (A cookbook is a book that includes recipes, or instructions for cooking.) As another example, take a word like *unknown*. You know the word *know* and you have seen the prefix *un-* in a word like *unhappy*. So you can figure out that *unknown* means something you do not know.

B. Use the Context
If the word itself doesn't help you, use the context in which you find it. The context can be:

- the words and sentences before and after the unknown word or expression;
- the general situation, or what the text is about—that is, the topic. Here is an example of how the topic helps you understand the meaning of a word. The word *field* can have a number of meanings. If the text is about sports, the word probably refers to a playing area (a baseball *field*). If the text is about agriculture, *field* probably means a growing area (a *field* of corn).

Step 5: Find help.
If you can't guess the meaning and you can't understand the idea without it, then ask someone for help or use a dictionary.

When you read a story, your purpose is usually to find answers to these questions: *Who is in the story? What happened? Where and when did the incident take place? What is important about this story?* If you can't answer these questions because you don't understand some of the words, then you can try using one (or more) of the five steps described on pages xii–xiii for handling unknown vocabulary.

Look at this example. The sentences come from the first paragraph of Selection One in Unit One, *My Early Memories*, by Colin Powell.

Text: I was born on April 5, 1937, at a time when my family was living on Morningside Avenue in <u>Harlem</u>.

Reader's Thinking: I suppose Harlem is where the Powells lived when Colin was born. That's all I need right now.

Text: My parents' first child, my sister, Marilyn, had been born five and a half years before. I have no <u>recollection</u> of the Harlem years.

Reader's Thinking: I don't know the word *recollection*, but the sentence doesn't seem to tell me anything important about what's happening, so I'll keep on reading.

Text: They say our earliest memories usually <u>involve a trauma</u>, and mine does.

Reader's Thinking: These words are important, but maybe if I keep reading I'll understand them later.

Text: I was four, and we had moved to the <u>South Bronx</u>. Gram Alice McKoy, my <u>maternal</u> grandmother, was <u>taking care of</u> me, since both my parents worked.

Reader's Thinking: The South Bronx is another place. I don't know the word *maternal*, but *grandmother* is enough. What do grandmothers sometimes do when parents work? Yes, *take care of* grandchildren.

Text: I was playing on the floor and <u>stuck</u> a <u>hairpin</u> into an electrical <u>outlet</u>. I remember the <u>blinding flash</u> and the <u>shock</u> almost lifting me off the floor.

Reader's Thinking: These words are important because they tell me what Colin did. There are no definitions, so let me try using what's in the text. He was playing on the floor with a *hairpin*, with something used for the hair. Maybe something his grandmother uses in her hair. What words go with *outlet*?—an *electrical outlet*. That must be where you put the electrical cord. I think he put a hairpin where the electrical cord goes, so *stuck* means something like *put. Flash* and *shock* must be something to do with electricity. This event was bad, so *trauma* means something bad.

Text: And I still remember Gram <u>scolding</u> and <u>hugging</u> me at the same time.

Reader's Thinking: *Scolding* and *hugging*. These verbs are important. They tell me what Gram did. No definitions; I really can't guess exactly what she did. Nobody is here to help me. Let's see what the dictionary says.

> **scold** /skoʊld/ *v* [T] to tell someone in an angry way that s/he has done something wrong: *Mom **scolded** me **for** wasting electricity.* —**scolding** *n* [C,U]

> **hug**[1] /hʌg/ *v* **-gged, -gging** [T] **1** to put your arms around someone and hold him/her tightly to show love or friendship

Gram talked angrily to Colin but at the same time she put her arms around him and held him tightly. That makes sense. She was angry at him and she loved him at the same time.

KEEPING A WORD BANK

Learning vocabulary is a gradual process that requires a lot of hard work. One way to help build a strong vocabulary is to begin a word bank on index cards, in a notebook, or in a word-processing file.

Look at the model for a word bank below. You may want to add a native language equivalent, especially in the case of idioms. An **idiom** is an expression which has a special meaning that you can't understand from knowing the meaning of the individual words in it.

Word in context	Definition
SCOLD (verb)	tell someone in an angry way that
Gram scolded Colin when	s/he has done something wrong
he stuck a hairpin in an outlet.	
HUG (verb)	put her arms around him
Gram also hugged him.	

 ## Comprehension Check

Number the five steps in the correct order from 1 to 5.

___ **a.** Find help.

___ **b.** Look for a definition in the text.

___ **c.** Locate the problem.

___ **d.** Recognize essential and non-essential vocabulary.

___ **e.** Use the information in the text.

Vocabulary

Vocabulary Review

Complete the following statements about the selection with the correct word or expression from the list below. Use each word or expression only once.

context	gradual	handle	non-essential
expression	guess	look for	similar

1. Building vocabulary is a _____ process that takes time.

2. This reading selection recommends five steps to help a person _____ new vocabulary.

3. The first step is to locate the problem. Sometimes the word looks _____ to a word in your native language, and there's no problem.

4. Sometimes a problem is a multi-word _____ which you have to learn as a unit.

5. Step 2 tells you that some words are _____, and you can understand the idea without knowing what they mean.

6. Step 3 tells you to _____ a definition in the text.

7. Step 4 says to use information in the text, including parts of the word or the _____, other words or information in the text.

8. If you can't _____ the meaning and you can't understand the idea without it, then ask someone for help or use a dictionary.

Sharing Your Thoughts

1. Which steps do you think will be easier to use? Which will be harder?
2. Which of the five steps have you been using? Which are new to you?
3. Apply the Five-Step approach to the end of the paragraph from Colin Powell's autobiography below.

Text: When my mother and father came home from work, much intense discussion occurred, followed by more scolding and fussing. My keenest memory of that day is not of the shock and pain, but of feeling important, being the center of attention, seeing how much they loved and cared about me.

Text Analysis

The information in "Five Steps for Handling Unknown Vocabulary" is in the form of a list. Presenting information in a numbered list helps the reader locate and remember important things. Lists can be organized in several ways. For example:

- in alphabetical order
- from most important to least important
- from least important to most important
- in the order in which something is done

How is the list of steps in the instructions organized?

 # Writing Task

1. Write a list of the things you read (such as newspapers or poetry) or topics you read about (such as sports or the environment). Begin by brainstorming the list, that is, write down everything you can think of without worrying about organization. Now organize your list in a logical way.

> **Paragraph**
> A **paragraph** is a set of sentences about a single topic.

2. Write two paragraphs—one about your ability to read in your native language, and one about your ability to read in English. You might want to begin your paragraphs like this:

   When I read in _____, . . .
   When I read in English, . . .

   Use these topics as a guide for each paragraph:

   - what you read
   - how much you read
   - how fast you can read
   - the way you handle unknown vocabulary
   - the enjoyment you get from reading

BUILDING ON BASICS

Growing Up

> *All my life I used to wonder what I would become when I grew up. Then about seven years ago, I realized that I never was going to grow up (that growing is an ever ongoing process).*
> —M. Scott Peck,
> *Further Along the Road Not Traveled*

FOCUS

➤ What are some of the ingredients of a happy childhood?

➤ What are some of the difficulties and pressures of growing up?

➤ What are these difficulties and pressures supposed to teach us?

➤ What does it mean to grow up?

Selection One

Before Reading

This selection is from Colin L. Powell's autobiography, *My American Journey*. Powell's parents came to New York City from Jamaica, an island nation located between North and South America, in the West Indies. When Powell was young, he didn't seem to have any special talents or a clear idea of what he wanted in life. That changed in college when he chose a career in the army. He became a general, and then he became the top military adviser to the president of the United States.

Discussion

Talk with your classmates about your early childhood memories. Think about family, school, hobbies, and playing with friends.

Previewing

You previewed Building Vocabulary in the Student's Introduction by first reading the title and section headings. **Previewing** also includes reading the first sentence of each paragraph. Sometimes the first sentence of a paragraph tells a lot about the content of the paragraph, but sometimes it does not. When you preview, you should also look at pictures and graphs and read their captions.

Preview this selection.

1. What does the title tell you about the content of this selection?

2. What, if anything, can you learn about the topic of paragraphs 2, 3, and 4 by reading only the first sentence?

   - Based on the first sentence, (it is clear / not clear) what paragraph 2 is about. Circle the correct choice.

   - Paragraph 3 is about Powell's ability in _____

   - Paragraph 4 is about Powell's ability in _____

Focus for the First Reading

Read these questions before you read the selection. You should be able to answer them after you finish the first reading.

1. What is Powell's earliest memory?

2. Does Powell believe his childhood was happy or unhappy?

3. What, if anything, was Powell exceptionally good at when he was a boy?

My Early Memories

by Colin L. Powell

1   I was born on April 5, 1937, at a time when my family was living on Morningside Avenue in Harlem. My parents' first child, my sister, Marilyn, had been born five and a half years

before. I have no recollection of the Harlem years. They say our earliest memories usually involve a trauma, and mine does. I was four, and we had moved to the South Bronx. Gram Alice McKoy, my maternal grandmother, was taking care of me, since both my parents worked. I was playing on the floor and stuck a hairpin into an electrical outlet. I remember the blinding flash and the shock almost lifting me off the floor. And I still remember Gram scolding and hugging me at the same time. When my mother and father came home from work, much intense discussion occurred, followed by more scolding and fussing. My keenest memory of that day is not of the shock and pain, but of feeling important, being the center of attention, seeing how much they loved and cared about me.

2   When I was nine, catastrophe[1] struck the Powell family. As a student at P.S. 39, I passed from the third to the fourth grade, but into the bottom form, called "Four Up," a euphemism meaning the kid is a little slow.[2] This was the sort of secret to be whispered with shaking heads in our family circle. Education was the escape hatch, the way up and out for West Indians. My sister was already an excellent student, destined for college. And here I was, having difficulty in the fourth grade. I lacked drive,[3] not ability. I was a happy-go-lucky[4] kid, amenable,[5] amiable,[6] and aimless.[7]

3   I was not much of an athlete either, though I enjoyed street games. One of my boyhood friends, Tony Grant, once counted thirty-six of them, stickball, stoopball, punchball, sluggo, and hot beans and butter among them. One day, I was playing baseball in an empty lot and saw my father coming down the street. I prayed he would keep on going, because I was having a bad day. But he stopped and watched. All the while Pop was there, I never connected. A swing and a miss, again and again, every time I was at bat. I can still feel the burning humiliation. It was always painful for me to disappoint my father. I imagined a pressure that probably was not there, since he rarely uttered a word of reproach[8] to me.

4   As a boy, I took piano lessons; but the lessons did not take with me, and they soon ended. I later studied the flute. Marilyn thought the noises coming out of it were hilarious.[9] I gave up the flute too. Apparently, I would not be a jock[10] or a musician. Still, I was a contented kid, growing up in the warmth and security of the concentric circles[11] my family formed. At the center stood my parents. In the next circle were my mother's sisters and their families. My father's only sibling[12] in America, Aunt Beryl, formed the next circle by herself. These circles rippled out in diminishing degrees of kinship,[13] but maintained considerable closeness. Family members looked out for, prodded,[14] and propped up[15] each other.

[1] **catastrophe**   a terrible event that causes destruction and suffering; as used here it is possibly an exaggeration for humor

[2] **slow**   slow to learn

[3] **lacked drive**   didn't have desire or motivation
[4] **happy-go-lucky**   without worries; carefree
[5] **amenable**   will listen to people; will do what people ask
[6] **amiable**   friendly
[7] **aimless**   without a clear purpose or direction

[8] **uttered a word of reproach**   said a critical word

[9] **hilarious**   very funny
[10] **jock**   athlete (slang)
[11] **concentric circles**

[12] **sibling**   brother or sister

[13] **kinship**   family relationship

[14] **prodded**   pushed; motivated
[15] **propped up**   helped; supported

Comprehension Check

A. First Reading

Circle the letter of the correct statement about each paragraph.

1. Paragraph 1
   a. Powell remembers a time when he did something dangerous.
   b. Powell remembers a time when he did something helpful.
   c. Powell remembers a time when he broke something.

2. Paragraph 2
   a. Powell was an excellent student in third and fourth grade.
   b. Powell was a better student than his sister.
   c. Powell was not an excellent student in third and fourth grade.

3. Paragraph 3
   a. Powell was an excellent athlete.
   b. Powell enjoyed games, but he wasn't an excellent athlete.
   c. Powell wanted to be a professional athlete someday.

4. Paragraph 4
   a. Powell was a happy child.
   b. Powell had an unhappy childhood.
   c. Powell was an only child.

B. Second Reading

1 *Read the selection again. Then show that you understand the main ideas by matching the idea on the left with the reason on the right.*

___ 1. Colin Powell got a shock, and Gram scolded him . . .

    a. because he wasn't a well-motivated student.

___ 2. Gram hugged him . . .

    b. because he didn't want to look bad in front of his father and disappoint him.

___ 3. Colin Powell passed to the bottom group in the fourth grade . . .

    c. because he put a metal hairpin in an electric outlet.

___ 4. Powell hoped his father wouldn't stop to watch him play baseball . . .

    d. because he lived in a circle of relatives who loved and supported him.

___ 5. Powell was basically a happy child . . .

    e. because she loved him and was worried about him.

2 *Which relatives go in concentric circles 1, 2, and 3 on page 3?*

 Vocabulary

 A. Vocabulary Building

Look at the underlined words or expressions in the sentences on the left. Find them in the reading selection. Then match them with the correct meaning on the right.

PARAGRAPH 1

___ **1.** I have no <u>recollection</u> of the Harlem years.

___ **2.** They say our earliest memories usually involve a <u>trauma</u>.

___ **3.** . . . my . . . grandmother was <u>taking care of</u> me.

___ **4.** The <u>shock</u> almost lifted me off the floor.

___ **5.** I still remember Gram <u>scolding</u> me.

___ **6.** I still remember Gram <u>hugging</u> me.

___ **7.** . . . they loved and <u>cared about me</u>.

a. talking in an angry way to someone

b. thought I was important

c. memory

d. putting one's arms around

e. something frightening

f. feeling of pain caused by electricity passing through the body

g. watching and helping

PARAGRAPH 3

___ **8.** I <u>was not much of an athlete</u> either.

___ **9.** One day, I was playing baseball in an <u>empty lot</u>.

___**10.** I <u>prayed</u> he would keep on going, because I was having a bad day.

___**11.** . . . I never connected. A swing and a <u>miss</u>. . .

___**12.** I can still feel the burning <u>humiliation</u>.

___**13.** It was always painful for me to <u>disappoint my father</u>.

h. hoped; wanted strongly

i. feeling of being small and unimportant; shame or embarrassment

j. piece of land with no buildings on it

k. not be able to do what my father wanted

l. had little ability in sports

m. no hit (when the baseball bat doesn't hit the ball)

PARAGRAPH 4

___**14.** . . . I <u>gave up</u> the flute too.

n. feeling of love

___**15.** . . . I was a <u>contented</u> kid. . .

o. stopped (playing)

___**16.** . . . growing up in the <u>warmth</u> . . . of the concentric circles my family formed.

p. feeling of safety

___**17.** . . . growing up in the . . . <u>security</u> of the concentric circles my family formed.

q. happy

B. Identifying Non-essential Vocabulary

Read each sentence, skipping the crossed-out words. Then try to answer the question that follows. If you can answer the question, the crossed-out words are not essential. If you can't, the crossed-out words are essential to understanding the sentence, and there may be an important word you need to look up in a dictionary.

1. As a student at P.S. 39, I passed from the third to the fourth grade, but into the bottom form, called "Four Up," a ~~euphemism~~ meaning the kid is a little slow. (¶ 2)
   • Was Powell one of the best students in the fourth grade?

2. This was the sort of secret ~~to be whispered with shaking heads~~ in our family circle. (¶ 2)
   • Did Powell's family feel good or bad that he was in "Four Up"?

3. Education was the escape ~~hatch~~, the way up and out for West Indians. (¶ 2)
   • Why was education important for West Indians?

4. My sister was already an excellent student, ~~destined~~ for college. (¶ 2)
   • Was Powell's sister a good student or not?

5. I took piano lessons; ~~but the lessons did not take with me~~, and they soon ended. (¶ 4)
   • Did Powell do well in his piano lessons?

6. These circles rippled out in diminishing degrees of kinship, but ~~maintained considerable~~ closeness. (¶ 4)
   • Were the members of the larger Powell family distant from each other?

C. Vocabulary Review

Complete the following statements about the reading selection with the correct word or expression from the list below. Use each word or expression only once.

athlete	contented	gave up	scolded
cared about	disappoint	an empty lot	shock

1. In Colin Powell's early memories, we see a normal little boy who played with an electric outlet and got a _____. His grandmother was angry and _____ him, but what he remembers most is that she hugged him because she loved and _____ him.

2. He wasn't an excellent student, a good musician, or a very good

   _____, but he loved to play games.

3. Once he was playing baseball in _____ when his father stopped to

   watch. He loved and respected his father and didn't want to _____

   him, but he never hit the ball.

4. He took flute lessons, but his sister laughed at him, so he _____

   the flute.

5. Even though he wasn't a star early in life, he was a _____, happy-

   go-lucky child who grew up in a loving circle of relatives.

Sharing Your Thoughts

1. What kinds of things make a child feel secure and happy?
2. What do you think are the values in the Powell family? What is important to them? What are your own family values? In what ways are they similar to or different from the Powells' values?
3. Why do you think the Powells, as an immigrant family, considered education very important?
4. How can high expectations of all kinds put both positive and negative pressure on children?
5. Ask three people who are not in your class to tell you about their earliest memory. Was it a happy event or a traumatic one? Compare your results with those of other students. Do most people seem to have earliest memories of happy or traumatic events?

Text Analysis

Narratives

Narrative writing is used to tell a story or describe events or incidents. When writers tell about incidents, they usually answer most of these questions:

1. Where did the incident happen?
2. When did it happen?
3. Who was there?
4. What happened? What did people do? Why?
5. How did people feel? Why?

Read paragraphs 1 and 3 in Selection One again. Then tell, or narrate, the incidents in your own words using the questions in the box on page 7 as a guide. You may want to answer the questions in a different order.

PARAGRAPH 1: One day when Colin Powell was four years old, his grandmother was taking care of him. *(Answers questions 2 and 3. Continue your narration with the answers to questions 1, 4, and 5.)*

Writing Task

1. Write the story of one of the two incidents you narrated in the Text Analysis exercise above. Imagine you are writing for a person who does not know anything about the reading selection. For example, the first time you refer to Colin Powell, use his name, not the pronoun *he*.

2. Write about your earliest memory or another important childhood memory. Before you begin writing, use the questions from the box on page 7 to help you plan the details that you want to include in your writing. Then decide in what order to answer the questions and write your sentences.

Selection Two

Before Reading

Laurence Steinberg is a professor of psychology at Temple University in Philadelphia. He and his colleagues, Bradford Brown from the University of Wisconsin and Sanford M. Dornbusch from Stanford University, studied American adolescents over a ten-year period. They collected information from more than 20,000 teenagers from nine high schools and spoke with many of their parents and teachers. This selection comes from the book *Beyond the Classroom*, which is about their research.

Discussion

People in our lives put pressure on us. They try to influence (affect) our behavior (actions), our thinking, and our decisions. We seem to feel and react to this pressure most during adolescence, the period between childhood and adulthood.

Look at the chart below. List three examples of people or groups that put pressure on young people. What do they try to influence: behavior or thinking? Give an example.

Who?	What they try to influence	Example
my mother	behavior	I can't say bad words around her.

Previewing: Reading Titles

Understanding the title of this selection will help you understand what it is about, but it contains difficult words. Look at the words in the title of Selection Two on page 10. Here are their dictionary entries.

peer[1] /pir/ *n* someone who is the same age as you
influence[1] /ˈinfluəns/ *n* someone or something that has an effect on other people or things
a·chieve·ment /əˈtʃivmənt/ *n* success in doing or getting what you worked for

From the title, what do you think this selection is about?
a. the effect of parents on schoolwork
b. the effect of friends on schoolwork

Focus for the First Reading

Read these questions before you read the selection. You should be able to answer them after you finish the first reading.

1. According to this study, who has the most influence on the schoolwork of American high school students: their parents, their friends, or their teachers?

2. In what aspect or area of social life is the influence of these people greatest?

Peer Influences on Achievement

by Laurence Steinberg

1   By tracking students over a three-year period, we were able to see how they were doing in school at the beginning of the time period, which friends they were spending time with, and whether their school performance[1] and behavior changed over time as a result. By comparing the academic careers of students who began high school with equivalent grades, but who had different sorts of friends during the school years, we were able to see whether the type of friends that adolescents have actually makes a difference in their school performance.

2   The answer is that it most certainly does, especially in two areas: academic performance and delinquency. Youngsters whose friends were more academically oriented—that is, whose friends had higher grades, spent more time on homework, had higher educational aspirations, and who were more involved in extracurricular activities[2]—did better over the course of high school than students who began school with similar records but who had less academically oriented friends. Similarly, students whose friends were more delinquent—who used more drugs and alcohol and who had more conduct problems—developed more problems themselves over time than did adolescents who began the study with the same behavior profile but who had friends who were less delinquent.

3   These findings tell us, then, that parents have legitimate reason to be concerned about the qualities and values of their children's friends, especially during early adolescence, when susceptibility to peer influence runs strong.[3] There is also reason to be concerned about the characteristics of the crowd[4] to which an adolescent belongs, since our study found that this influence matters, too. All other things being equal, adolescents who are members of more academically oriented crowds do better in school than other students, whereas those who are members of more alienated[5] crowds do worse and are more likely[6] to get into trouble.

4   How large a difference do friends make? In one set of analyses, we were able to contrast the influence of best friends with the influence of parents on two important outcomes: the grades in school that the adolescent was getting, and the adolescent's amount of drug and alcohol use. At least by high school, the influence of friends on school performance and drug use is more substantial than the influence of parents' practices at home. Parents may influence their children's long-term educational plans, but when it comes to day-to-day influences on schooling—whether students attend class, how much time they spend on homework, how hard they try in school, and the grades they bring home—friends are more influential than parents.

---

[1] **school performance**   academic work; grades
[2] **extracurricular activities**   activities outside classes (sports, music groups, clubs)
[3] **when susceptibility to peer pressure runs strong**   when the person is easily affected by peer influence
[4] **crowd**   group with common interests, attitudes, and activities (not necessarily friends), for example, the athletic, social, or intellectual crowd
[5] **alienated**   not belonging to a group; not in favor with most other students
[6] **likely**   probable

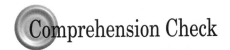

Comprehension Check

A. First Reading

Circle the letter of the choice that correctly completes the sentence.

1. According to this study, _____ have the most influence on the schoolwork of American high school students.

   a. parents
   b. friends
   c. teachers

2. In addition to school achievement, this group has the greatest influence on _____.

   a. religious beliefs
   b. career choice
   c. drug and alcohol use

B. Second Reading

*Read the selection again. Then mark the statements **T** (true) or **F** (false). Be prepared to show evidence in the selection that supports your answers.*

1. T F   The researchers compared groups of students with similar grades.

2. T F   They compared the students' grades at the beginning of the school year with their grades at the end of the year.

3. T F   Students who had academically oriented friends had better grades over the course of high school.

4. T F   Students who had less academically oriented friends had worse grades.

5. T F   Close friends and crowds both had an important influence on students' grades and behavior.

6. T F   Parents and peers had a similar influence on students' grades.

Vocabulary

A. Vocabulary Building

Look at the underlined words or expressions in the sentences on the left on page 12. Find them in the reading selection. Then match them with the correct meaning on the right.

_____ **1.** . . . we were able to see . . . <u>whether</u> their school performance and behavior changed over time . . . (¶ 1)

a. have an effect

_____ **2.** students . . . with <u>equivalent</u> grades, but who had different sorts of friends . . . (¶ 1)

b. research results

_____ **3.** . . . the type of friends that <u>adolescents</u> have actually makes a difference in their school performance. (¶ 1)

c. worried about

_____ **4.** These <u>findings</u> tell us . . . that parents have . . . reason to be concerned . . . (¶ 3)

d. equal in value; the same

_____ **5.** . . . parents have . . . reason to be <u>concerned about</u> the qualities and values of their children's friends . . . (¶ 3)

e. get lower grades

_____ **6.** . . . adolescents who are members of more academically oriented crowds <u>do better</u> in school . . . (¶ 3)

f. if

_____ **7.** . . . those who are members of more alienated crowds <u>do worse</u> . . . (¶ 3)

g. teenagers

_____ **8.** . . . when it comes to day-to-day influences on schooling . . . friends <u>are</u> more <u>influential</u> than parents. (¶ 4)

h. get higher grades

B. Identifying Essential and Non-essential Vocabulary

Read the sentences, skipping the shaded words. Which shaded words or phrases are essential, that is, which ones do you need to know in order to understand the sentence? Which ones are not essential? Mark them **E** for essential and **NE** for non-essential.

1. (¶ 1) We were able to see how they (students) were doing . . . at the
                                       a. __E__
beginning of the time period.
              b. __NE__

2. (¶ 1) By comparing the academic careers of students who began high school

with equivalent grades, but who had different sorts of friends during the
      a._____   **b.**_____
school years, we were able to see whether the type of friends that

adolescents have actually makes a difference in their school performance.

3. (¶ 2) Similarly, students whose friends were more delinquent . . . developed more problems themselves over time than did adolescents who began the study with the same behavior profile but who had friends who were less delinquent.
      a._____ b._____

4. (¶ 3) These findings tell us, then, that parents have legitimate reason to be
      a._____
   concerned about the qualities and values of their children's friends. . . .
   b._____

5. (¶ 4) In one set of analyses, we were able to contrast the influence of best
      a._____
   friends with the influence of parents on two important outcomes: the grades
      b._____
   in school that the adolescent was getting, and the adolescent's amount of

   drug and alcohol use.

C. Vocabulary Review

Complete the following statements about the reading selection with the correct word or expression from the list below. Use each word or expression only once.

behavior	do better	influential	whether
concerned about	findings	peers	

1. The researchers who did this study wanted to know _____ parents or friends had a greater influence on the academic performance and _____ of adolescents.

2. The _____ of the study show that friends are more _____ than parents, at least during high school.

3. Parents should be _____ who their children's friends are, because youngsters who have more academically oriented friends _____ in school.

4. This research showed the importance of _____ in young people's lives.

Sharing Your Thoughts

1. On the basis of the findings in his study, Steinberg comments that parents should be concerned about the friends their children choose. What, if anything, do you think parents can do to help their children choose the right friends?

2. There are a lot of influences on young people in today's world. Here are some of them. Add others you can think of.

parents

close friends

teachers

religious leaders

television and movie stars

singers and musicians

other: _____

3. Which of the people mentioned above has the most influence on young people in the areas listed below? Think about yourself and your culture. Compare your responses with those of your classmates.

a. clothing and hair styles _____

b. free-time activities _____

c. music preferences _____

d. choice of friends _____

e. dating; who young people can
    and cannot go out with _____

f. the amount of studying students do _____

g. career choice _____

h. part-time employment _____

i. alcohol or drug use _____

j. criminal behavior _____

Text Analysis

A. Topic and Main Idea

> **Topic:** Every piece of writing—a book, a newspaper article, even a paragraph—has a subject, or a topic. Topics can be general (for example, *Baseball* or *Drugs*) or more specific (for example, *The problems between baseball players and team owners* or *The increase in teenage drug use in the United States*).
>
> **Main Idea:** There is always one idea about the topic that is the most central. This is the main idea.

Choose the best topic and main idea for Selection Two.

1. Topic
    a. Parental pressure to get good grades
    b. Influence of peers on academic work and behavior
    c. Research results in American schools

2. Main Idea

    a. Students in American schools don't value academic achievement, and they abuse alcohol and drugs.

    b. Parents should help their children choose their friends and stop them from using drugs and drinking alcohol.

    c. Research shows that during high school, friends have a greater effect on an adolescent's grades and use of alcohol and drugs than parents do.

B. Finding the Writer's Definition

When writers have a specific meaning for a word or expression, they often include the definition between dashes (— . . . —). Refer to the indicated paragraph, and copy the author's definition. The first one has been started for you.

1. (¶ 2) By *academically oriented*, the writer means a student whose friends

    had higher grades.

2. (¶ 2) By *delinquent*, the writer means a student who

    _____

3. (¶ 4) By *day-to-day influences on schooling*, the writer means

    _____

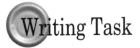

Writing Task

1. Write about your reaction to the findings of this study. Use these questions as a guide.

    What were the findings of this study?
    Did these findings surprise you? Why or why not?

2. Write your interpretation of the cartoon below. Use these questions as a guide.

    What reason does the son give his mother for wearing his clothes the way he does?
    Look at the last frame. What is the real reason the son wears his clothes the way he does?
    How does this cartoon relate to the study described in Selection Two?

Selection Three

Before Reading

Angie Erickson was in the ninth grade when she wrote this essay, which appeared in *Newsweek* on October 24, 1994.

Discussion
Discuss the title and subtitle of the article. What is a disability? With your classmates, list some disabilities you know of.

Why do some children make fun of people with disabilities? Are these children being mean or unkind, or is there another explanation?

Previewing: Scanning

When you pass your eyes quickly over a text to locate specific information, you are **scanning**.

Scan the first two paragraphs of this article to find out what Angie's disability is. Share what you know about this disability with your classmates.

Do you know enough about it to imagine some of the problems she has?

Focus for the First Reading
Read these questions before you read the selection. You should be able to answer them after you finish the first reading.

1. How did Angie's disability affect her mental and physical abilities?

2. How did it affect her friendships?

It's OK to Be Different

Stop Making Fun of My Disability

by Angie Erickson

1   Why me? I often ask myself. Why did I have to be the one? Why did I get picked to be different? Why are people mean to me and always treating me differently? These are the kinds of questions that I used to ask myself. It took more than ten years for me to find answers and to realize that I'm not *more* different than anyone else.

2   I was born on June 29, 1978. Along with me came my twin sister, Stephanie. She was born with no birth defects,[1] but I was born with cerebral palsy.[2] For me, CP made it so I shake a little; when my sister began to walk, I couldn't. The doctors knew it was a minor case of cerebral palsy. But they didn't know if I'd

---

[1] **birth defects**   imperfections you are born with
[2] **cerebral palsy (CP)**   an illness caused by damage to a baby's brain before it is born, which makes its muscles permanently weak

ever walk straight or do things that other kids my age could do.

3   At first my disability did not bother me, because when you're a toddler,[3] you do things that are really easy. When it took me a little longer to play yard games, because I couldn't run that well, my friends just thought I was slow. My disability was noticed when other children were learning how to write and I couldn't. Kids I thought were my friends started to stay away from me because they said I was different. Classmates began commenting on my speech. They said I talked really weird. Every time someone was mean to me, I would start to cry and I would always blame myself for being different.

4   People thought I was stupid because it was hard for me to write my own name. So when I was the only one in the class to use a typewriter, I began to feel I was different. It got worse when the third graders moved on to fourth grade and I had to stay behind. I got held back because the teachers thought I'd be unable to type fast enough to keep up. Kids told me that was a lie and the reason I got held back was because I was a retard.[4] It really hurt to be teased by those I thought were my friends.

5   After putting up with everyone making fun of me and me crying about it, I started sticking up for myself when I was ten, in fourth grade. I realized if I wanted them to stop, I would have to be the person who made them stop. I finally found out who my real friends were, and I tried to ignore the ones who were mean. Instead of constantly thinking about the things I couldn't do, I tried to think about the things I *could* do, and it helped others, and myself, understand who I really was. When there was something I couldn't do, such as play Pictionary, I sat and I

watched or I would go find something else to do. A few people still called me names and made fun of me, but after a while, when they saw they didn't get a reaction, they quit, because it wasn't fun anymore. What they didn't know was that it did still hurt me. It hurt me a lot more than they could ever imagine.

6   It took a lot of willpower on my part and a lot of love from family and friends to get where I am today. I learned that no one was to blame for my disability. I realize that I can do things and I can do them very well. Some things I can't do, like taking my own notes in class or running in a race, but I will have to live with that. At sixteen, I believe I've learned more than many people will learn in their whole lives. I have worked out that some people are just mean because they're afraid of being nice. They try to prove to themselves and others that they are cool, but, sooner or later, they're going to wish they hadn't said some of those hurtful things. A lot of people will go through life being mean to those with disabilities because they don't know how to act or what to say to them—they feel awkward with someone who's different.

7   Parents need to teach their children that it's all right to be different and it's all right to be friends with those who are. Some think that the disabled should be treated like little kids for the rest of their lives. They presume we don't need love and friends, but our needs are the same as every other human being's.

8   There are times when I wish I hadn't been born with cerebral palsy, but crying about it isn't going to do me any good. I can only live once, so I want to live the best I can. I am glad I learned who I am and what I am capable of doing. I am happy with who I am. Nobody else could be the Angela Marie Erickson who is writing this. I could never be, or ever want to be, anyone else.

---

[3] **toddler**   child learning to walk

[4] **retard**   offensive slang for a person who develops more slowly than usual; comes from *mental retardation*

Comprehension Check

A. First Reading

*Mark the statements **T** (true) or **F** (false). Be prepared to show evidence in the selection that supports your answers.*

1. T   F   Cerebral palsy affected Angie's ability to think. She wasn't as smart as the other children in her class.

2. T   F   Angie had problems making friends. Other children laughed at her and were mean to her because she was different.

B. Second Reading

1 *Read the selection again. Then mark the statements **T** (true) or **F** (false). Be prepared to show evidence in the selection that supports your answers.*

1. T   F   Angie had a serious case of cerebral palsy.

2. T   F   Her disability first became a real problem for her in school.

3. T   F   She didn't pass to the fourth grade because she wasn't smart enough.

4. T   F   Angie learned that if she didn't react, kids stopped making fun of her.

5. T   F   According to Angie, one reason people are mean to others with disabilities is that they don't feel comfortable with someone who is different.

6. T   F   Angie thinks disabled people have different emotional needs from other people.

2 *Angie had a disability that affected her life. For each item below, circle all the correct results and be prepared to show evidence in the selection.*

1. Angie had a mild case of CP. As a result she
    a. shook a little
    b. started walking later than her twin sister
    c. couldn't walk or run very well
    d. couldn't write very easily
    e. couldn't talk at all

2. Kids teased and made fun of Angie. As a result she
    a. talked to the teacher about them
    b. cried
    c. felt hurt
    d. blamed herself for her problems

3. Angie was the only child in class to use a typewriter, so she
   a. felt different
   b. was held back in the third grade
   c. could write faster on her typewriter

4. Angie's life was not easy. As a result she learned things. The difficulties taught her
   a. that to stop the teasing she had to ignore the mean kids
   b. that she could do anything she wanted
   c. who her real friends were
   d. that she should focus on what she could do and not what she couldn't do

 Vocabulary

 A. Vocabulary Building

Look at the underlined words or expressions in the sentences below. Find them in the selection. Then choose the correct meaning for the context.

1. Why are people <u>mean</u> to me and always treating me differently? (¶ 1)
   a. kind
   b. helpful
   c. cruel

2. It took more than ten years for me to find answers and to <u>realize</u> that I'm not *more* different than anyone else. (¶ 1)
   a. imagine
   b. understand
   c. guess

3. . . . when my sister began to walk, I <u>couldn't</u>. (¶ 2)
   a. was not able (to walk)
   b. was too lazy (to walk)
   c. didn't want (to walk)

4. They said I talked really <u>weird</u>. (¶ 3)
   a. strange
   b. loud
   c. soft

5. Every time someone was mean to me, I would start to cry and I would always <u>blame myself</u> for being different. (¶ 3)
   a. accept myself
   b. place responsibility on myself
   c. make myself feel better

6. . . . I tried to <u>ignore</u> the ones who were mean. (¶ 5)

   a. say mean things to

   b. appreciate

   c. not pay attention to

7. A lot of people . . . feel <u>awkward</u> with someone who's different. (¶ 6)

   a. uncomfortable

   b. afraid

   c. concerned

  B. Multi-word Expressions

① *Look at the underlined multi-word expressions in the sentences below. Find them in the selection. Then choose the correct meaning for the context.*

1. Stop <u>making fun of</u> my disability. (title)

   a. enjoying

   b. laughing at

   c. talking about

2. Kids . . . started to <u>stay away from</u> me because they said I was different. (¶ 3)

   a. keep a distance from

   b. give help to

   c. visit

3. . . . when the third graders moved on . . . I had to <u>stay behind</u>. (¶ 4)

   a. leave school

   b. get help

   c. repeat (third grade)

4. . . . the teachers thought I'd be unable to type fast enough to <u>keep up</u>. (¶ 4)

   a. continue typing

   b. go at the same speed as the group

   c. be able to pay attention to the class

5. Kids told me . . . the reason I <u>got held back</u> was because I was a retard. (¶ 4)

   a. passed to the next grade

   b. didn't pass to the next grade

   c. was expelled from school

② *Find three multi-word expressions in paragraph 5, and write them on the lines to the right of the numbers. Match each with its correct meaning on the lines to the left of the numbers.*

___ **1.** _____   **a.** learned; discovered

___ **2.** _____   **b.** accepting; tolerating

___ **3.** _____   **c.** defending

C. Vocabulary Review

Complete the following statements about the reading selection with the correct word or expression from the list below. Use each word or expression only once.

awkward	couldn't	keep up	mean	stay behind
blamed	ignore	made fun of	realized	weird

1. Angie had a minor case of cerebral palsy, and there were some things she _____ do.

2. Kids who didn't understand her disability were _____ to her and _____ her.

3. Angie tried to _____ the kids who said that she talked _____.

4. Teachers didn't help the situation when they said she had to _____ in third grade. They thought she couldn't type fast enough to _____ with the other children.

5. For a long time, Angie _____ herself for being different.

6. When she was in the fourth grade, she finally _____ that many people feel _____ with someone who is different. This helped her understand herself and her situation.

Sharing Your Thoughts

1. Who do you think helped Angie most to grow and change: her parents, her real friends, her teachers, or Angie herself? How did they help her?

2. What do you think is the most important thing she learned?

3. Would Angie get the same reactions from children in your culture? Why or why not?

4. What, if anything, do you admire about Angie? What might you learn from her?

5. What kind of adult do you think Angie has become? Explain.

6. Disabilities are one serious problem that makes growing up difficult. List other problems that make growing up difficult. What activities or organizations can help children if they have a disability or other kind of problem? Talk about the ways these organizations try to help children with problems.

Text Analysis

A. Topics and Main Ideas in Personal Essays

Personal essays like Selection Three also have topics and main ideas. Choose the best topic and main idea for this selection.

1. Topic
   a. American schools
   b. Mean kids
   c. Living with a disability
2. Main Idea
   a. People with disabilities should always ask for help because they can't do everything by themselves.
   b. Angie learned to accept herself and learned to live with being different.
   c. Kids can be cruel to others without knowing they are hurting them.

B. Paragraph Topics

A piece of writing is divided into paragraphs. Each **paragraph** is a group of sentences with a specific topic that relates to the main idea of the essay. Sometimes more than one paragraph can be on a single topic.

Match paragraphs 2 through 7 from Selection Three with their topics.

PARAGRAPH TOPIC

¶ 1 Introduction

¶ 2 _____

¶ 3 _____
    a. Angie's early years and the beginning of her problems

¶ 4 _____
    b. what Angie learned and how she changed

¶ 5–6 _____
    c. the conditions of Angie's birth

¶ 7 _____
    d. Angie's comments for parents

¶ 8 Conclusion
    e. people's reactions to Angie

Writing Task

1. Select one sentence from Angie Erickson's essay that you consider special or particularly meaningful. Explain why you chose it and what the sentence means to you. You might begin this way:

   > There are several sentences in Angie Erickson's essay, "It's OK to be Different," which I like, but the one that is the most meaningful to me is "..."

2. Write about a person who is different from others in some way. Perhaps this person has a disability; perhaps he or she has a special talent. Write two paragraphs; each paragraph will have a different topic.

   - *Topic for paragraph 1*: the person and his or her "difference" (Identify and describe the person. Tell how he or she is different and what he or she can and cannot do.)

   - *Topic for paragraph 2*: how people treat the person, and his or her reaction to this treatment.

Selection Four

Before Reading

Amy Tan is a contemporary American writer. This selection is from her novel *The Joy Luck Club*, which tells the stories of four mothers and their daughters. The mothers were born in China and emigrated to San Francisco, California, where they raised their families.

Discussion

Parents want things for their children; they have expectations for them. For example, many parents expect their children to behave in a certain way or to study for a certain career. These expectations put pressure on the children.

Talk with your classmates about different parental expectations and the pressures parents put on children. Continue to list some of these expectations and pressures.

Many parents expect their children to do well in school. There is pressure to get good grades.

Now talk about how children and young people often react when there are very strong pressures on them.

For example, how would you feel and what might you do if your mother or father expected you to be a *prodigy*—that is, to have exceptional abilities at an early age (like the composer Mozart, who wrote music and gave piano concerts when he was four years old)?

Previewing: Identifying the Narrator of a Story

This selection comes from a novel, which is a long work of fiction. Stories and novels have **narrators**, or people who tell the story. Sometimes the narrator is the writer; sometimes it is a character in the story.

Read the first sentence of the selection. Who is the narrator—the author, one of the mothers, or one of the daughters?

Focus for the First Reading

The narrator is a young girl named Jing-Mei. Jing-Mei's mother believes a person "can be anything in America." Just before this excerpt from the novel, Jing-Mei's mother has told her that she can be a prodigy (she "can be best anything").

Read these questions before you read the selection. You should be able to answer them after you finish the first reading.

1. What did Jing-Mei's mother do that made Jing-Mei feel pressure?
2. What does Jing-Mei decide at the end?

Two Kinds

by Amy Tan

1   In the beginning, I was just as excited as my mother, maybe even more so. I pictured this prodigy part of me as many different images, trying each one on for size. I was a dainty ballerina girl standing by the curtains, waiting to hear the right music that would send me floating on my tiptoes. I was like the Christm child[1] lifted out of the straw manger, crying with holy indignity. I was Cinderella[2] stepping from her pumpkin carriage with sparkly cartoon music filling the air.

2   In all of my imaginings, I was filled with a sense that I would soon become *perfect*. My mother and father would adore me. I would be beyond reproach.[3] I would never feel the need to sulk[4] for anything.

3   But sometimes the prodigy in me became impatient. "If you don't hurry up and get me out of here, I'm disappearing for good,"[5] it warned. "And then you'll always be nothing."

4   Every night after dinner, my mother and I would sit at the Formica kitchen table. She would present new tests, taking her examples from stories of amazing children she had read in *Ripley's Believe It or Not*, or *Good Housekeeping*, *Reader's Digest*, and a dozen other magazines she kept in a pile in our bathroom. My mother got these magazines from people whose houses she cleaned. And since she cleaned many houses each week, we had a great assortment. She would look through them all, searching for stories about remarkable children.

5   The first night she brought out a story about a three-year-old boy who knew the capitals of all the states and even most of the European countries. A teacher was quoted as saying the little boy could also pronounce the names of the foreign cities correctly.

6   "What's the capital of Finland?" my mother asked me, looking at the magazine story.

7   All I knew was the capital of California, because Sacramento was the name of the street we lived on in Chinatown. "Nairobi!" I guessed, saying the most foreign word I could think of. She checked to see if that was possibly one way to pronounce "Helsinki" before showing me the answer.

8   The tests got harder—multiplying numbers in my head, finding the queen of hearts in a deck of cards, trying to stand on my head without using my hands, predicting the daily temperatures in Los Angeles, New York, and London.

[1] **Christ child**   the baby Jesus, whose birth is celebrated by Christians on December 25
[2] **Cinderella**   fairy tale character who goes from cleaning the house for her evil stepmother to being a princess

[3] **beyond reproach**   perfect; impossible to criticize
[4] **sulk**   show you are upset, especially by not talking to others

[5] **for good**   permanently; forever

9   One night I had to look at a page from the Bible for three minutes and then report everything I could remember. "Now Jehoshaphat had riches and honor in abundance and . . . that's all I remember, Ma," I said.

10   And after seeing my mother's disappointed face once again, something inside of me began to die. I hated the tests, the raised hopes[6] and failed expectations.[7] Before going to bed that night, I looked in the mirror above the bathroom sink and when I saw only my face staring back—and that it would always be this ordinary face—I began to cry. Such a sad, ugly girl! I made high-pitched noises like a crazed animal, trying to scratch out[8] the face in the mirror.

11   And then I saw what seemed to be the prodigy side of me— because I had never seen that face before. I looked at my reflection, blinking so I could see more clearly. The girl staring back at me was angry, powerful. This girl and I were the same. I had new thoughts, willful thoughts, or rather thoughts filled with lots of won'ts. I won't let her change me, I promised myself. I won't be what I'm not.

[6] **raised hopes**   the mother's high hopes, or desires, for her daughter
[7] **failed expectations**   the mother's beliefs about the daughter that weren't coming true
[8] **scratch out**   use fingernails or claws (like an animal) to eliminate or erase

Comprehension Check

A. First Reading

Fill in the blanks with an appropriate word or phrase.

Jing-Mei's mother wanted her daughter to be a _____, "best
(1)
anything." She gave Jing-Mei a lot of _____. They didn't make Jing-
(2)
Mei better at anything; they only made her _____ . In the end, Jing-
(3)
Mei decided that she would not let her mother _____ her.
(4)

B. Second Reading

1   *Read the selection again. Then mark the statements **T** (true) or **F** (false). Be prepared to show evidence in the selection that supports your answers.*

1.   T   F   In the beginning, Jing-Mei wanted to please her parents.

2.   T   F   Jing-Mei first imagined herself graceful and beautiful.

3.   T   F   In the beginning, Jing-Mei was confident about her future.

4.   T   F   The mother's tests were tests of thinking ability.

5.   T   F   Jing-Mei did well on her mother's tests.

6.   T   F   Jing-Mei didn't like her reflection in the mirror at first.

2 *What did Jing-Mei do while she was looking in the mirror? Act out what she did.*

3 *Jing-Mei changes during the course of this story. Complete the chart below to show the changes.*

Before	After
1. Jing-Mei wanted to please her mother and be a prodigy.	She is going to be herself.
2. She saw her face as ordinary, even ugly.	
3. She is confused about herself and who she is.	

 Vocabulary

 A. Vocabulary Building

Look at the underlined words or expressions in the sentences on the left. Find them in the reading selection. Then match them with the correct meaning on the right.

___ **1.** I pictured this prodigy part of me . . . (¶ 1)

___ **2.** . . . I would soon become perfect. (¶ 2)

___ **3.** . . . searching for stories about remarkable children. (¶ 4)

___ **4.** . . . after seeing my mother's disappointed face . . . (¶ 10)

___ **5.** I hated the tests . . . (¶ 10)

___ **6.** I had new thoughts, willful thoughts . . . (¶ 11)

a. unusual; noticeable in a way that deserves attention

b. with nothing wrong; without defects

c. with a mind of your own; doing what you want even when people tell you not to do it

d. strongly disliked

e. imagined

f. unhappy; showing that what a person wanted to happen didn't happen

B. Vocabulary Review

Complete the following statements about the reading selection with the correct word or expression from the list below. Use each word or expression only once.

disappointed	hated	pictured	willful
expectations	perfect	remarkable	

1. Jing-Mei's mother had great _____ for her daughter; she

   wanted her to be some kind of prodigy.

2. In the beginning, Jing-Mei liked this idea. She _____ herself as a ballerina or Cinderella.

3. She imagined she could become _____ if she worked hard enough.

4. Jing-Mei's mother was always comparing her to _____ children whom she read about in magazines.

5. She gave Jing-Mei tests from magazines and got a _____ look on her face when Jing-Mei didn't answer correctly.

6. Jing-Mei _____ the tests her mother gave her.

7. In the end, Jing-Mei decided that she was not ordinary but strong, powerful, and _____.

Sharing Your Thoughts

1. Why do you think Jing-Mei's mother pressured her daughter to be some kind of prodigy?

2. Why do you think Jing-Mei hated the tests?

3. What do you think began to die in Jing-Mei when she saw her mother's disappointed face?

4. What do you think will happen next in Jing-Mei's life?

5. Why do parents sometimes want their children to have certain friends, prepare for a certain career, or be a certain kind of person? In what cases is parental pressure good, and in what cases is it bad?

6. In his book *What Preteens Want their Parents to Know*, Ryan Holladay says, "Listening is one of the best ways to show me you love me" and "Don't begin sentences with 'When I was your age. . . .'" Discuss things you would like to tell parents about how to make parent-child relationships better.

7. What similarities (and differences) do you see in the lives of Jing-Mei and Angie Erickson?

 Text Analysis

Finding Similarities and Differences

Good readers see **similarities** and **differences** in the things they read. This requires looking closely at the texts. A Venn diagram, two overlapping circles, helps to organize information you read.

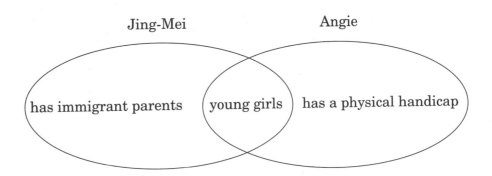

Jing-Mei · Angie

has immigrant parents · young girls · has a physical handicap

Make a Venn diagram to show similarities and differences between Jing-Mei and Angie. (Think about the discussion you had in Sharing Your Thoughts, question 7). Fill in facts about each person on the appropriate side of the diagram. When you find things they have in common, write them in the middle section. Remember that there is more than one way to fill in a Venn diagram. It helps to organize your thinking.

 Writing Task

1. You read about Jing-Mei's feelings. Imagine you are her mother, and a close friend asks you the three questions below about Jing-Mei. What would you say? Write the complete conversation, including a brief opening and a closing to the conversation.

   How is Jing-Mei doing?
   Why are you giving Jing-Mei these tests?
   What do you want her to be someday?

2. Write a paragraph about the similarities between Angie and Jing-Mei, using the information in the center section of your Venn diagram. Use the suggestions below to help you organize your writing.

   Angie and Jing-Mei are similar in (two/three/four) ways.

   First, _____. Second, _____. Finally, _____.

Selection Five

Linda Pastan is a contemporary American poet. This poem was published in 1988.

Discussion

Talk about how you think parents feel as they watch their children grow up. Make a list of their feelings, and give an example of when they might feel this way.

How they feel	When
proud	When children graduate from school
worried	

Focus for the First Reading

Read these questions before you read the selection. You should be able to answer them after you finish the first reading.

1. Who are the people in this poem?

2. What are they doing?

To a Daughter Leaving Home

by Linda Pastan

1 When I taught you
at eight to ride
a bicycle, loping[1] along
beside you
5 as you wobbled[2] away
on two round wheels,
my own mouth rounding
in surprise when you pulled
ahead down the curved
10 path of the park,
I kept waiting
for the thud
of your crash as I
sprinted[3] to catch up,

[1] **loping**   moving easily and quickly with long steps (usually used to describe animals)

[2] **wobbled**   moved in an unbalanced way from side to side

[3] **sprinted**   ran very fast

15 while you grew
   smaller, more breakable
   with distance,
   pumping, pumping[4]
   for your life, screaming
20 with laughter,
   the hair flapping
   behind you like a
   handkerchief waving
   goodbye.

[4] **pumping**   moving the legs rapidly up and down

Comprehension Check

A. First Reading

Answer the questions. Be prepared to show evidence in the selection that supports your answers.

1. How old was the daughter when this incident happened?
2. What were the daughter and parent doing?

B. Second Reading

Read the poem again. Then answer the questions. Be prepared to show evidence in the selection that supports your answers.

1. Why was the parent surprised by the daughter? What did the parent expect?
2. How does the parent feel?
3. How do you know the parent couldn't catch up?
4. How did the daughter feel? How do you know she felt that way?
5. How did the daughter look to the parent?
6. Draw a picture of the scene described in this poem.

Sharing Your Thoughts

1. Reread the title of the poem. Is the poem only about teaching a child to ride a bike? How might leaving home and learning to ride a bicycle be related in the poet's mind?
2. What does this poem suggest parents must do to help their children grow up? Is this easy or hard for parents to do? Explain.

3. Do you think the parent in this poem is the mother or the father? Explain.

4. Would most parents have the same feelings about a boy in a similar situation? Why or why not?

 Writing Task

1. Imagine what happens immediately after the scene described in the poem. Write a short conversation between the parent and daughter. Have each person speak at least three times.

2. Learning to ride a bicycle is a step toward independence. What do you remember as an important step toward independence in your life? Perhaps you have a clear memory of getting your driver's license, getting your first job, taking a trip for the first time without your parents. Write about the experience. Use these questions as a guide.

> How old were you?
> What did you do?
> Who else was there, if anyone?
> How did you feel? How did your parents feel?
> What was the importance of this event to you?

A Final Look

Discussion

1. Work with a classmate, in a small group, or as a whole class. Drawing on all five selections in this unit, discuss the focus questions on page 1.

2. Reread the quote on page 1 and put it in your own words. M. Scott Peck is a doctor and writer. In what ways could he still be growing? In what ways could the parents in this unit still be learning things and growing?

3. Think about the parents in this unit. What kinds of support did they give their children? What kinds of pressure did they put on them? Discuss the kinds of support and pressure you think might be helpful to children. What kinds of support and pressure might not be helpful?

4. Which of the people in these selections—either child or parent—did you identify with most? In what way or ways do you share their feelings or ideas?

5. Share stories of things that happened to you while you were growing up. They may be important or unimportant, serious or funny, but they taught you something. Tell your story and explain what it taught you.

Unit Project

Step 1 *Working with classmates, write several questions about growing up to ask someone who is forty years old or older.*

Step 2 *Interview two or three adults, using the questions you wrote. Report back to your classmates any interesting things said by the people you interviewed.*

Step 3 *Write about your interviews. Use these questions as a guide. The number of questions you choose to answer and the amount of information you give will determine the number of paragraphs you write.*

Who did you talk with? Where and when did they grow up?

Did the people you talked to say the same or different things about growing up?

What one comment do you remember more than all the others? Why?

Did you have fun talking to these people? Did they seem to have fun talking to you? Describe the interview.

UNIT 2 — *Looking for Love*

> *Though pop singers may croon "I love you," lasting relationships depend more on "I like you."*
>
> —Catherine Houck
> *What Makes a Marriage Last*

FOCUS

➤ How do people meet marriage partners?

➤ When is the best age to marry? Why?

➤ What are important characteristics in a partner?

➤ What contributes to a successful relationship?

Selection One

Before Reading

Richard Feynman won the Nobel Prize for Physics in 1965. He also served on the presidential commission to investigate the accident that destroyed the space shuttle *Challenger* on January 28, 1986. This selection comes from his autobiographical book *What Do You Care What Other People Think?*

Discussion

Discuss with your classmates what you know about dating in the United States and in other countries where dating is a custom.
How do people meet? At what age do they start dating? Where do they go on dates?

Previewing

In Unit One you previewed selections by reading and thinking about the title and headings and by reading the first sentence of paragraphs. Previewing can also include reading the first one or two paragraphs of a selection, and sometimes also the last paragraph or two.

Read the first two paragraphs of this selection. What do you think the rest of the reading will be about?

Focus for the First Reading

Read this question before you read the selection. You should be able to answer it after you finish the first reading.

How did Feynman feel about his first date when he was a young teenager?

Untitled

by Richard Feynman

1   When I was a young fella,[1] about thirteen, I had somehow gotten in with a group of guys who were a little older than I was, and more sophisticated. They knew a lot of different girls, and would go out with them—often to the beach.

2   One time when we were at the beach, most of the guys had gone out on some jetty with the girls. I was interested in a particular girl a little bit, and sort of thought out loud: "Gee, I think I'd like to take Barbara to the movies. . ."

3   That's all I had to say, and the guy next to me gets all excited. He runs out onto the rocks and finds her. He pushes her back, all the while saying in a loud voice, "Feynman has something he wants to say to you, Barbara!" It was most embarrassing.

[1] **fella**   informal pronunciation of *fellow* (male)

4   Pretty soon the guys are all standing around me, saying, "Well, *say* it, Feynman!" So I invited her to the movies. It was my first date.

5   I went home and told my mother about it. She gave me all kinds of advice on how to do this and that. For example, if we take the bus, I'm supposed to get off the bus first, and offer Barbara my hand. Or if we have to walk in the street, I'm supposed to walk on the outside.[2] She even told me what kinds of things to say. She was handing down a cultural tradition to me: the women teach their sons how to treat the next generation of women well.

6   After dinner, I get all slicked up[3] and go to Barbara's house to call for her. I'm nervous. She isn't ready, of course (it's always like that) so her family has me wait for her in the dining room, where they're eating with friends—a lot of people. They say things like, "Isn't he cute!" and all kinds of other stuff. I didn't feel cute. It was absolutely terrible!

7   I remember everything about the date. As we walked from her house to the new, little theater in town, we talked about playing the piano. I told her how, when I was younger, they made me learn piano for a while, but after six months I was still playing "Dance of the Daisies," and couldn't stand it anymore. You see, I was worried about being a sissy,[4] and to be stuck for weeks playing "Dance of the Daisies" was too much for me, so I quit. I was so sensitive about being a sissy that it even bothered me when my mother sent me to the market to buy some snacks called Peppermint Patties and Toasted Dainties.

8   We saw the movie, and I walked her back to her home. I complimented her on the nice, pretty gloves she was wearing. Then I said goodnight to her on the doorstep.

9   Barbara says to me, "Thank you for a very lovely evening."[5]

10   "You're welcome!" I answered. I felt terrific.

11   The next time I went out on a date—it was with a different girl—I say goodnight to her, and she says, "Thank you for a very lovely evening."

12   I didn't feel quite so terrific.

13   When I said goodnight to the third girl I took out, she's got her mouth open, ready to speak, and I say, "Thank you for a very lovely evening!"

14   She says, "Thank you—uh—Oh!—Yes—uh, I had a lovely evening, too, thank you!"

[2] **on the outside**   nearer to the traffic

[3] **get all slicked up**   take special care in getting dressed up

[4] **sissy**   a boy who looks or acts like a girl

[5] **Thank you for a very lovely evening** when Feynman was young, girls usually used this polite phrase at the end of a date; sometimes it indicated that they weren't interested in going out with the boy again

Comprehension Check

A. First Reading

*Mark the statements **T** (true) or **F** (false). Be prepared to show evidence in the selection that supports your answers.*

1. T F Feynman felt good when his friends forced him to invite Barbara to the movies.

2. T F He felt uncomfortable while he was waiting for Barbara at her house.

3. T F He enjoyed his first date.

B. Second Reading

*Read the selection again. Then mark the statements **T** (true) or **F** (false). Be prepared to show evidence in the selection that supports your answers.*

1. T F Feynman's friends were boys who were the same age he was.

2. T F Feynman wasn't interested in asking Barbara out on a date.

3. T F His mother told him the correct things to do on a date.

4. T F Feynman worried that people might think he was a sissy.

5. T F Feynman felt good when Barbara thanked him for the evening.

Vocabulary

A. Vocabulary Building

Three of the words in each row are similar in meaning, at least for this context. Each of them could complete the sentence without changing its original meaning. Circle the three words that are similar. Use a dictionary if necessary.

1. When I was . . . about thirteen, I had somehow gotten in with a group of _____ who were a little older than I was . . . (¶ 1)

   a. guys

   b. fellas

   c. girlfriends

   d. boys

2. It was most _____ (when they forced Feynman to invite Barbara to the movies). (¶ 3)

   a. humiliating

   b. uncomfortable

   c. embarrassing

   d. interesting

3. My mother gave me all kinds of _____ on how to do this and that. (¶ 5)

   a. advice

   b. correction

   c. suggestions

   d. recommendations

4. . . . if we have to walk in the street, I'm _____ walk on the outside. (¶ 5)

   a. expected to

   b. supposed to

   c. asked to

   d. required to

5. (Barbara's parents and their friends) say things like, "Isn't he _____ !" (¶ 6)

   a. ugly

   b. nice-looking

   c. cute

   d. attractive

6. . . . after six months I was still playing "Dance of the Daisies," and _____ it . . . (¶ 7)

   a. hated

   b. liked

   c. couldn't stand

   d. couldn't tolerate

7. . . . to be stuck for weeks playing "Dance of the Daisies" was too much for me, so I _____. (¶ 7)

   a. continued

   b. quit

   c. stopped

   d. gave up

8. I was so _____ about being a sissy that it even bothered me when my mother sent me to the market to buy . . . Peppermint Patties and Toasted Dainties. (¶ 7)

   a. easily embarrassed

   b. strong

   c. sensitive

   d. worried

B. Vocabulary Building

Look at the underlined words or expressions in the sentences below. Find them in the selection. Then choose the correct meaning for the context. List words from the selection or ideas from the context that helped you understand the meaning. The first two have been done as examples.

1. When I was a young fella, about thirteen, I had somehow gotten in with a group of guys who were a little older than I was, and more <u>sophisticated</u>. They knew a lot of different girls, and would go out with them—often to the beach. (¶ 1)

   a. well dressed

   ⓑ experienced in social life

   c. athletic

   Context that helps: *were a little older; knew a lot of different girls, and would go out with them*

2. She was <u>handing down</u> a cultural tradition to me . . . (¶ 5)

   a. pushing

   b. taking

   ⓒ passing on/giving

   Context that helps: *the general situation that this is coming from a mother to a son*

3. After dinner, I . . . go to Barbara's house to <u>call for her</u>. (¶ 6)

   a. call her on the telephone

   b. go to her house to get her

   c. ask her questions

   Context that helps: _____

4. . . . to be <u>stuck</u> for weeks playing "Dance of the Daisies" was too much for me . . . (¶ 7)

   a. not making progress

   b. enjoying

   c. not practicing

   Context that helps: _____

5. I <u>complimented</u> her on the nice, pretty gloves she was wearing. (¶ 8)

   a. said something nice to her

   b. said something mean or cruel to her

   c. made conversation with her

   Context that helps: _____

C. Vocabulary Review

Complete the following statements about the reading selection with the correct word or expression from the list below. Use each word or expression only once.

advice	**cute**	**guys**	**supposed to**
called for	**embarrassing**	**sensitive**	

1. Some of the other _____ forced Feynman to invite
   Barbara to the movies. It was an _____ situation for him.

2. His mother helped him by giving him _____ about things
   boys are _____ do on a date.

3. When he _____ Barbara at her house, she wasn't ready.

4. He didn't like it when her parents and their friends said he was
   _____ because he thought that was not masculine, and he
   was very _____ about being a sissy.

Sharing Your Thoughts

1. This selection doesn't have a title. What title would you give it? Why?

2. Why do you think Feynman "didn't feel quite so terrific" when the second girl he took out said, "Thank you for a very lovely evening"? What happened at the end of the third date? Was dating getting easier or harder for him?

3. This selection gives us ideas about dating customs in the 1940s when Feynman was growing up. Work with a classmate or a small group, and complete the two lists. Is dating the same or different today? Explain.

THINGS BOYS WERE SUPPOSED TO DO	THINGS GIRLS WERE SUPPOSED TO DO
a. ask girls out	**a.** not be ready when the boy arrives
b.	**b.**
c.	**c.**
d.	**d.**

4. Below is a list of types of dates. Add any others you know of from personal experience or knowledge about other cultures. Discuss the advantages and disadvantages of each with your classmates. If dating is a custom in your culture, which of the types of dates are most common?

   a. single dating (the couple goes out alone)

   b. double dating (two couples go out together)

   c. blind dates (the two people don't know each other; a mutual friend arranges the date)

   d. going out in groups

   e. going out with a chaperone (another person, usually older, accompanies the couple and watches their behavior)

   f. _____

5. In some cultures dating is not a custom. Share what you know about how marriage partners are chosen in different cultures.

 **Text Analysis**

Using Present Tense in Narratives

Writers sometimes use a **present tense** (simple present or present continuous) to tell about past events because it makes the events come to life. In paragraphs 3 and 4, for example, Feynman tells about being forced to ask Barbara out when he was thirteen years old:

- . . . the guy next to me gets all excited. (simple present)
- Pretty soon the guys are all standing around me . . . (present continuous)

Find three more examples of this use of the present or present continuous in Feynman's writing.

   a. _____

   b. _____

   c. _____

Writing Task

1. Choose *a*, *b*, or *c*, and write a paragraph to answer the question.

   a. What do you like or what don't you like about American dating customs?

   b. What are dating customs in your country?

   c. If dating is not a custom in your country, how are marriage partners chosen?

2. Write about a person you have seen and find attractive but have not spoken to, at least not much. Use these questions as a guide.

   Where did you first see this person?

   What attracted you to him or her?

   What does he/she look like?

   How do you hope this relationship will develop?

Selection Two

Before Reading

This selection is an adaptation of a research report that appeared in the magazine *USA Today*.

Discussion

Talk with your classmates about the title of this article. It includes the expression "love conquers all," which means that love can solve all problems. Do you think love can solve all problems? Explain.

Previewing

From the title alone, what do you think the researchers studied? Now read the first paragraph. Answer these questions.

1. Who were the participants in the study?

2. What did they believe?

Focus for the First Reading

Read these questions before you read the selection. You should be able to answer them after you finish the first reading.

1. Do the researchers also believe "love conquers all"?

2. Do the researchers believe that it is good when young people are very optimistic about their relationships and about marriage?

Students Think Love Conquers All

USA Today Staff

1   When it comes to relationships, the honeymoon[1] never ends, at least not in the minds of college students who were part of a study to measure what they expected from their relationships. The researchers found that students believed their relationships would keep getting better and better over time.

2   "These kinds of expectations are like something you would find in a 1950s Doris Day–Rock Hudson[2] movie. But they are contrary to what research suggests about marital satisfaction,[3]" according to Andrew I. Schwebel, professor of psychology, Ohio State University. He says that such optimistic expectations can result in marital dissatisfaction later in life.

3   "Someone might think, for instance, 'Well, I'm not really happy with my partner right now, but since things are going to get better, I'll go ahead and marry him or her.'"

---

[1] **honeymoon**   trip a couple takes after the wedding; also refers to happiness in the first months of marriage
[2] **Doris Day and Rock Hudson**   American actress and actor who appeared together in a number of romantic films in the 1950s
[3] **marital satisfaction**   happiness in marriage

4   Schwebel and his student Bryce Sullivan studied 238 students ranging in age from 18 to 34. All were single, although more than a quarter were dating only one person and had discussed marriage with their partner.

5   Each student was asked to complete two questionnaires. One measured their beliefs about dysfunctional relationships;[4] the other asked for their expectations for four different stages of a relationship: casual[5] dating, engagement,[6] five years of marriage, and fifteen years of marriage. The students also were asked what they thought the average[7] American's relationship would be like at these same stages.

6   Based on their answers, researchers could see that students felt their own relationships would be much better in the future than those of other couples. In some ways, Schwebel says, such beliefs can be helpful. "We want people to have positive expectations because this leads them to try harder. On the other hand,[8] there's probably some cutoff point where their expectations are unrealistically[9] high."

7   "For example," Sullivan suggests, "people who think they are never going to have any trouble in their marriage may be setting themselves up for disappointment.[10] It would be much better if they realized[11] that marriage can be tough, and they're going to have to work pretty hard to make it succeed."

---

[4] **dysfunctional relationships**   relationships that do not work
[5] **casual**   informal; not serious
[6] **engagement**   period between deciding to marry and actually getting married
[7] **average**   typical

[8] **on the other hand**   this expression indicates that an opposing idea comes next
[9] **unrealistically**   impossibly (what they expect will probably not happen)
[10] **setting themselves up for disappointment**   asking for disappointment later (their marriage probably won't be as good as they expect)
[11] **realized**   understood

Comprehension Check

A. First Reading

*Mark the statements **T** (true) or **F** (false). Be prepared to show evidence in the selection that supports your answers.*

1.   T   F   The researchers agree that "love conquers all."

2.   T   F   The researchers believe that expecting too much from a relationship can result in disappointment.

B. Second Reading

Read the selection again. Then answer the questions. Be prepared to find evidence in the selection that supports your answers.

1.   Who did the study?

2.   Where do you think the study was done?

3.   How many people participated in the study?

4.   How old were the participants? Were they married or single?

5. What did the researchers ask the students to respond to?

   a. a questionnaire about _____

   b. a questionnaire about their expectations for their relationships at four stages:

      1. _____

      2. _____

      3. _____

      4. _____

   c. They also asked the students what they thought _____
_____ would be like at these same stages.

6. The students believe that their own relationships will

   a. get better

   b. get worse

7. The students believe that the average person's relationship is

   a. better than their own

   b. not as good as their own

8. Which statement would Professor Schwebel agree with?

   a. When people think a bad relationship is going to get better, it usually will get better.

   b. People should expect their partners to change, because they probably will.

   c. High expectations are good for a relationship up to a point.

9. Which statement would Sullivan agree with?

   a. If you have high expectations for your marriage, it will succeed.

   b. Marriage is difficult, and it takes work to make it succeed.

   c. Marriage partners usually learn to handle their problems.

 **Vocabulary**

 A. Vocabulary Building

Look at the underlined words or expressions in the sentences below. Find them in the selection. Then choose the correct meaning for the context.

   1. . . . the honeymoon never ends, at least not in the minds of college students who were part of a study to measure what they <u>expected</u> from their relationships. (¶ 1)

      a. thought was going to happen

      b. were sure was going to happen

2. . . . students believed their relationships would <u>keep</u> getting better and better over time. (¶ 1)

   a. stop

   b. continue

3. But they (these kinds of expectations) are <u>contrary</u> to what research suggests . . . (¶ 2)

   a. similar

   b. opposite

4. . . . such <u>optimistic</u> expectations can result in marital dissatisfaction later in life. (¶ 2)

   a. positive

   b. negative

5. "Someone might think, <u>for instance</u>, 'Well I'm not really happy with my partner . . .'" (¶ 3)

   a. for example

   b. right away

6. All were <u>single</u> . . . (¶ 4)

   a. not twins

   b. not married

7. One measured their <u>beliefs</u> about dysfunctional relationships . . . (¶ 5)

   a. opinions

   b. hopes

8. "We want people to have positive expectations because this <u>leads</u> them to try harder." (¶ 6)

   a. causes

   b. forces

9. "It would be much better if they realized that marriage can be <u>tough</u> . . ." (¶ 7)

   a. fun

   b. difficult

10. ". . . they're going to have to work pretty hard to make it <u>succeed</u>." (¶ 7)

    a. happen

    b. work well

B. Word Analysis

Parts of Speech

There are four major parts of speech: *nouns, verbs, adjectives*, and *adverbs*.

Nouns give the name of a person, place, thing, or abstract concept; they answer the questions *Who?* or *What?*

Verbs refer to an action (*run*), mental activity (*think*), or state of being (*be, have*).

Adjectives add information about a noun, that is, they modify nouns; they answer the questions *Which?* or *What kind of?*

Adverbs add information about a verb; they answer the questions *Where? When? How?* or *How often?*

Suffixes Indicating Parts of Speech

Word endings, called **suffixes**, often help us determine the part of speech of a word. See the italicized parts of the words in the chart below. Note that if a box is blank, either there is no word to fill it or the word is missing because it is not one you need to worry about now.

Nouns	Verbs	Adjectives	Adverbs
belief	believe	believ*able*	believab*ly*
expecta*tion*	expect		
optim*ism*		optimis*tic*	optimistic*ally*
optim*ist*			
discuss*ion*	discuss		
marriage	marry	marri*ed*	
	get married		
		unrealis*tic*	unrealistic*ally*
disappoint*ment*	disappoint	disappoint*ed*	
success	succeed	success*ful*	successful*ly*

Using the sets of related words from the chart above, choose the word that correctly completes these sentences.

1. If you _____ (belief/believe) things will turn out well, you are an

    _____ (optimism/optimistic) person.

2. Students are optimistic. They _____ (expect/expectation) their

    relationships to keep getting better.

3. We all hope that our _____ (married/marriage) will be happy; in other words, we hope it will be a _____ (success/succeed).

4. Unfortunately some people will be _____ (disappoint/disappointed) because not all marriages are _____ (success/successful).

5. Some people have _____ (unrealistic/unrealistically) expectations, and they may be setting themselves up for _____ (disappoint/ disappointment) later on.

C. Vocabulary Review

Complete the following statements about the reading selection with the correct word or expression from the list below. Use each word or expression only once.

average	**disappointment**	**optimistic**	**succeed**
believe	**honeymoon**	**realize**	**tough**

1. The researchers found that the college students they studied are unrealistically _____ about their relationships.

2. The students _____ that their relationships will keep getting better, and the _____ will never end.

3. They have higher expectations for themselves than for the _____ American couple.

4. Their positive attitude can be good, up to a point, but it can set them up for _____ later in life.

5. Couples should _____ that marriage can be _____ and that spouses have to work hard to make the relationship _____.

Sharing Your Thoughts

1. Why do you think people expect their own relationships to be better than other people's relationships?

2. In a small group, discuss what you consider important in a partner. Begin by deciding the importance of the items in the chart on page 50. Add other items you can think of.

Partner	Very Important	Important	Not Very Important	Not Important at All
is good-looking				
is rich				
is hard-working				
is sociable				
is intelligent				
has the same ethnic or religious background				
has similar political beliefs				
has a sense of humor				
(other)				

3. Suppose your partner has different ideas from you in areas such as the following:

     how to spend money

     attitude toward working

     how many children to have

     how clean the house should be

     ways to spend leisure time

     (other areas you may think of) _____

Is it reasonable to expect your partner to change in any of these areas? If so, which ones? Give your reasons.

 Text Analysis

Making Connections

In clear writing, ideas are connected to each other. Understanding the connections in writing will help you understand the writer's ideas. Using words that refer to something else in the text is one way to make connections.

Show what the underlined words connect to by answering the question below each item. Refer to the paragraph for the context. The first one has been done for you.

1. "<u>These kinds of expectations</u>" (¶ 2)

   What expectations are the authors referring to?

   They are referring to the students' expectations that their relationships would keep getting better and better (See the end of ¶ 1)

2. But <u>they</u> are contrary to what research suggests . . . (¶ 2)

   What does *they* refer to?

   _____

   _____

3. <u>All</u> were single . . . (¶ 4)

   Who does *all* refer to?

   _____

   _____

4. <u>One</u> measured their beliefs about dysfunctional relationships; <u>the other</u> asked for their expectations for four different stages of a relationship . . . (¶ 5)

   What does *one* refer to? *One* what?

   _____

   _____

   What does *the other* refer to? *The other* what?

   _____

   _____

5. . . . students felt their own relationships would be much better in the future than <u>those</u> of other couples. (¶ 6)

   What does *those* refer to?

   _____

   _____

6. In some ways, Schwebel says, <u>such beliefs</u> can be helpful. (¶ 6)

   What does *such beliefs* refer to?

   _____

   _____

7. <u>It would be much better</u> if they realized that marriage can be tough . . . (¶ 7)

   It would be much better to do what?

   _____

   _____

Writing Task

1. In Sharing Your Thoughts on pages 49–50 you talked about the things you consider important in a partner. Write a paragraph about three things you think are important in choosing a partner.

   Start with a sentence like the one below and use words like *first, second,* and *finally* that help the reader follow your thoughts:

   There are at least three things that I think are important characteristics a partner should have. First, . . .

2. Study the data in the table below. Then answer the questions about the number of marriages and divorces.

Marriages and Divorces in the United States: 1970–1995

Year	Number of Marriages	Number of Divorces and Annulments[1]
1970	2,159,000	708,000
1980	2,390,000	1,189,000
1985	2,413,000	1,190,000
1990	2,443,000	1,182,000
1995	2,336,000	1,169,000

[1] an official statement that there was no marriage

SOURCE: U.S. Bureau of the Census, *Statistical Abstract of the United States, 1997* (117th edition), Washington, D.C., 1997.

   a. Has the number of marriages in the United States been increasing constantly?

   b. What happened to the marriage rate between 1990 and 1995?

   c. Has the number of divorces and annulments in the United States been increasing constantly?

   d. What happened to the number of divorces and annulments between 1985 and 1990?

Write a paragraph. Use the statements below and information in the table to support the information in your paragraph.

   Like the students in "Students Think Love Conquers All," a lot of people in the United States believe in marriage. (Support with numbers.)
   However, not all marriages in the United States are successful. (Support with numbers.)
   In conclusion, . . . (Conclude your paragraph with a comment relating the statistics in the table and the attitude of the students described in the selection.)

Selection Three

Before Reading

In this selection, which is an adaptation of Cheryl Lavin's column in the *Chicago Tribune*, "Tales from the Front," you will read about real-life experiences of people who married young.

Discussion

Talk with your classmates about what you think is the ideal age to get married, and explain why.

Previewing

Read the first paragraph and skim the rest of the selection.

1. This selection is about

    a. romantic stories of people who lived happily ever after

    b. the advantages and disadvantages of getting married young

2. The selection includes

    a. examples of six individuals who tell their own stories

    b. the author's comments about six different marriages

Focus for the First Reading

When you read this selection for the first time, you should be able to categorize the six individuals into two groups: the people who were happy that they got married young, and the people who were not happy that they got married young

Getting Married Young

by **Cheryl Lavin,** *Chicago Tribune*

1   Some people discover that getting married when they are young and "in love" does not always turn out happily. Others, however, say that getting married young gives them more good years together and they have no regrets. If you ask people to talk about their experiences marrying young, here are some of the things you will hear.

2   *Charles:* "The best decision I ever made was marrying Helen when we were only 19. Would I have been better off financially[1] if I'd waited till 25? Probably, but we were in love. Because we married so young, my wife lived to see all four of our children finish college and her first grandchild. She left us with millions of wonderful memories. She has been gone five years, and I've never regretted a day of the 38 years we had together. If we'd waited till we were 25, I would only have had 32 years with her."

3   *Carol:* "In 1970, at the age of 18, I got married. He was 19. I had graduated from high school, and we both had fairly good

---

[1] **financially**   in terms of money

jobs. It was the era of Woodstock, Vietnam and women's lib.[2] I was very happy that the Homecoming King[3] chose me and glad that I didn't have to think about choices like college, career and independence anymore.

4   "On the day of my large, expensive wedding, I clearly remember feeling scared enough to question my coming marriage. I realize now that I wasn't in love with my fiancé;[4] I was in love with love. I was much too young and immature to make a life commitment.[5]

5   "Seven years and two children later, I wanted more, and my husband was satisfied. I wanted college, freedom, no more children. He was hurt and unhappy.

6   "We got divorced, and I raised my children alone. His anger turned him against his sons for nearly 15 years. We all got through this difficult time thanks to help from my parents and brothers and sisters."

7   *Alicia:* "This year my husband and I will celebrate our eighth wedding anniversary. We met in college and dated nearly four years before we got married. I was 23, Bill was 24. Like many career-minded women in the '80s, I never thought I'd marry young. I had a life plan, which included establishing a career, finding a husband before 30 and then starting a family. Well, I met Bill and my plans went out the window. Do I regret it? Absolutely not. The best part about having found Bill so early is that I've always had someone to share in my successes and support me when things don't go quite as planned."

8   *Lisa:* "My husband and I got married when I was 22 and he was 24. I was a senior in college, and he had just graduated. He took a less-than-ideal job because he was tired of looking.

9   "After the excitement was gone, we argued about bills, the dishes, who forgot to put gas in the car and even whose responsibility it was to get the mail.

10   "After five years of trying to make it work, we talked about divorce. But court costs are $500 and lawyers want another $500 just to file the papers. Then I was told that this process[6] could take six months.

11   "Getting into a marriage should be as hard as getting out. Then silly young people who feel lovey-dovey won't make a quick decision that will affect them the rest of their lives. Before 25, you don't even know who you are much less can you promise yourself to someone till 'death do you part.'[7] I have changed, and so has my husband. We don't like the new person either has become."

12   *Sarah:* "I married my high school sweetheart when I was 19. I'm now 23 and have a 2-year-old boy. Even though I love my husband and child, I wish I had waited. I thought I was so grown up and knew everything there was to know, but now I realize that even now, I know just a fraction about life and what it's about.

13   "I recommend that anyone who is thinking of getting married at a young age should wait. If it's right, it will happen. Why rush life, marriage and parenting? Take this time to be nice to yourself. Believe me, I wish I had taken my own advice."

14   *Robert:* "We were 23 when we got married, and we'll celebrate 15 years in November. I work with a lot of singles, and all I hear about from the women are the slimy[8] guys they run into in bars. From the guys, all I hear about are the psycho[9] women they've dated. AIDS testing? My wife and I have been monogamous[10] since 1978. She is my love, my best friend and the mother of my children. I have what so many of my friends are searching for."

---

[2] **era of Woodstock, Vietnam and women's lib**   late 1960s and 1970s—known today for a rock concert at Woodstock, New York; the Vietnam War, disliked by many Americans; and the women's liberation movement

[3] **Homecoming King**   the most important male student at a celebration in honor of past students (graduates)

[4] **fiancé**   person to whom one is engaged to marry

[5] **commitment**   a promise to be loyal to someone or something

[6] **process**   series of steps; things one has to do to get a divorce

[7] **'death do you part'**   death separates you (words from traditional western marriage ceremony)

[8] **slimy**   unpleasant; repulsive; disgusting; bad

[9] **psycho**   crazy (short for *psychotic*)

[10] **monogamous**   having only one sexual partner

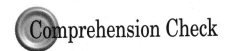

Comprehension Check

A. First Reading

Write the names of the people you read about on the appropriate line.

People who were happy that they married young:

_____

People who regretted that they married young:

_____

B. Second Reading

1 *Read the selection again. Then mark the statements **T** (true) or **F** (false). Be prepared to show evidence in the selection that supports your answers.*

1. T   F   Charles and Helen waited until they were twenty-five to get married.

2. T   F   When Carol and her husband got divorced, they both continued to have a good relationship with their children.

3. T   F   Alicia thinks that age twenty-three is a young age to marry.

4. T   F   Alicia followed her life plan.

5. T   F   Lisa and her husband are divorced.

6. T   F   Sarah believes that people still have a lot to learn at age twenty-three.

7. T   F   Robert misses the life of the single man.

2 *Find two more advantages and disadvantages of getting married young that are mentioned in this selection and add them in the chart below.*

Advantages	Disadvantages
1. have someone for support when things go wrong: Alicia	1. later may want more from life than husband or wife, for example, going to college: Carol
2.	2.
3.	3.

 Vocabulary

 A. Vocabulary Building

Look at the underlined words or expressions in the sentences below. Find them in the selection. Then choose the correct meaning for the context.

1. Some people discover that getting married when they are young and "in love" does not always <u>turn out</u> happily. (¶ 1)
   a. end
   b. start out

2. Others . . . <u>have no regrets</u>. (¶ 1)
   a. are not rich
   b. are not sorry

3. Would I have been <u>better off</u> financially if I'd waited til 25? (¶ 2)
   a. in need
   b. in better condition

4. She left us with millions of <u>wonderful</u> memories. (¶ 2)
   a. mysterious
   b. very good

5. On the day of my large, expensive wedding, I clearly remember feeling <u>scared</u> enough to question my coming marriage. (¶ 4)
   a. afraid
   b. sad

6. I was much too young and <u>immature</u> to make a life commitment. (¶ 4)
   a. like a child
   b. like an adult

7. . . . I wanted more, and my husband was <u>satisfied</u>. (¶ 5)
   a. lazy (about working harder on the marriage)
   b. happy (with the marriage as it was)

8. . . . I've always had someone to share in <u>my successes</u> . . . (¶ 7)
   a. good things that happened to me
   b. bad things that happened to me

9. He took a <u>less-than-ideal job</u> because he was tired of looking. (¶ 8)
   a. a job that was not perfect
   b. a job that was easy

10. . . . we <u>argued</u> about bills . . . (¶ 9)
    a. forgot
    b. fought

11. I married my high school <u>sweetheart</u> when I was 19. (¶ 12)
    a. boyfriend (or girlfriend)
    b. best friend

B. Using a Dictionary

Sometimes the same word, without any change in form (such as the addition of a suffix), can be more than one part of speech. Therefore, to locate the correct dictionary entry, you have to know how the word is used in the sentence. Is it a noun, verb, adjective, or adverb? Once you identify the part of speech, read all the dictionary entries for that part of speech until you find the one that makes sense for the context. Many times the first definition will work, but sometimes you need to read several definitions before you find the correct one.

When you are looking up a phrasal verb, marked *phr v* (a verb with two or three words—for example, *get into*), you need to look under the entry for the main verb (*get*). Even though phrasal verbs contain two or three words, you should think of them as one vocabulary item.

Find the dictionary entry and the correct definition for the underlined words. The first one has been partly done as an example.

1. ... I clearly remember feeling scared enough to <u>question</u> my coming marriage. (¶ 4)

    Question can be a noun or a verb.

    Which is it in this sentence? N _____ V _____

    Which definition fits this sentence? Definition #_____

ques·tion[1] /ˈkwɛstʃən, ˈkwɛʃtʃən/ *n* **1** a type of phrase used in order to ask for information: *I have a **question about** the math homework.*|*Do you mind if I ask you a personal question?* **2** a subject that needs to be discussed or a problem that needs to be solved; ISSUE: *The question is whether more troops should be sent.*|*a debate on **the question of** tax cuts* **3** a feeling of doubt about something: *The recent fighting has **called into question** (=made people have doubts about) the government's power to keep the peace.* **4 without question a)** definitely: *Their weapons technology is without question a threat to us.* **b)** without complaining or asking why: *They accepted our demands without question.* **5 in question** the person or thing that is in question is the one that is being discussed: *The document in question is a report dated June 18, 1948.* **6 be out of the question** used in order to emphasize that what someone wants to do is not possible or not allowed: *A career in basketball is out of the question, unless he works harder at it.* **7 (that's a) good question!** SPOKEN said when you are admitting you do not know the answer to a question: *"If we don't have enough people to help, how can we finish the job?" "Good question!"*

question[2] *v* [T] **1** to ask someone questions, especially about a crime: *Police are questioning three men about the murder.* **2** to stop trusting someone or start to have doubts about something: *Are you questioning my honesty?* —see usage note at ASK

2. . . . I've always had someone to . . . <u>support</u> me when things don't go quite as planned. (¶ 7)

N_____ V_____ Definition # _____

> **sup·port**[1] /səˈpɔrt/ *v* [T] **1** to say that you agree with an idea, group, person etc. and want him, her, or it to succeed: *The union will support workers' demands for a pay raise.* **2** to hold the weight of something in order to prevent it from falling: *an arch supported by two columns* **3** to help and encourage someone: *I appreciate your supporting me during my divorce.* **4** to provide enough money for someone to live: *How can Brad support a family on his salary?* **5** to get money in order to pay for a bad habit: *He's started stealing to support his drug habit.* **6** to prove that something is true: *There is now enough data to support the theory.*
> **support**[2] *n* **1** [U] the things people do to help an idea, plan, group etc. succeed, or the act of encouraging it: *The proposal has won the support of local businesses.* **2** [U] help and encouragement that you give someone: *My parents have **given** me a lot of **support**.* **3** [C,U] an object that holds up something else: *supports for the roof*

3. Getting into a marriage should be as hard as <u>getting out</u>. (¶ 11)

Definition # _____

> **get out** *phr v* **1** [I] to escape from a place: *How did the dog **get out of** the yard?* **2** [T **get sth ↔ out**] to produce or publish something: *We have to **get** the book **out** next month.*

4. Why <u>rush</u> life, marriage and parenting? (¶ 13)

N _____ V _____ Definition # _____

> **rush**[1] /rʌʃ/ *v* **1** [I,T] to move or do something very quickly: *It's an important decision; don't rush it.* | *There's no need to rush - we have plenty of time.* | *Everyone was **rushing to** catch the last bus.* **2** [T] to take or send something somewhere very quickly: *We had to **rush** Helen **to** the hospital.* **3** [T] to try to make someone do something quickly: *Don't rush me - let me think.*
> **rush around** *phr v* [I] to try to do a lot of things quickly in a short period of time
> **rush into** sth *phr v* [T] to get involved in something quickly without thinking carefully about it: *My mother's worried that I'm **rushing into** getting married.*
> **rush** sth ↔ **through** *phr v* [T] to get something such as a new law approved more quickly than usual
> **rush**[2] *n* **1** [singular] a sudden fast movement of things or people: *They all made a rush for the door.* **2** [singular, U] a situation in which you need to hurry, especially because a lot of people want to do or get something: *There's a big **rush to** get tickets.* **3** the rush the time when a place or group of people are very busy: *the Christmas rush for shoppers* **4** INFORMAL a strong, usually pleasant feeling that you get from taking a drug or from doing something exciting

C. Vocabulary Review

Complete the following statements about the reading selection with the correct word or expression from the list below. Use each word or expression only once.

better off	immature	satisfied	turn out
commitment	rush	support	wonderful

1. Most people are usually very optimistic about the idea of getting married; they expect everything will _____ well, and they think they are ready to make a long-term _____.

2. Some young people are too _____ for marriage and should wait. They shouldn't _____ into making such an important decision.

3. There are _____ things about marriage such as having someone to share good times with. Also, partners _____ each other in hard times.

4. Despite a high divorce rate, many people are really very _____ with married life and feel they are _____ married than single.

Sharing Your Thoughts

1. Lisa thinks that "getting into a marriage should be as hard as getting out." Do you agree with her? How hard or easy should it be to get married? How hard or easy should it be to get divorced?

2. What would Lisa think of the research findings described in Selection Two? What does she say that supports your answer?

3. In a small group, talk about marriages that you know of. How old were the couple when they got married? Are they still married? Why was their marriage successful or unsuccessful?

4. What, if anything, do you learn from this selection about how people and relationships change over time? Give specific reasons why some of these people are not as optimistic as the students described in Selection Two were.

5. Talk to five people who are not in your class. Ask them the following questions:

   Are you married? If not, have you ever been married?
   What do you think is the ideal age to marry? Why?

As a class, record the total number of people who chose each age group in the chart below.

Best Age to Marry	Respondents Who Have Been Married	Respondents Who Have Never Been Married	Total
Under 20			
20–24			
25–29			
30–34			
35–44			
Above 45			

Study your findings and answer these questions:

Which age group was chosen most often?

Do answers differ depending on whether the respondent has ever been married or not?

 Text Analysis

Evaluating Inferences

*Sometimes you can infer things about people even though they may not state things directly. Decide whether the statements below are reasonable (**R**) or unreasonable (**U**) inferences. Circle your choices. Give the evidence in the selection that supports your answers. The first one has been done as an example.*

1. **(R)** U   Money is not very important to Charles.

EVIDENCE: <u>Charles has no regrets that he got married when he was nineteen. He says he</u>
<u>probably would have been better off financially if he had waited. But he is not</u>
<u>sorry that he got married young and had less money, so money must not be</u>
<u>very important to him.</u>

2. R   U   Carol's husband probably does not think education is very important.

EVIDENCE: _____

_____

_____

3. R   U   Alicia probably puts her husband first and her career second.

EVIDENCE: _____

_____

_____

4. R   U   Lisa and her husband have probably made a lot of money.

EVIDENCE: _____

_____

_____

5. R   U   Robert would probably like to spend a lot of time in singles bars.

EVIDENCE: _____

_____

_____

Writing Task

1. Write a "Tale from the Front." Think of someone you know who got married young. Use these questions as a guide.

   How old were they when they got married?
   Were they happy that they got married young, or did they regret it? Explain.

2. Answer these questions with information from the table on page 62.

   At what ages did most women marry in 1980?
   Did the number of women marrying when they were under 20 years of age increase or decrease between 1980 and 1990?
   At what ages did most men marry in 1980?
   Did the number of men marrying before they were 30 years old increase or decrease between 1980 and 1990?
   Overall, has the age at first marriage increased or decreased between 1980 and 1990?

Write a paragraph about the ages at which men and women marry for the first time.

Percentage Distribution of First Marriages by Age and Sex, 1980–1990							
	Under Age 20	20–24	25–29	30–34	35–44	45–64	Over Age 65
Women							
1980	30.4	47.3	16.0	4.0	1.6	0.6	0.1
1990	16.6	40.8	27.2	10.1	4.5	0.7	0.1
Men							
1980	12.7	50.0	25.7	7.5	2.9	1.1	0.1
1990	6.6	36.0	34.3	14.8	7.1	1.1	0.1

SOURCE: U.S. Bureau of the Census, *Statistical Abstract of the United States, 1997* (117th edition), Washington, D.C., 1997.

Selection Four

Before Reading

Gary Soto, a poet and short story writer, grew up in Fresno, California. He teaches English and Chicano Studies at the University of California. "Finding a Wife" is from his collection, *Small Faces*.

Discussion

Talk with your classmates about how your parents and other married relatives met each other. If you are married, tell how you met your partner. As a class, make a list of the ways couples often meet.

Previewing

Read the title and the first three paragraphs of this story. Answer these questions.

1. The narrator, the person who is telling the story, is a . . .

    a. literature professor.

    b. student.

    c. marriage counselor.

2. He keeps thinking about the statement "It's easy to find a wife" because . . .

    a. he thinks he said something stupid.

    b. he might give others the wrong impression.

    c. what he said may sound strange, but perhaps it's true.

3. Beginning with paragraph 3, the story . . .

    a. continues in the same time frame.

    b. shifts to the future.

    c. shifts to the past.

Focus for the First Reading

Read these questions before you read the selection. You should be able to answer them after you finish the first reading.

1. How did the narrator find his wife?

2. Was it easy, as he said in the first sentence of the story, or did they have problems along the way?

Finding a Wife

by Gary Soto

1 It's easy to find a wife, I told my students. Pick anybody, I said, and they chuckled and fidgeted in their chairs. I laughed a delayed laugh, feeling hearty and foolish as a pup[1] among these young men who were in my house to talk poetry and books. We talked, occasionally making sense, and drank cup after cup of coffee until we were so wired we had to stand up and walk around the block to shake out our nerves.

2 When they left I tried to write a letter, grade papers, and finally nap on the couch. My mind kept turning to how simple it is to find a wife, that we can easily say after a brief two- or three-week courtship, "I want to marry you."

3 When I was twenty, in college and living on a street that was a row of broken apartment buildings, my brother and I returned to our apartment from a game of racquetball to sit in the living room and argue whether we should buy a quart of beer. We were college poor, living off the cheap blessings of rice, raisins, and eggs that I took from our mom's refrigerator when Rick called her into the back yard about a missing sock from his laundry—a ploy from the start.

4 "Rick, I only got a dollar," I told him. He slapped his thigh and told me to wake up. It was almost the end of the month. And he was right. In two days our paychecks from Zak's Car Wash would burn like good report cards in our pockets.[2] So I gave in. I took the fifteen cents—a dime and five pennies—he had plucked from the ashtray of loose change in his bedroom, and went downstairs, across the street and the two blocks to Scott's Liquor. While I was returning home, swinging the quart of beer like a lantern,[3] I saw the Japanese woman who was my neighbor, cracking walnuts on her front porch. I walked slowly so that she looked up, smiling. I smiled, said hello, and continued walking to the rhythm of her hammer rising and falling.

5 In the apartment I opened the beer and raised it like a chalice[4] before we measured it in glasses, each of us suspicious that the other would get more. I rattled sunflower seeds onto a plate, and we pinched fingersful, the beer in our hands cutting loose a curtain of bubbles. We were at a party with no music, no host, no girls. Our cat, Mensa, dawdled in, blinking from the dull smoke of a sleepy afternoon. She looked at us, and we looked at her. Rick flicked a seed at her and said, "That's what we need—a woman!"

6 I didn't say anything. I closed my eyes, legs shot out in a V from the couch, and thought of that girl on the porch, the rise and fall of her hammer, and the walnuts cracking open like hearts.

[1] **pup** puppy; playful young dog

[2] **would burn like good report cards in our pockets** record of school grades sent home for parents; children would hurry to take a good report card out of their pockets to show to their parents

[3] **lantern**

[4] **chalice**

7 I got up and peeked from our two-story window that looked out onto a lawn and her apartment. No one. A wicker chair, potted plants, and a pile of old newspapers. I looked until she came out with a broom to clean up the shells. "Ah, my little witch," I thought, and raced my heart downstairs, but stopped short of her house because I didn't know what to say or do. I stayed behind the hedge[5] that separated our yards and listened to her broom swish across the porch, then start up the walk to the curb.[6] It was then that I started to walk casually from behind the hedge and, when she looked at me with a quick grin, I said a hearty hello and walked past her without stopping to talk. I made my way to the end of the block where I stood behind another hedge, feeling foolish. I should have said something. "Do you like walnuts," I could have said, or maybe, "Nice day to sweep, isn't it?"—anything that would have my mouth going.

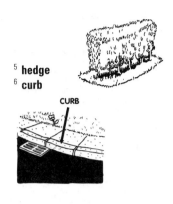

⁵ **hedge**
⁶ **curb**

CURB

8 I waited behind that hedge, troubled by my indecision. I started back up the street and found her bending over a potted geranium, a jar of cloudy water in her hand. Lucky guy, I thought, to be fed[7] by her.

⁷ **fed** given food

9 I smiled as I passed, and she smiled back. I returned to the apartment and my bedroom, where I stared at my homework and occasionally looked out the window to see if she was busy on the porch. But she wasn't there. Only the wicker chair, the plants, the pile of newspapers.

10 The days passed, white as clouds. I passed her house so often that we began to talk, sit together on the porch, and eventually snack on sandwiches that were thick as Bibles, with tumblers of milk to wash down her baked sweet bread flecked with tiny crushed walnuts.

11 After the first time I ate at her house, I hurried to the apartment to brag about my lunch to my brother, who was in the kitchen sprinkling raisins on his rice. Sandwiches, I screamed, milk, cold cuts,[8] chocolate ice cream! I spoke about her cupboards, creaking like ships weighed down with a cargo of rich food, and about her, that woman who came up to my shoulder. I was in love and didn't know where to go from there.

⁸ **cold cuts** thin slices of cold, cooked meat

12 As the weeks passed, still white as clouds, we saw more of each other. Then it happened. On another Saturday, after browsing at a thrift shop[9] among gooseneck lamps and couches as jolly as fat men, we went to the west side of Fresno for Mexican food—menudo[10] for me and burritos[11] for her, with two beers clunked down on our table. When we finished eating and were ready to go, I wiped my mouth and plucked my sole five-dollar bill from my wallet as I walked to the cashier. It was all the big money I had. I paid and left the restaurant as if it were nothing, as if I spent such money every day. But inside I was thinking. "What am I going to do?"

⁹ **thrift shop** store that sells used merchandise at low prices
¹⁰ **menudo** popular dish among Mexican Americans made of beef stomach
¹¹ **burritos** beans and/or meat wrapped in a tortilla

13 Scared as I was, I took Carolyn's hand into mine as we walked to the car. I released it to open the door for her. We drove and

drove, past thrift shops she longed to[12] browse through, but I didn't want to stop because I was scared I would want to hold her hand again. After turning corners aimlessly, I drove back to her house where we sat together on the front porch, not touching. I was shivering, almost noticeably. But after a while, I did take her hand into mine and that space between us closed. We held hands, little tents opening and closing, and soon I nuzzled my face into her neck to find a place to kiss.

14 I married this one Carolyn Oda, a woman I found cracking walnuts on an afternoon. It was a chance meeting: I was walking past when she looked up to smile. It could have been somebody else, a girl drying persimmons on a line, or one hosing down her car, and I might have married another and been unhappy. But it was Carolyn, daughter of hard workers, whom I found cracking walnuts. She stirred them into dough that she shaped into loaves, baked in the oven, and set before me so that my mouth would keep talking in its search of the words to make me stay.

[12] **longed to**   wanted to; had a strong desire to

Comprehension Check

A. First Reading

*Mark the statements **T** (true) or **F** (false). Be prepared to show evidence in the selection that supports your answers.*

1. T   F   A neighbor introduced the narrator to Carolyn.

2. T   F   The narrator and Carolyn didn't seem to have serious problems while they were dating.

B. Second Reading

Read the selection again. Then answer the questions. Be prepared to show evidence in the selection that supports your answers.

1. List details that show that the narrator and his brother didn't have much money when they were in college.

2. The narrator does things that show he is interested in Carolyn. For example, he walked past her house slowly so she might notice him. List other details that show he is interested in her.

3. What, if anything, did Carolyn do to help the relationship develop?

4. What happened on their first date?

 Vocabulary

 A. Vocabulary Building

Look at the underlined words or expressions in the sentences on the left. Find them in the selection. Then match them with the correct meaning on the right.

___ **1.** <u>Pick</u> anybody . . . (¶ 1)

a. without direction

___ **2.** We . . . drank cup after cup of coffee until we were so <u>wired</u> . . . (¶ 1)

b. breaking open

___ **3.** . . . we can easily say after a <u>brief</u> . . . <u>courtship</u> . . . (¶ 2)

c. choose

___ **4.** . . . I saw . . . my neighbor, <u>cracking</u> walnuts . . . (¶ 4)

d. smile

___ **5.** . . . when she looked at me with a quick <u>grin</u>, I said a hearty hello . . . (¶ 7)

e. awake; stimulated

___ **6.** . . . we began to talk, sit together on the porch, and eventually <u>snack on</u> sandwiches . . . (¶ 10)

f. short period of dating

___ **7.** . . . I hurried to the apartment to <u>brag</u> about my lunch to my brother . . . (¶ 11)

g. eat, but not a big meal

___ **8.** After turning corners <u>aimlessly</u> . . . (¶ 13)

h. accidental; unplanned

___ **9.** I was <u>shivering</u>, almost noticeably. (¶ 13)

i. tell in a proud way

___ **10.** It was a <u>chance</u> meeting . . . (¶ 14)

j. trembling (because of cold or nervousness)

 B. Identifying Non-essential Vocabulary

Read each sentence, skipping the crossed-out words. Then try to answer the question that follows. If you can answer the question, the crossed-out words are not essential. If you can't, the crossed-out words are essential to understanding the sentences, and there may be an important word you need to look up in a dictionary.

1. I took the fifteen cents—a dime and five pennies—he had ~~plucked~~ from the ashtray ~~of loose change~~ in his bedroom . . . (¶ 4)
   • What did he take? Where was it?

2. I ~~rattled~~ sunflower seeds onto a plate, and we pinched fingersful, the beer in our hands ~~cutting loose a curtain of bubbles.~~ (¶ 5)
- What were the men eating with their beer?
- Were they eating them from a bag, a jar, or a plate?

3. A ~~wicker~~ chair, ~~potted~~ plants, and a ~~pile~~ of old newspapers. (¶ 7)
- What was on the neighbor's porch?

4. . . . we began to talk, sit together on the porch, and eventually snack on sandwiches . . . with ~~tumblers~~ of milk ~~to wash down~~ her baked ~~sweet~~ bread ~~flecked~~ with ~~tiny crushed~~ walnuts. (¶ 10)
- What did Carolyn and the narrator eat and drink? What was in the bread?

5. On another Saturday, after ~~browsing~~ at a thrift shop among ~~gooseneck~~ lamps and couches . . . (¶ 12)
- Where were Carolyn and the narrator?
- What are two things sold there?

6. . . . we went to the west side of Fresno for Mexican food—menudo for me and burritos for her, with two beers ~~clunked down~~ on our table. (¶ 12)
- Where were the beers?

7. . . . and soon I ~~nuzzled~~ my face into her neck to find a place to kiss. (¶ 13)
- Where did the narrator kiss Carolyn?

C. Vocabulary Review

Complete the following statements about the reading selection with the correct word or expression from the list below. Use each word or expression only once.

bragged	**courtship**	**pick**
chance	**cracking**	**snack**

1. This story is about how the narrator met his wife. He told his students it was easy. "_____ anybody," he said.

2. One day he saw his neighbor _____ walnuts on her front porch. Little by little they started talking to each other. She invited him to _____ on sandwiches and other good food she prepared. He invited her to a Mexican restaurant for dinner.

3. He was scared but also excited about this relationship and _____ about it to his brother.

4. His _____ of Carolyn was brief. It's surprising how such an important thing, like finding a wife, can develop from a _____ meeting.

Sharing Your Thoughts

1. What similarities and differences are there between (1) the narrator and Carolyn's meeting and first date, and (2) Feynman and Barbara's date in Selection One? Consider things like age and customs of the times (1940s versus 1980s).

2. Before reading this selection, you talked about ways couples you know met each other. Is it unusual for serious relationships to develop from informal, casual beginnings like the one described in this story?

3. How long do you think a couple should know each other before considering marriage? What should they know about each other?

4. The couple in this story is an intercultural couple: Chicano and Japanese. What special problems, if any, might an intercultural couple have?

Text Analysis

A. Grammar-Meaning Connection: Using *could have, might have, should have*

Could have, might have, and *should have* are useful phrases for communicating about things that didn't happen in the past.

Read these examples. Answer the question below each one.

1. I *should have said* something. (¶ 7)

    Did he say something?

2. "Do you like walnuts?" I *could have said*, . . . (¶ 7)

    Did he say, "Do you like walnuts?"

3. It *could have been* somebody else . . . (¶ 14)

    Did he marry Carolyn or somebody else?

4. . . . I *might have married* another and been unhappy. (¶ 14)

    Did he marry another?

5. In these sentences the narrator shows that . . .

    a. what happens in life is often a matter of chance.

    b. we plan and control what happens to us in life.

B. Figurative Language: Similes

Writers often create word pictures for the reader by using similes—phrases beginning with *like* or *as*—which show similarities between two things that aren't obviously similar.

Read the following examples from this story, try to draw a picture of some of the images the writer has created, and share your drawings. If you don't know a word that seems important to get the picture, consult a dictionary. The first picture is provided for you.

1. While I was returning home, <u>swinging the quart of beer</u> *like a lantern*, I saw the Japanese woman who was my neighbor, cracking walnuts on her front porch. (¶ 4)

2. . . . I opened the beer and <u>raised it</u> *like a chalice* before we measured it in glasses . . . (¶ 5)

3. . . . sandwiches that were <u>thick</u> *as Bibles* . . . (¶ 10)

4. . . . her <u>cupboards, creaking</u> *like ships weighed down with a cargo of rich food* . . . (¶ 11)

5. . . . <u>couches as jolly</u> *as fat men* (¶ 12)

Writing Task

1. Imagine and write the first conversation between the narrator and Carolyn as they were standing in front of her house. Have each person speak at least three times.

2. Imagine you are Carolyn. Write a letter to your sister or a girlfriend. Tell her about the man you have met. You might focus on how you met, your first date, or your feelings about him.

3. Gary Soto uses similes to describe furniture, cabinets, sandwiches, and other physical things. Brainstorm similes to describe a room that is familiar to you. For example:

   the room is empty/messy/neat/clean as a _____

   the room is quiet/noisy, light, sunny/dark as a _____

   imagine furnishings—a table as old/new as a _____

   Write a paragraph that describes the room and incorporates some of the similes.

Selection Five

Before Reading

Phil Hey writes and teaches writing at Briar Cliff College in Sioux City, Iowa. This poem is from the collection *Going Over to Your Place*, compiled by Paul Janeczko.

Discussion
Suppose a romantic relationship ends. Talk with your classmates about the kinds of things a person might have to remind himself or herself of the lover.

Focus for the First Reading
Read these questions before you read the poem. You should be able to answer them after you finish the first reading.

1. What makes the poet remember his old sweetheart?

2. Approximately how old were they when the poet last thought of this sweetheart?

Sweetheart

by Phil Hey

1   Looking in a thicket[1]
  of forgotten papers, I find
  a love letter of yours.
  Seventeen years it's been
5   since I last thought of you.
  Somewhere a perfect stranger
  with your name nears forty,
  like me, but these few words
  show me all I want to know:
10   like locust[2] skin, the shape
  you had to leave behind
  to grow away from here.

[1] **thicket**   packet; bunch; literally dense plant growth

[2] **locust**   insect that destroys crops; it loses its skin as it changes from one stage to another

Comprehension Check

A. First Reading

Complete the sentences with an appropriate word or phrase.

The poet finds a _____ from his old sweetheart. They have not seen each
             (1)

other for at least _____ years. Since they are almost forty now, they were
            (2)

about _____ years old when their relationship ended.
     (3)

B. Second Reading

Read the poem again. Then answer the questions.

1. The poet uses a simile: He says the words in the letter are "like locust skin." What does this show him? Does this suggest why the relationship ended?

2. How do you think the poet feels about the ending of this relationship as he looks back on it now? Do you think he has regrets? Why or why not?

Sharing Your Thoughts

1. Do you think this couple did the right thing to end their relationship when they did? Explain.

2. How is the couple in the poem different from the students who believe "love conquers all" in Selection Two? How do you think those students would react to this poem?

3. Talk about some of the ways couples grow apart. Think of your own experiences and those of other people you know. Think about Carol and Lisa in Selection Three.

4. How do individuals usually feel immediately after a relationship ends? How do they feel years later?

Writing Task

1. Write your version of the letter that the poet found.

2. Write about a relationship of yours that ended. Use these questions as a guide.

> Why did the relationship end?
> How did you feel at the time?
> How do you feel about it now?
> Do you think you did the right thing?

A Final Look

Discussion

1. Work with a classmate, in a small group, or as a whole class. Drawing on all five selections in this unit, discuss the focus questions and quote on page 35.

2. Gail Sheehy notes in her book, *New Passages*, that men and women in the United States born after 1945 are marrying later and having fewer children. What explanations for this can you find in the readings you have done and in your own experience?

3. This unit focuses on finding a partner. That may not be the right decision for everyone. Also, not everyone is lucky enough to find the right partner. What are some of the reasons people might live alone, either by choice or by necessity? If people in your culture are not married, would they be expected to live alone, with family, or with other unmarried people?

Unit Project

As a class, conduct a survey of adults who are married. Each member of the class will ask five people these three questions.

1. How did you meet your partner?

2. How old were you when you met your partner?

3. How long did you know each other before you got married?

Step 1 *Prepare a piece of paper with question numbers and space to write the person's responses. Include a place to indicate the person's sex.*

Step 2 *Interview your five people and record their answers on the answer sheets you prepared.*

Step 3 *To analyze the data, form three groups of students, one for each question.*

Group 1 will list the most common ways couples meet each other. They might create categories such as "introduced by a friend or relative." After counting the number of people in each category, order the list from most common *ways to meet to* less common *ways.*

Groups 2 and 3 will review their data and fill in the following information.

GROUP 2

Age at which partners met

    average age, men _____

    average age, women _____

    average age, total _____

    range from youngest to oldest _____

GROUP 3

Length of time partners knew each other before they got married

    average length of time in years and months for men _____

    for women _____

    total _____

    range from shortest to longest time _____

Step 4 *Put together a class report. Each group will write a summary of its findings. As a class, write an introductory paragraph about the survey. Follow it by the three group reports.*

Finding Your Way

Martina
Navratilova

Buckminster
Fuller

Koffi Annan

Maria
Callas

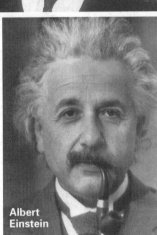

Albert
Einstein

FOCUS

➤ What is intelligence? What does it mean to say that some people are more intelligent than others?

➤ How do people differ in intelligence and abilities?

➤ How can understanding our abilities help us in making career or lifestyle choices?

➤ What can schools do to help children develop their abilities?

Happiness, or feeling satisfied with life, is unrelated to health, age, money, or most of the other things we'd expect. What really matters is working hard and achieving a goal in an area that challenges you, no matter what your level of accomplishment or walk of life.
—Gilbert Brim, *Ambition: How We Manage Success and Failure Throughout Our Lives*

Selection One

 Before Reading

This selection comes from Thomas Armstrong's book, *Multiple Intelligences in the Classroom*. In it, Armstrong presents some of Howard Gardner's ideas on multiple intelligences and offers ways teachers can apply his theory in the classroom. Howard Gardner is a professor of education at Harvard University.

Discussion

Talk with your classmates about which of the people pictured on page 75 you think are intelligent. Why do you think they are intelligent?

Previewing: Headings

Long pieces of writing are usually divided in some way. Books are divided into chapters. Chapters and articles are often divided into sections. **Headings**, which are section titles, indicate the topic of sections and subsections. Headings are often in darker print, called boldface.

1. *Read the two section headings in this selection. Which section will contain the following type of information?*

   • Support for the idea of multiple intelligences _____1 2

   • Definitions of the intelligences _____1 2

2. *Scan the boldfaced names of the intelligences and look at the diagram on page 77. Does anything about these seven intelligences surprise you? If so, what?*

Focus for the First Reading

Read these questions before you read the selection. You should be able to answer them after you finish the first reading.

1. What are the seven intelligences?

2. Why does Gardner use the word *intelligences*?

Multiple Intelligences

by Thomas Armstrong

The Seven Intelligences Described

1   **Linguistic Intelligence:** The ability to use words effectively, whether orally (e.g., as a storyteller, orator, or politician) or in writing (e.g., as a poet, playwright, editor, or journalist).

2   **Logical[1]-Mathematical Intelligence:** The ability to use numbers effectively (e.g., as a mathematician, tax accountant, or statistician) and to reason[2] well (e.g., as a scientist, computer programmer, or logician).

3   **Spatial Intelligence:** The ability to perceive the visual-spatial[3] world accurately (e.g., as a hunter, scout, or guide) and to perform transformations upon[4] those perceptions (e.g., as an interior decorator, architect, artist, or inventor). This intelligence includes sensitivity to color, line, shape, form, space, and the relationships that exist between these elements.

4   **Bodily-Kinesthetic Intelligence:** Skill in using one's whole body to express ideas and feelings (e.g., as an actor, a mime, athlete, or a dancer) and ability to use one's hands to produce or transform things (e.g., as a craftsperson, sculptor, mechanic, or surgeon).

5   **Musical Intelligence:** The ability to perceive (e.g., as a music aficionado[5]), discriminate (e.g., as a music critic), transform (e.g., as a composer), and express (e.g., as a performer) musical forms.

6   **Interpersonal Intelligence:** Sensitivity to the moods, intentions, motivations, and feelings of other people. This can include sensitivity to facial expressions, voice and gestures; the ability to discriminate among many different kinds of interpersonal cues; and the ability to respond effectively to those cues.

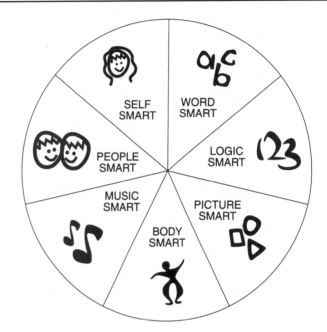

7   **Intrapersonal Intelligence:** Self-knowledge and the ability to act adaptively on the basis of that knowledge. This intelligence includes having an accurate picture of oneself (one's strengths and limitations); awareness of inner moods, intentions, motivations, temperaments, and desires; and the capacity for self-discipline, self-understanding, and self-esteem.

The Theoretical Basis for MI Theory[6]

8   Many people look at the above categories—particularly musical, spatial,

---

[1]   **logical**   related to logic, the science of thinking carefully
[2]   **reason**   think logically
[3]   **visual-spatial**   related to seeing—related to position, size, or shape

[4]   **perform transformations upon**   make changes to
[5]   **aficionado**   lover or fan of something (from Spanish)
[6]   **theory**   an idea that explains something but is not yet proven

and bodily-kinesthetic—and wonder why Howard Gardner insists on calling them intelligences, not *talents* or *aptitudes*. Gardner realized that many people are used to hearing expressions like "He's not very intelligent, but he has a wonderful aptitude for music"; thus, he was quite conscious of his use of the word[7] *intelligence* to describe each category. He said in an interview that he wanted to make people think and talk about the idea of intelligences. If he had said that there are seven kinds of competencies,[8] people would have yawned and said, 'Yeah, yeah.' But by calling them 'intelligences,' he was saying that we have tended to put on a pedestal[9] one variety called intelligence, and there are actually several of them, and some are things we have never thought of as 'intelligence' at all.

9 Gardner set up certain basic "tests" that each intelligence had to meet to be considered a full-fledged intelligence and not simply a talent, skill, or aptitude. The first test is related to work he did in hospitals. At the Boston Veterans Administration, he worked with individuals who had suffered accidents or illnesses that affected only specific areas of the brain. For example, a person with a lesion[10] in Broca's area (left frontal lobe) might have a substantial portion of his linguistic intelligence damaged, and thus experience great difficulty speaking, reading, and writing. Yet he might still be able to sing, do math, dance, reflect on feelings, and relate to others. In these cases, brain lesions seemed to have selectively affected one intelligence and not others.

---

[7] **conscious of his use (of the word)**   used on purpose or knowingly
[8] **competencies**   abilities; skills

[9] **put on a pedestal**   put in a high place or position; idolize
[10] **lesion**   a wound; a cut, for example

Comprehension Check

A. First Reading

1 *Match the name of each intelligence on the left with an ability on the right.*

___ **1.** linguistic

___ **2.** logical-mathematical

___ **3.** spatial

___ **4.** bodily-kinesthetic

___ **5.** musical

___ **6.** interpersonal

___ **7.** intrapersonal

a. ability in understanding and getting along with other people

b. ability in using the parts of one's body

c. ability with numbers, clear thinking

d. ability in understanding yourself

e. ability with language

f. ability in singing, playing an instrument

g. ability with color, line, space

2 *Circle the correct reason.*

Gardner uses the word *intelligence* because:

   a. he wants people to understand what he is talking about.

   b. he wants people to change their definition of intelligence.

   c. he thinks it is easier to understand than similar words.

B. Second Reading

*Read the selection again. Then mark the statements **T** (true) or **F** (false). Be prepared to show evidence in the selection that supports your answers.*

1. T F Giving students opportunities to write is the only way to develop their linguistic intelligence.

2. T F A computer programmer has to have strong interpersonal intelligence.

3. T F A painter or sculptor needs both spatial and bodily-kinesthetic intelligence.

4. T F To have musical intelligence, a person has to be able to play an instrument.

5. T F A person with good interpersonal intelligence makes a good team member.

6. T F People with strong intrapersonal intelligence know themselves but cannot change.

7. T F Studying what people can and can't do after they suffer a head injury is one test Gardner used to show that there are separate intelligences.

8. T F Gardner found that when a part of the brain is damaged, certain intelligences are affected but not others.

Vocabulary

A. Vocabulary Building

*Look at the underlined words or expressions in the sentences on the left. Find them in the selection. Then match them with the correct meaning on the right. Match **1–5** with **a–e** and continue with sentences **6–10** on page 80.*

___ **1.** The ability to perceive the visual-spatial world <u>accurately</u> . . . (¶ 3)

    a. body movements that show what you mean or how you feel

___ **2.** This intelligence includes <u>sensitivity</u> to color . . . (¶ 3)

    b. ability to perceive or notice something

___ **3.** Sensitivity to the <u>moods</u> . . . and feelings of other people. (¶ 6)

    c. correctly

___ **4.** . . . sensitivity to facial expressions, voice and <u>gestures</u> . . . (¶ 6)

    d. signals; hints

___ **5.** . . . the ability to discriminate among many different kinds of interpersonal <u>cues</u> . . . (¶ 6)

    e. a person's mental state (happy, sad) at a particular time

Match 6–10 with f–j.

___ **6.** Self-knowledge and the ability to <u>act adaptively</u> on the basis of that knowledge. (¶ 7)

f. strong points; things a person is good at

___ **7.** This intelligence includes having an accurate picture of oneself (one's <u>strengths</u> and limitations) . . . (¶ 7)

g. ability to control your actions

___ **8.** This intelligence includes having . . . <u>awareness</u> of inner moods . . . (¶ 7)

h. change

___ **9.** This intelligence includes having . . . the capacity for <u>self-discipline</u> . . . (¶ 7)

i. respect or admiration for yourself

___ **10.** This intelligence includes having . . . the capacity for <u>self-esteem</u>. (¶ 7)

j. knowledge; consciousness

 B. Word Analysis

> Words can have several parts. A **prefix** is a part that comes at the beginning of a word and changes the meaning of the basic word, for example, *un-* in the word *unhappy*. A **suffix**, as you learned in Unit Two, is a part that comes at the end of a word and changes its meaning or function, for example, the suffix *-ly* in *happily* changes an adjective (*happy*) to an adverb.

1 *Look at the two important prefixes in this selection. They come from Latin.*

inter- = between

interpersonal = involving relationships between people

intra- = within

intrapersonal = within or inside one person

Explain the meaning of the following:

1. international flight
2. interplanetary travel
3. intravenous feeding (*ven-* = veins, from Latin)
4. interracial problems
5. interstate highway
6. intramural sports (*mur-* = wall, from Latin; referring here to the walls of a school)

2 *This selection includes many examples of words that include or can add the common suffix -tion / -sion, which changes a verb to a noun. Complete each of the sentences with the correct form of the word.*

1. express (v) / expression (n)
   a. People's faces _____ emotions.
   b. What does that _____ on your face mean?

2. perceive / perception
   a. I don't _____ the problem in the same way that you do.
   b. Your _____ is not the same as mine.

3. transform / transformation
   a. Wow! What a _____ in your appearance!
   b. It's amazing how a new hairstyle can _____ the way you look.

3 *Selection One does not use both the verb and noun forms for the following words. Fill in the missing form. Check a dictionary if you need to. Then complete the sentences with the correct word.*

1. discriminate / _____
   a. I took a hearing test. They called it a test of auditory _____.
   b. I found out I can't _____ sounds very well.

2. _____ / intention
   a. I'm sorry. I didn't _____ to hurt your feelings.
   b. That was not my _____.

3. _____ / limitation
   a. Having a broken arm will _____ what you can do.
   b. Fortunately, this _____ will not last forever.

4. _____ / motivation
   a. Why does he act that way? I wonder what his _____ is.
   b. What _____ him to act that way?

5. produce / _____
   a. A new factory will begin _____ next month.
   b. They are going to _____ radios.

4 *This selection mentions many occupations. Search the text to find occupations with the following suffixes:*

-er storyteller (find five more) _____

_____

-or (find six) _____

_____

-ian (find four) _____

_____

-ist (find three) _____

_____

C. Vocabulary Review

Complete the following statements about the reading selection with the correct word or expression from the list below. Use each word or expression only once.

accurately	interpersonal	logical	performers	self-esteem
express	limitations	moods	reason	theory

1. Over many years, Howard Gardner developed his _____ of multiple intelligences.

2. Gardner knew that when people say someone is intelligent, they mean the person is "school smart"—good at reading, math, and _____ thinking.

3. But people have other intelligences in addition to the ability to use words and numbers and to _____ well.

4. For example, spatial intelligence is the ability to perceive the physical world _____.

5. Dancers have bodily-kinesthetic intelligence; they use their bodies to _____ ideas and feelings.

6. Some people with musical intelligence are composers who write music; others are _____ and play an instrument.

7. _____ intelligence is the ability to perceive the _____ , intentions, motivations, and feelings of other people.

8. If you have good intrapersonal intelligence, you know yourself. You know your strengths and _____. You value yourself; you have _____.

Sharing Your Thoughts

1. Schools generally emphasize the linguistic and logical-mathematical intelligences. Think about the schools you have attended. How good have they been in developing all seven intelligences in students?

2. Imagine you are in a parents' group. You all have preschool children. What kind of activities will you plan for your children to develop each of the seven intelligences?

3. How well developed are your own seven intelligences? Evaluate your intelligences using this scale. Put a check (√) in the appropriate box.

Multiple Intelligences Evaluation Form

	Linguistic	Logical-mathematical	Spatial	Bodily-kinesthetic	Musical	Inter-personal	Intra-personal
5—very strong							
4—fairly strong							
3—moderate							
2—fairly weak							
1—weak							

4. Move around the classroom and try to find a classmate with a similar self-evaluation of the seven intelligences. Compare interests and things you like to do in your free time. Are your free-time activities similar?

 Text Analysis

Brief Examples

The letters *e.g.* are an abbreviation for the Latin words *exempli gratia*, meaning *for example*. They are often used to mark short examples.

1. What kind of brief examples does Armstrong give to help you understand the seven different intelligences? Why are the examples he chooses appropriate for each intelligence?

2. What punctuation convention does the writer use to separate the examples from the text?

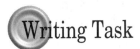 Writing Task

1. Write a paragraph in which you define and illustrate one of the first six intelligences. You can get vocabulary help from the selection, but write in your own words. For example:

   INTRAPERSONAL INTELLIGENCE
   Intrapersonal intelligence is knowing yourself. You have to know your strengths and your limitations. If you have good intrapersonal intelligence, you can understand why you do things and why you are in a good mood or a bad mood. You also have the ability to change the things you do not like about yourself.

2. Write a paragraph about your intelligences, based on the self-evaluation you did in Sharing Your Thoughts on pages 82–83. Consider answering one or more of the questions below. Use these questions as a guide.

Which do you think is your strongest intelligence?
What are one or two things you can do well because of this intelligence?
When did you first notice you had this intelligence?
What have you done in your life that has helped you develop this intelligence?

Selection Two

Before Reading

This selection is an excerpt from a professional journal article by psychologist Robert Sternberg. It was published in *Language Testing*, November 1995.

Discussion

In Selection One, Armstrong gave examples of types of work or careers that were compatible with, or match, different intelligences. In addition to intelligences and abilities, what makes a person a good fit, or match, for a type of work?

Think of a type of work or career which is a good fit for the following people and one which would be a bad fit.

- a person who likes to be active
- a person who likes to plan and organize things
- a person who does not like to follow instructions

Previewing

Preview the selection by reading the title, the first paragraph, the first sentence of paragraphs 2–9, and the last paragraph. Answer these questions.

1. Are styles and abilities the same thing?

2. You only learn some of the following facts about Alex, Bill, and Curt from your preview.

   Check the ones you do learn.

___a. Alex was a good student.

___b. Alex is happy in his work and personal life.

___c. Bill became a scientist.

___d. Curt, Alex, and Bill had similar abilities.

3. Which idea will the writer illustrate, using Alex, Bill, and Curt as examples?

   a. People have different abilities and different styles.

   b. People can have similar abilities but different styles.

Focus for the First Reading

Read these questions before you read the selection. You should be able to answer them after you finish the first reading.

1. What is each person's occupation?

2. Why is each person good at his job?

Styles of Thinking and Learning

by **Robert Sternberg**

1   A style is a way of thinking. It is not an ability, but rather how we use the abilities we have. We do not have *a* style, but rather a *profile*[1] of styles. People may be almost identical in their abilities, and yet have very different styles. Consider, for example, three friends: Alex, Bill and Curt (who are real people—only the names are changed).

2   Alex was a model student[2] all the way through his senior year of college. He received outstanding grades, and went to a highly prestigious college. The first time he had academic problems was when he was in his senior year of college. For the first time, he had to really think for himself. Up to then, he had been able to get As by doing what the teachers told him to do. But his senior essay was an independent project, and now he found himself at a loss. He was fine so long as[3] other people told him what to do, but was in trouble when he had to come up with his own ideas. He probably could have come up with his own ideas if he really wanted to: he just didn't like doing it, and didn't feel comfortable doing things differently from others. So he was smart and able, just so long as there was someone to guide him.

3   Alex had thought about being a historian or possibly a writer. He certainly had the ability to follow either of those careers. But his style of thinking was much better suited to the career he actually chose: today he is a contracts lawyer, and a highly successful one.

When people ask him what he does, he describes his work as directed by others. Investment bankers decide on a deal,[4] and then instruct Alex to draw up a contract. Thus the bankers set the structure[5] and Alex works within it. But if the bankers decide to modify their deal, they have to pay Alex to do it. So every time they have an idea or change one, they have to pay Alex. He has found a job that is a good fit for his style of thinking. The important thing to remember is that Alex had the ability to do a lot of things, but found a career that was a good fit to the way he likes to use his abilities. As a result, he is happy with his career.

4   Alex is also happy in his personal life, which in many ways is compatible with his professional life. Alex and his wife have 2.5 children (well, three actually), and live in a comfortable suburb[6] in a major metropolitan area. They keep up with the Joneses,[7] and take their cues in their life from what others do. They do not question much why they do what they do, but rather fall into the patterns set for them by others.

5   Bill matched Alex in abilities, but not in school achievement. Bill's primary style is quite different from Alex's, and is one that schools don't usually reward. Most schools value an Alex, the bright child who does what he or she is told; fewer value a Bill, a child who is bright but who wants to do things his or her own way. Indeed, children like Bill are

---

[1] **profile**   group or variety
[2] **model student**   example of a good student
[3] **so long as**   as long as; if
[4] **deal**   business agreement

[5] **set the structure**   determine the form of the whole
[6] **suburb**   residential area outside the center of the city
[7] **keep up with the Joneses**   do or have what their neighbors do or have

often seen as behavior problems, or as lacking in ability.

6   Bill's experience was the opposite of Alex's. He got a mediocre[8] grade in his introductory science course. He came into his own when he could work independently and come up with his own ideas. He first began to feel successful when he started his career as a research scientist. As a scientist, he was in a position to come up with his own ideas—his own theories, his own experiments. He no longer had to follow the instructions of a teacher or supervisor.

7   Bill's personal life has also showed his style of thinking. Bill's first marriage, to the 'right' woman from the 'right' background, ended in divorce. The marriage was a model of what society says a marriage should be, but Bill was extremely bored. He had the right house in the right neighbourhood with the right schools, and his wife thought he was crazy to be dissatisfied. In his second marriage, however, Bill lives the kind of life that he prefers, in the wrong neighbourhood with the wrong spouse, and he is happier than ever before. He's doing it his way, which is what he always wanted.

8   Curt was similar in abilities to Alex and Bill, but his predominant style was different. As a college student, he was editor of the college-course critique,[9] and as a result was in charge of evaluating every course taught at the college. When he went out on dates, he even gave his dates a test of values— which they did not know they were taking. If they passed the test, he continued to go out with them; if not, that was the end of the relationship. Today, Curt is in his mid-40s and, perhaps predictably, is still not married.

9   But Curt, like Alex and Bill, has found a job that is a good fit to his predominant style of thinking. Curt always liked to evaluate people and things, and today he is a highly successful psychotherapist who evaluates people and their problems, and prescribes courses of therapy[10] for them. Curt had the ability to do many things, but he found a job that was compatible with his style.

10   Alex, Bill and Curt are the lucky ones. But go to any high school or college reunion,[11] and you will meet scores of people[12] who went into the wrong job for them. Perhaps they did what their guidance or career counsellor told them to do, based on abilities or even interests, but many of them are in careers where they feel they are at a dead end.[13] People often feel at a dead end when the work they do isn't a good fit with the best uses of their talents. Understanding styles can help people better understand why some activities fit them and others do not, and even why some people fit them and others do not.

---

[8] **mediocre**   neither good nor bad

[9] **college-course critique**   pamphlet in which students evaluate the courses in their college or university

[10] **therapy**   treatment of a mental or emotional problem

[11] **college reunion**   party for graduates years after they have graduated

[12] **scores of people**   many people (one score = twenty)

[13] **dead end**   end of a road that goes nowhere

Comprehension Check

A. First Reading

Complete the statements with the person's occupation and predominant, or most common, style of thinking or working. Choose from:

- contracts lawyer, psychotherapist, or research scientist
- evaluating people and things, thinking for himself, or carrying out other people's instructions

1. Alex is a successful _____. He is good at _____.
2. Bill is a successful _____. He is good at _____.
3. Curt is a successful _____. He is good at _____.

B. Second Reading

Read the selection again. Then show that you understand the major ideas by matching the idea on the left with the reason on the right.

___ 1. Alex had trouble with his senior project . . .

___ 2. Alex is happy as a contracts lawyer . . .

___ 3. Bill felt successful as a research scientist . . .

___ 4. Curt has probably not married . . .

___ 5. Alex, Bill, and Curt are the lucky ones . . .

___ 6. Many people feel at a dead end in their work . . .

___ 7. Understanding your profile of styles is important . . .

a. because he is always evaluating people and finding something wrong with them.

b. because it helps you choose the right lifestyle and partner.

c. because he is good at following the instructions of the people who hire him.

d. because each went into the correct job for his style of thinking.

e. because he had to think independently, and that wasn't his style.

f. because he could think independently and use his own ideas.

g. because they have jobs which don't fit their styles of thinking.

Vocabulary

 A. Vocabulary Building

Look at the underlined words or expressions in the sentences on the left. Find them in the selection. Then match them with the correct meaning on the right.

___ **1.** He (Alex) received <u>outstanding</u> grades . . . (¶ 2)

___ **2.** So he was smart and able, just so long as there was someone to <u>guide</u> him. (¶ 2)

___ **3.** He certainly had the ability to follow either of those <u>careers</u>. (¶ 3)

___ **4.** Investment bankers . . . instruct Alex to draw up a <u>contract</u>. (¶3)

___ **5.** Alex is also happy in his personal life, which . . . is <u>compatible</u> with his professional life. (¶ 4)

___ **6.** Bill's primary style . . . is one that schools don't usually <u>reward</u>. (¶ 5)

___ **7.** Most schools <u>value</u> an Alex . . . (¶ 5)

___ **8.** . . . the <u>bright</u> child who does what he or she is told . . . (¶ 5)

___ **9.** . . . but Bill was extremely <u>bored</u>. (¶ 7)

___**10.** (Curt) . . . was in charge of <u>evaluating</u> every course . . . (¶ 8)

a. tired or impatient because something is uninteresting

b. a good fit

c. smart; intelligent

d. excellent; superior

e. saying if something is good or bad; identifying strengths and limitations

f. have a high opinion of

g. legal written agreement between people, companies, etc.

h. type of work a person has been trained for and plans to do for a long time

i. give something (e.g., good grades) because work is well done

j. show the way; direct

  B. Multi-word Expressions

Underline the multi-word expressions in the sentences below. Find them in the selection. Then choose the correct meaning for the context. The first one has been done as an example.

1. But his (Alex's) senior essay was an independent project, and now he found himself <u>at a loss</u>. (¶ 2)

   a. knowing what to do

   b. not knowing what to do

2. He (Alex) was fine so long as other people told him what to do, but was in trouble when he had to come up with his own ideas. (¶ 2)

   a. think of; invent

   b. enter; come in

3. Investment bankers . . . instruct Alex to draw up a contract. (¶ 3)

   a. sign

   b. write

4. They do not question much why they do what they do, but rather fall into the patterns set for them by others. (¶ 4)

   a. start following

   b. make or determine

5. He (Bill) came into his own when he could work independently . . . (¶ 6)

   a. found himself and his way

   b. got lost

6. As a college student, he (Curt) . . . was in charge of evaluating every course taught at the college. (¶ 8)

   a. responsible for

   b. worried about

7. . . . but many of them (people at class reunions) are in careers where they feel they are at a dead end. (¶ 10)

   a. very successful

   b. with nowhere to go

C. Vocabulary Review

Complete the following statements about the reading selection with the correct word or expression from the list below. Use each word or expression only once.

at a loss	**come up with**	**evaluate**	**model**
came into his own	**compatible**	**guide**	**styles**

1. Robert Sternberg illustrates personal _____ by describing the academic, professional, and personal lives of three men.

2. Alex was a _____ student, but he found himself _____ when he had to do an independent project in his senior year.

3. He decided on a career as a contracts lawyer because he prefers to have someone else _____ his work.

4. Bill is just the opposite. Bill didn't do well in his early science courses, but he _____ when he could work independently.

5. He is a research scientist and likes his work because he has to

_____ his own theories.

6. Curt is happy as a psychotherapist because he likes to _____

people and their problems.

7. Alex, Bill, and Curt are lucky because their jobs are _____

with their personal styles.

Sharing Your Thoughts

1. Sternberg suggests that these three men are all smart or intelligent. Which of the seven intelligences in Selection One do you think each one has?

2. Is your style more like Alex's or Bill's? On a scale of 1 to 4, circle the number that indicates how well the statements below describe you.

	True of me		Not true of me	
a. I don't care much what other people think of me.	4	3	2	1
b. I can take orders from a boss.	4	3	2	1
c. I like someone to guide me in projects I do.	4	3	2	1
d. I feel comfortable doing what people around me do.	4	3	2	1
e. I like to come up with my own ideas for projects.	4	3	2	1
f. I don't like working for other people.	4	3	2	1
g. What other people think of me is important to me.	4	3	2	1
h. I feel comfortable being different from people around me.	4	3	2	1

Now add the numbers you circled for **a**, **b**, **e**, and **h**. Then add the numbers you circled for **c**, **d**, **f**, and **g**. You are more like Alex if the total for **a**, **b**, **e**, and **h** is greater than the total for **c**, **d**, **f**, and **g**.

3. Talk with your classmates about other personal styles you think people have. Look at the list below (continued on pg. 92). Add to this list. Then list jobs that are compatible with these personal styles.

OTHER PERSONAL STYLES	COMPATIBLE JOBS
a. likes to work alone	_____
b. likes to work with other people	_____
c. likes to work with details	_____

d. likes to work with the larger, moregeneral situation

_____

e. likes to work on a conventional 9–5 time schedule

_____

f. likes to work on a flexible time schedule

_____

g. _____

_____

h. _____

_____

4. Alex and his wife had similar personal styles and a successful marriage. Bill and his first wife had different personal styles and ended up getting divorced. Think of couples you know. How important is it for spouses to have similar personal styles?

5. Which have you experienced: schools that value students who do what they are told, or schools that help students follow their own ways? What are the advantages and disadvantages of each?

 Text Analysis

Extended Examples

In paragraph 1, Sternberg defines style. How well do you understand personal styles from this brief definition? If someone asked you to explain a personal style, what would you say?

Sternberg knows that without the examples of Alex, Bill, and Curt, his definition is not clear enough.

Complete the chart with details about the academic, professional, and personal lives of these men. This will illustrate how the lives of people with similar abilities can be very different because of different styles.

	Alex	**Bill**	**Curt**
Style		likes to think for himself	
Academic life	had trouble with his senior project		
Professional life			is a psychotherapist
Personal life		first marriage ended in divorce	

Writing Task

1. Describe a person you know. Include characteristics such as the ones in the list below. To make your description come alive, give specific examples of things the person does. The number of paragraphs you write will depend on the number of characteristics you choose and the amount of information you give about each.

   is curious about everything

   likes to be physically active

   likes to plan and organize things

   works well under pressure / works best without pressure

   likes to work alone / with other people

   likes / doesn't like routine

   likes / doesn't like to follow instructions

2. Write a paragraph about either **a** or **b**.

   a. If you have not begun your career, write a paragraph about a type of work or career that you want someday. Use these questions as a guide.

      What work or career do you want in the future?
      Why will it be a good fit with your abilities or personal styles?

   b. If you are working and happy with your work, explain how your work fits your abilities and styles. If you are not happy in your career, write about a career change you would like to make. Explain why you think it will be better for you.

Selection Three

Before Reading

This selection is an excerpt from an article entitled "Why Schools Flunk Biology" by LynNell Hancock that appeared in *Newsweek*, February 19, 1996.

Discussion

Talk with your classmates about your elementary school education.

What subjects did the school teach?

What kind of class activities were there for learning math, history, and language?

What activities did you participate in outside of class?

What kind of activities do you think you learned the most from?

Which of the seven intelligences described in Selection One did your school develop most?

Previewing

Read the title of the selection. From the title, you know that the article is about what children should study in school. Scan the article and name the school subjects mentioned in it.

Focus for the First Reading

Read these questions before you read the selection. You should be able to answer them after you finish the first reading.

1. What are two classes that American schools should not cut according to education research?

2. What does research suggest about physical activity?

Windows of Opportunity:

What Students Should Study and When

by LynNell Hancock

1   Plato[1] once said that music "is a more potent[2] instrument than any other for education." Now scientists know why. Music, they believe, trains the brain for higher forms of thinking. Researchers at the University of California, Irvine, studied the power of music by observing two groups of preschoolers. One group took piano lessons and sang daily in chorus. The other did not. After eight months the musical 3-year-olds were expert puzzlemasters, scoring 80 percent higher than their playmates did in spatial intelligence—the ability to visualize the world accurately.

2   This skill later translates into complex math and engineering skills. "Early music

---

[1] **Plato**   ancient Greek philosopher
[2] **potent**   powerful

training can enhance a child's ability to reason," says Irvine physicist Gordon Shaw. Yet music education is often the first "frill"[3] to be cut when school budgets shrink. Schools on average have only one music teacher for every 500 children, according to the National Commission on Music Education.

3   Then there's gym—another expendable hour by most school standards. Only 36 percent of schoolchildren today are required to participate in daily physical education. Yet researchers now know that exercise is good not only for the heart. It also juices up the brain, feeding it nutrients in the form of glucose and increasing nerve connections—all of which make it easier for kids of all ages to learn. Neuroscientist William Greenough confirmed this by watching rats at his University of Illinois at Urbana-Champaign lab. One group did nothing. A second exercised on an automatic treadmill.[4] A third was set loose in a Barnum & Bailey[5] obstacle course[6] requiring the rats to perform acrobatic feats. These "supersmart" rats grew "an enormous amount of gray matter"[7] compared with their sedentary partners, says Greenough.

4   Of course, children don't ordinarily run such gantlets[8]; still, Greenough believes, the results are significant. Numerous studies, he says, show that children who exercise regularly do better in school.

5   The implication for schools goes beyond simple exercise. Children also need to be more physically active in the classroom, not sitting quietly in their seats memorizing subtraction tables. Knowledge is retained longer if children connect not only aurally[9] but emotionally and physically to the material, says University of Oregon education professor Robert Sylwester in "A Celebration of Neurons."

6   Good teachers know that lecturing on the American Revolution is far less effective than acting out a battle. Angles and dimensions are better understood if children chuck their work sheets and build a complex model to scale. The smell of the glue enters memory through one sensory system, the touch of the wood blocks another, the sight of the finished model still another. The brain then creates a multidimensional mental model of the experience—one easier to retrieve. "Explaining a smell," says Sylwester, "is not as good as actually smelling it."

7   Scientists argue that children are capable of far more at younger ages than schools generally realize. People obviously continue learning their whole lives, but the optimum "windows of opportunity for learning" last until about the age of 10 or 12, says Harry Chugani of Wayne State University's Children's Hospital of Michigan. Chugani determined this by measuring the brain's consumption of its chief energy source, glucose. (The more glucose it uses, the more active the brain.) Children's brains, he observes, gobble up[10] glucose at twice the adult rate from the age of 4 to puberty.[11] So young brains are as primed[12] as they'll ever be to process new information. Complex subjects such as trigonometry or foreign language shouldn't wait for puberty to be introduced. In fact, Chugani says, it's far easier for an elementary-school child to hear and process a second language—and even speak it without an accent. Yet most U.S. districts wait until junior high to introduce Spanish or French—after the "windows" are closed.

---

[3] **frill**   something extra or not essential

[4] **treadmill**   wheel that rats exercise on

[5] **Barnum & Bailey**   a circus company

[6] **obstacle course**   line of objects to jump over, go under, etc.

[7] **gray matter**   brain tissue

[8] **run such gantlets**   do such incredible physical activity (also *gauntlets*)

[9] **aurally**   through hearing

[10] **gobble up**   eat fast and completely

[11] **puberty**   stage of life when a child becomes physically capable of having children

[12] **primed**   ready

Comprehension Check

A. First Reading

Circle the letters of the choices that correctly complete each sentence.

1. Even though education research suggests that it is not a good idea, American schools often cut
   a. math
   b. music
   c. physical education

2. Research suggests that physical activity is
   a. good for the heart
   b. good for the brain
   c. good for both the heart and the brain

B. Second Reading

1 *Read the selection again. Then show that you understand the major ideas by matching the idea on the left with the reason on the right.*

___ 1. Music instruction is important for children . . .

a. because knowledge is retained longer and retrieved more easily when a child has a multi-dimensional mental model.

___ 2. Exercise in physical education (PE) class is important . . .

b. because it is easy for elementary school children to learn one.

___ 3. Schools often cut subjects like music . . .

c. because it prepares the brain for higher thinking, for example, the skills required in math and engineering.

___ 4. Children should learn by using all their senses, not just by listening . . .

d. because it increases glucose to the brain.

___ 5. Children can learn more at younger ages . . .

e. because their budgets shrink.

___ 6. Schools shouldn't wait for children to reach puberty to introduce a foreign language . . .

f. because their brains are getting twice as much glucose as adult brains.

2 *This reading selection includes summaries of two research studies, one in ¶ 1 and one in ¶ 3. Answer as many of these questions as possible about each research study.*

1. Who did the research?
2. What did they study
3. Who were the subjects?

4. How many groups were there? What did each group do?

5. How long did the treatment last?

6. What were the findings of the study?

 Vocabulary

 A. Vocabulary Building

Academic writing uses formal and technical vocabulary. Find a formal or technical word in the reading selection that means the same as the words or expressions below.

1. watching (¶ 1) _____

2. see (¶ 1) _____

3. increase (¶ 2) _____

4. a fixed amount of money (¶ 2) _____

5. food; chemicals that help living things grow (¶ 3) _____

6. showed something is true; proved (¶ 3) _____

7. important; meaningful (¶ 4) _____

8. meaning; message (¶ 5) _____

9. remembered (¶ 5) _____

10. remember; bring back to one's conscious mind (¶ 6) _____

11. best (¶ 7) _____

12. proved; established (¶ 7) _____

 B. Vocabulary Building

Look at the underlined words or expressions in the sentences below. Find them in the selection. Then choose the correct meaning for the context.

1. Music . . . <u>trains</u> the brain for higher . . . thinking. (¶ 1)
   a. moves
   b. prepares

2. This skill . . . <u>translates into</u> complex math and engineering skills. (¶ 2)
   a. becomes
   b. speaks

3. ... <u>complex</u> math and engineering skills (¶ 2)

   a. simple

   b. complicated

4. Yet music education is often the first "frill" to be cut when school budgets <u>shrink</u>.(¶ 2)

   a. get smaller

   b. get larger

5. Then there's gym—another <u>expendable</u> hour by most school standards. (¶ 3)

   a. unnecessary

   b. necessary

6. It (exercise) also <u>juices up</u> the brain, feeding it nutrients . . . (¶ 3)

   a. destroys

   b. increases energy to

7. ... <u>feeding</u> it (the brain) nutrients (¶ 3)

   a. giving

   b. taking from

8. These "supersmart" rats grew "an <u>enormous</u> amount of gray matter" compared with their sedentary partners . . . (¶ 3)

   a. large

   b. small

9. . . . compared with their <u>sedentary</u> partners . . . (¶ 3)

   a. active

   b. inactive

10. Good teachers know that <u>lecturing</u> . . . is far less effective than acting out a battle. (¶ 6)

    a. talking about something

    b. thinking about something

11. . . . if children <u>chuck</u> their work sheets . . . (¶ 6)

    a. keep using

    b. throw away

C. Vocabulary Review

Complete the following statements about the reading selection with the correct word or expression from the list below. Use each word or expression only once.

budgets	confirms	nutrients	trains
complex	lecture	retain	windows of opportunity

1. Schools often cut music and gym classes when their _____

   shrink, but these "frills" are very important classes.

2. Music _____ children to reason, to think logically, and to visualize the world accurately.

3. Physical exercise increases the amount of glucose that goes to the brain, and when brains get a lot of _____, they are ready for learning _____ things like trigonometry or a foreign language.

4. Children should be active in all classes and learn by using all their senses. If teachers just _____ to young children, the students don't _____ as much as if they use more senses in the learning process.

5. Research _____ that children can learn a lot of things when they are very young. It's a mistake not to take advantage of the _____ for early learning.

Sharing Your Thoughts

1. Explain what "windows of opportunity" are in the context of learning. How does this idea relate to the main idea of this selection?

2. What are some advantages and disadvantages of teaching children *more* at a younger age?

3. This article suggests that young children learn better when they are active and use several senses. Do you think this is also true for older students? As a student, what changes in your own classes do you think would help you learn better?

4. In your culture, how important are the common elementary school subjects in the list below? Mark them **EI** (extremely important), **I** (important), or **LI** (less important). If you have classmates from other cultures, compare your evaluation to theirs.

_____ art

_____ foreign or second languages

_____ mathematics

_____ music

_____ physical education

_____ reading and writing in the native language

_____ science

_____ social studies

Text Analysis

Sources of Information

> When writers give you a statistic or make a claim that something is true, they should give you the **source**; they should tell you where the statistic comes from or who makes the claim.
>
> When you are reading, you should notice whether the article gives you sources for statistics, claims, and quotes. It is not a good idea to believe everything you read. Would you believe someone who told you that music class increases math ability *without some evidence*?

Check the selection and find the source of the following facts, claims, and quotes. One has no clear source.

> **EXAMPLE:** Music is a more potent instrument than any other for education.
> _____Plato_____

1. Three-year-olds with musical training scored 80 percent higher on a test of spatial intelligence than those without musical training. _____

2. Early music training can enhance a child's ability to reason. _____

3. Schools on average have only one music teacher for every 500 children. _____

4. Only 36 percent of schoolchildren today are required to participate in daily physical education. _____

5. Exercise makes it easier for kids of all ages to learn. _____

6. Explaining a smell is not as good as actually smelling it. _____

7. Windows of opportunity for learning last until about the age of 10 or 12. _____

8. Children's brains use twice the glucose of adult brains from age 4 to puberty. _____

9. It's far easier for an elementary-school child to hear and process a second language—and even speak it without an accent—before junior high school. _____

Writing Task

1. Write about a time you really enjoyed learning something. Use these questions as a guide.

   > What did you enjoy learning?
   > Where and when did you learn it?
   > Who helped you learn it, or did you teach yourself?
   > How did you learn it? What steps did you follow? Did it take long? Did it take a lot of practice?
   > Why did you enjoy learning this?

2. Your local school board is going to cut the funds for all music classes in elementary schools. It is also going to cut physical education to once every two weeks. Write a letter to your school board saying that you are against this plan. In your own words, report some of the information from this selection to support your opinion. Be sure to give credit to your source, as illustrated in the example.

   > **EXAMPLE:** I am opposed to your decision to reduce physical education classes because, as reported by LynNell Hancock in "Why Schools Flunk Biology" (*Newsweek*, February 19, 1996), exercise increases nutrients to the brain, which helps children learn. Furthermore . . .

Selection Four

Before Reading

In his writing, Robert Fulghum expresses his thoughts on the ordinary things that have happened to him in his life as father, neighbor, cowboy, folk singer, IBM salesman, and minister, among others. This selection comes from his third book, *Uh Oh: Some Observations from Both Sides of the Refrigerator Door.*

Discussion

Think about yourself and your life when you were about five years old.
 What kind of person were you at that age?
 What did you like to do?
 How did the world look to you?
Complete these sentences and share them with your class.
 When I was about five, I was a / an _____ person.
 I loved to _____.
 The world looked _____ to me.

Previewing: Making Predictions

> While reading, efficient readers form ideas and **make predictions** about what is coming next. As they read, they check to see if their predictions are correct. If they are not correct, they make changes in their ideas and continue reading.

1. *Read the first sentence of the selection. Which is the better prediction? Why?*

   a. Fulghum will write only about young children.

   b. Fulghum will write about young children and young adults.

2. *Read the second and third sentences. What will follow?*

   a. examples of similarities between kindergartens and colleges

   b. examples of differences between kindergartens and colleges

3. *Read to the end of the paragraph. What will follow?*

   a. examples of how kindergarten children and college students are similar

   b. examples of how kindergarten children and college students are different

Focus for the First Reading

Read these questions before you read the selection. You should be able to answer them after you finish the first reading.

1. What difference does Fulghum see between kindergarten children and college students?

2. What does Fulghum want to know at the end of the selection?

Untitled

by Robert Fulghum

1   Over the last couple of years I have been a frequent guest in schools; most often invited by kindergartens and colleges. The environments[1] differ only in scale.[2] In the beginners' classroom and on university campuses the same opportunities and facilities exist. Tools for reading and writing are there—words and numbers; areas devoted to scientific experiment—labs and work boxes; and those things necessary for the arts—paint, music, costumes, room to dance—likewise[3] present and available. In kindergarten, however, the resources are in one room, with access for all. In college, the resources are in separate buildings, with limited availability. But the most apparent difference is in the self-image of the students.

2   Ask a kindergarten class, "How many of you can draw?" and all hands shoot up. Yes, of course we can draw—all of us. What can you draw? Anything! How about a dog eating a fire truck in a jungle? Sure! How big you want it?

3   How many of you can sing? All hands. Of course we sing! What can you sing? Anything! What if you don't know the words? No problem, we make them up. Let's sing! Now? Why not!

4   How many of you dance? Unanimous again. What kind of music do you like to dance to? Any kind! Let's dance! Now? Sure, why not?

5   Do you like to act in plays? Yes! Do you play musical instruments? Yes! Do you write poetry? Yes! Can you read and write and count? Yes! We're learning that stuff now.

6   Their answer is Yes! Over and over again, Yes! The children are confident in spirit, infinite in resources,[4] and eager to learn. Everything is still possible.

7   Try those same questions on a college audience. A small percentage of the students will raise their hands when asked if they draw or dance or sing or paint or act or play an instrument. Not infrequently, those who do raise their hands will want to qualify their response with their limitations: "I only play piano, I only draw horses, I only dance to rock and roll, I only sing in the shower."

8   When asked why the limitations, college students answer they do not have talent, are not majoring in[5] the subject, or have not done any of these things since about third grade, or worse, that they are embarrassed for others to see them sing or dance or act. You can imagine the response to the same questions asked of an older audience. The answer: No, none of the above.

9   What went wrong between kindergarten and college?

10   What happened to YES! of course I can?

---

[1] **environments**   all the things that are around you; your surroundings
[2] **in scale**   in size or amount

[3] **likewise**   also

[4] **infinite in resources**   inventive; can always think of something to do and how to do it

[5] **majoring in**   studying something as your main subject at a college or university

Comprehension Check

A. First Reading

Circle the letter of the correct answer.

1. Which is the most essential difference between kindergartners and college students, according to Fulghum?

   a. a difference in their knowledge of the world

   b. a difference in the way they think about themselves

   c. a difference in the way they think about the world

2. Fulghum asks "What went wrong between kindergarten and college? What happened to YES! of course I can?" Which is the best paraphrase of his questions?

   a. Why have so many college students lost the ability to learn?

   b. Why have so many college students lost the desire to learn?

   c. Why have so many college students lost confidence in their ability to learn?

B. Second Reading

Read the selection again. Think about the similarities and differences between the two groups of students. Follow the directions below.

1. Make a Venn diagram showing the similarities and differences that Fulghum mentions between kindergartens / kindergarten students and colleges / college students. Consider opportunities and tools for learning, facilities, resources, and self-image of the students.

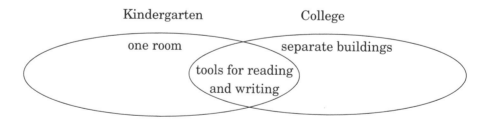

2. Sort the words and expressions into two categories: those that apply to kindergartners (mark these **K**) and those that apply to college students (mark these **C**).

   _____Anything!   _____No problem!

   _____not majoring in the subject   _____Of course!

   _____confident in spirit   _____qualify responses with their limitations

   _____eager to learn

   _____embarrassed   _____Sure, why not?

   _____have not done any of these things since about third grade   _____they do not have talent

         _____Yes!

Vocabulary

 A. Vocabulary Building

*Look at the underlined words or expressions in the sentences on the left. Find them in the selection. Then match them with the correct meaning on the right. Match 1–7 with **a–g**.*

___ **1.** . . . the <u>resources</u> are in one room . . . (¶ 1)

a. chance or right to use something

___ **2.** . . . in one room, with <u>access</u> for all. (¶ 1)

b. easily seen

___ **3.** . . . in separate buildings, with <u>limited availability</u>. (¶ 1)

c. the way they see themselves

___ **4.** But the most <u>apparent</u> difference is . . . (¶ 1)

d. invent

___ **5.** . . . in the <u>self-image</u> of the students. (¶ 1)

e. make pictures with pencil or pen

___ **6.** How many of you can <u>draw</u>? (¶ 2)

f. materials

___ **7.** No problem, we <u>make</u> them <u>up</u> (¶ 3)

g. not for everyone to use at all times

*Match 8–14 with **h–n**.*

___ **8.** We're learning <u>that stuff</u> now. (¶ 5)

h. What happened to cause this bad change?

___ **9.** The children are <u>confident</u> in spirit . . . (¶ 6)

i. nervous or uncomfortable in front of other people

___ **10.** . . . and <u>eager</u> to learn. (¶ 6)

j. restrictions on what they can do

___ **11.** . . . those who do raise their hands will want to qualify their response with their <u>limitations</u> . . . (¶ 7)

k. studying as their main subject

___ **12.** . . . they . . . are not <u>majoring in the subject</u> . . . (¶ 8)

l. sure they can do something well

___ **13.** . . . they are <u>embarrassed</u> for others to see them sing or dance or act. (¶ 8)

m. having a strong desire to do something; excited

___ **14.** <u>What went wrong</u> . . . ? (¶ 9)

n. those things (informal)

B. Vocabulary Review

Complete the following statements about the reading selection with the correct word or expression from the list below. Use each word or expression only once.

apparent	eager	majoring in	self-image	went wrong
confident	embarrassed	make up	stuff	

1. Fulghum sees a big difference between kids in kindergarten and college students. The most _____ difference is in the way they view themselves, their _____.

2. Little kids are full of enthusiasm and self-confidence, but older kids are _____ about doing things that they think they can't do well.

3. Not being perfect in something doesn't stop little kids. They are _____ to learn all kinds of _____.

4. They are imaginative and will _____ the words to a song if they don't know them all.

5. When you ask kindergartners if they can do something, they say they can do anything. College students, on the other hand, will say they can't do things because they aren't _____ the subject.

6. Fulghum seems to wish that college students could be as _____ as kindergartners. He wonders what _____ between kindergarten and college.

Sharing Your Thoughts

1. What title would you give to this selection? Explain.

2. Were you similar to or different from the kindergartners that Fulghum describes? Explain.

3. Would Fulghum agree or disagree with the following statements? Write **A** if he would agree and **D** if he would disagree. Explain your answers.

   a. It is sad that college students feel embarrassed to do something that they are not very good at.   ____

   b. Kindergarten children should be seen and not heard.   ____

   c. Schools should cut music and art programs as budgets shrink.   ____

   d. The windows of opportunity close too soon for most people.   ____

   e. College students should only take courses related to their majors.   ____

4. Fulghum asks, "What happened to Yes! of course I can?" Based on your own experience, what do you think the answer to this question is? What do you think of the reasons below, which are suggested by Selections One, Two, and Three in this unit?

a. Schools concentrate too much on the linguistic and logical-mathematical intelligences.

b. Schools don't pay enough attention to the children's different styles of thinking and learning.

c. Schools don't take advantage of the early windows of opportunity—schools don't teach children material when their brains are most ready to learn.

d. Schools don't give children enough opportunities for active learning—for making models, putting on plays, and so on.

5. Fulghum is concerned that people lose confidence in their own abilities as they grow older. What negative effects, if any, could this loss of confidence have on their adult lives and careers?

 Text Analysis

A. Using Exact Words

In paragraphs 2 through 5, Fulghum shows the self-image of children by giving their responses to his questions instead of telling us about them. For example, he doesn't say, "The children were very enthusiastic." Instead he uses their exact words, "Yes! We can!"

Divide a piece of paper into two columns. On the left, list Fulghum's questions. On the right, write the children's answers. Paragraph 2 is done as an example.

FULGHUM'S QUESTIONS	CHILDREN'S ANSWERS
How many of you can draw?	Yes, of course we can draw—all of us.
What can you draw?	Anything!
How about a dog eating a fire truck in a jungle?	Sure! How big do you want it?

Do the same thing for paragraphs 3–5. Study the children's answers. Which of their words, in your opinion, show the following characteristics?

1. They are positive about their abilities.

2. They see no limitations.

3. They are imaginative and creative.

B. Contrast

When we contrast things, we show differences. The focus of this selection is a contrast between kindergartners and college students. Show how Fulghum organizes the contrast by matching each paragraph or set of paragraphs with its contribution to the whole piece of writing.

___ ¶ 1

a. asks questions to make the reader think about the meaning of the contrast

___ ¶ 2–6

b. describes the college students' responses to his questions

___ ¶ 7–8

c. presents Fulghum's general observations about kindergartens and colleges

___ ¶ 9–10

d. gives examples of kindergartners' responses to his questions

 Writing Task

Writing a Summary

A **summary** presents the most important ideas and examples in a shortened form. To write an effective summary, it helps to see the major parts of a text as you did in Text Analysis B. Then you look for the writer's main idea in each part and include the main ideas in your summary.

1. Write a one-paragraph summary of this selection by completing the sentences in your own words with information from the selection. The paragraph numbers indicate the parts of the selection that each of your sentences summarizes.

   (¶ 1) In "Untitled" Robert Fulghum observes that kindergartners and college students have quite similar resources and facilities, but . . .

   (¶ 2–6) When he asks kindergartners if they can draw, sing, dance, or act in plays, they . . .

   (¶ 7–8) When you ask college students the same questions, they . . .

   (¶ 9–10) Fulghum ends by asking his readers . . .

2. Write about something you did as a child but have stopped doing. Use these questions as a guide.

   What did you use to do?
   Why did you stop?
   Did someone criticize you?
   Did someone make fun of you?
   Did you lose interest?
   Did you stop because you didn't have time anymore?
   How do you feel about giving up this activity? Are you happy or sad that you don't do it anymore?

Selection Five

Before Reading

Mel Glenn, a high school English teacher, has written many poems about fictional high school students, but they were inspired by real students he has taught over the years.

Discussion
Have you ever tried to write a poem, a play, a song, or do some other creative work? How did you feel about showing it to someone else? Why did you feel that way?

Focus for the First Reading
Read these questions before you read the poem. You should be able to answer them after you finish the first reading.

1. What did Elizabeth McKenzie create?
2. What did she do with it?

Elizabeth McKenzie
by Mel Glenn

1   Late at night and in secret
    So as to avoid stupid questions
    From insensitive friends
    And questioning parents,
5   I wrote a play in two acts.
    I was afraid to show it to my English teacher,
    Afraid he wouldn't like any of it
    And would rip it apart,[1]
    Afraid he'd like it so much that
10 He wouldn't criticize it at all.
    For days I circled his desk after class
    And talked to him about everything except
    My play.
    When my ramblings[2] became longer
15 And his replies more curtly[3] polite,
    I stopped going up to his desk.
    Instead, I took my play home
    And stuffed it in a bottom drawer
    With the clothes I no longer wear.
20 Maybe, one day, I'll have the courage to
    Get my acts[4] together.[5]

[1] **rip . . . apart**   tear into pieces; criticize

[2] **ramblings**   long talk which doesn't seem to have a purpose
[3] **curtly**   speaking with few words, suggesting rudeness

[4] **acts**   sections of a play
[5] **get my acts together**   suggests the idiomatic expression "Get your act together," meaning do things in a more organized way

Comprehension Check

A. First Reading

Fill in the blanks with an appropriate word or phrase.

Elizabeth McKenzie wrote a two-act _____ in secret. On many
(1)

occasions, she went to talk with her English teacher after _____ , but
(2)

she talked about everything except what she had written. After a while, she

stopped going up to his _____. She took her play home and stuffed it
(3)

in a _____ with some clothes she didn't wear anymore.
(4)

B. Second Reading

Read the poem again. Then answer the questions.

1. When did Elizabeth write her play?
2. Why did she write at that time?
3. What are two reasons she was afraid to show it to her English teacher?
4. Which of the following adjectives would you use to describe Elizabeth's
    feelings about showing the play to her English teacher? What details in the
    poem suggest that the words you chose describe her well?

    confident

    eager to share it

    embarrassed

    happy

    nervous

    proud

    scared

    timid

Sharing Your Thoughts

1. Do you think this is the first time Elizabeth has written something like a play? What in the poem supports your answer?

2. What do the last two lines say about Elizabeth's self-image?

3. Elizabeth didn't get help from her English teacher. How do you think things might have turned out if she had gotten help?

4. Which of the other selections in this unit, if any, does this poem remind you of? What connection do you see?

Writing Task

1. Write a conversation between Elizabeth and one of the people listed below. Have each person speak at least three times.

   a. a friend who found out that she wrote a play

   b. a parent who found out that she wrote a play

   c. her English teacher, the first or last time she goes to see him

2. Write about a time you were embarrassed about showing work you had done to others or about taking credit for something you did. Use these questions as a guide.

   What did you create or do? When, where, why?
   How did you feel about your work? Why?
   How did you feel about showing it to others?

A Final Look

Discussion

1. Work with a classmate, in a small group, or as a whole class. Drawing on all five selections in this unit, discuss the title of the unit and the focus questions on page 75.

2. Reread the quote on page 75. Have you learned anything in this unit that you think might help you find your way in life and live more happily?

3. How does the following quote from Quotable Quotes, *Reader's Digest* (July 1995), relate to this unit as a whole?

   "You don't get harmony when everybody sings the same note."
   —Doug Floyd, Spokane, WA

4. We tend to do things we are good at. What, if anything, might you gain by doing things as hobbies and recreational activities that you are *not* really good at? What, if anything, do you do for a hobby or recreational activity that you are not particularly good at? Why do you do it? What kind of satisfaction do you get from it?

5. Robert Fulghum suggests that many adults have lost the ability to play, to have fun, to be creative and imaginative. Take a few moments to have fun and be creative. How many different things can these drawings be? Invent a similar drawing to test the imagination of your classmates.

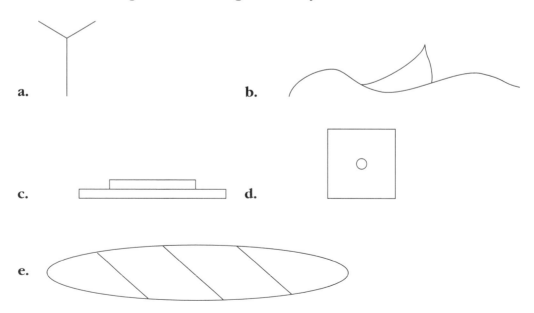

Unit Project

Step 1 *Respond to this inventory individually.*

MULTIPLE INTELLIGENCES INVENTORY
Check the statements that apply to you in each intelligence category.

LINGUISTIC INTELLIGENCE
_____ Books are very important to me.
_____ I enjoy word games like Scrabble, Anagrams, or Password.
_____ Social studies, history, and my native language class were easier for me in school than math and science.
_____ When I drive down a freeway, I pay more attention to the words written on billboards than to the scenery.
_____ My conversation includes references to things that I've read or heard.

LOGICAL-MATHEMATICAL INTELLIGENCE
_____ Math and / or science were among my favorite subjects in school.
_____ I enjoy playing games or solving problems that require logical thinking.
_____ I'm interested in new developments in science.
_____ I sometimes think in clear, abstract, wordless, imageless ideas.
_____ I like finding logical errors in things that people say and do at home and work.

SPATIAL INTELLIGENCE
_____ I often see clear visual images when I close my eyes.
_____ I'm sensitive to color.
_____ I enjoy doing jigsaw puzzles, mazes, and other visual puzzles.
_____ I can generally find my way around unfamiliar territory.
_____ I like to draw or doodle.

BODILY-KINESTHETIC INTELLIGENCE
_____ I play at least one sport or do some physical activity on a regular basis.
_____ I find it difficult to sit still for long periods of time.
_____ I like working with my hands at concrete activities such as sewing, weaving, carving, carpentry, or model building.
_____ I need to touch things in order to learn more about them.
_____ I would describe myself as well coordinated.

MUSICAL INTELLIGENCE
_____ I frequently listen to music on radio, records, cassettes, or compact discs.
_____ I play a musical instrument.
_____ I can easily keep time to a piece of music with a simple percussion instrument.
_____ I know the tunes to many different songs or musical pieces.
_____ If I hear a musical selection once or twice, I am usually able to sing it back fairly accurately.

INTERPERSONAL INTELLIGENCE
_____ I'm the sort of person that people come to for advice and counsel at work or in my neighborhood.
_____ When I have a problem, I'm more likely to ask another person for help than try to work it out on my own.
_____ I have at least three close friends.
_____ I like to get involved in social activities connected with my work, church, or community.
_____ I would rather spend my evenings at a lively party than stay at home alone.

INTRAPERSONAL INTELLIGENCE
_____ I regularly spend time alone meditating, reflecting, or thinking about important life questions.
_____ I can respond to problems in life without too much difficulty.
_____ I have a realistic view of my strengths and weaknesses or limitations.
_____ I keep a personal diary or journal to record the events of my inner life.
_____ I am self-employed or have at least thought seriously about starting my own business.

Step 2 *Think about what your answers to the inventory tell about yourself. Which of your intelligences are stronger or better developed? Which are weaker or less developed? What, if anything, surprised you about what the inventory showed about your intelligences? Compare your response on this inventory with the profile that you got when you did Sharing Your Thoughts on page 83.*

Step 3 *Write a summary of what the inventory shows about your intelligences. You may want to write two paragraphs, one about your better-developed intelligences and one about your less-developed intelligences.*

Between Two Worlds

FOCUS

➤ Why do people sometimes leave their country?

➤ How do they feel about leaving?

➤ What are some of the changes and problems they might face in a foreign country?

➤ How do immigrants feel about the change in their lives?

➤ What contributions do immigrants make to the countries they migrate to?

> *between these two worlds*
> *I am happy, confused, angry*
> *and in pain—all at the same time,*
> *for I am a door*
> *caught between two rooms.*
> *I see and feel both of them*
> *But I don't seem to belong to either.*
> — Nagesh Rao,
> excerpt from
> *I am a door*

115

Selection One

Before Reading

This selection is adapted from an article by Peter Stalker which appeared in the magazine *World of Work*, a publication of the International Labour Organization in Geneva, Switzerland.

Discussion

When people leave their homelands, they migrate; they become immigrants in a new country.

Think of people you know who migrated to a foreign country. Make a list of the reasons they left their homeland; add other reasons you can think of that people might leave their homelands.

Previewing

1. Efficient readers get information from maps and tables before they start to read.
   Look at the world map and the table under it.
   What countries are people leaving? What countries are they going to?

2. Below the title of some magazine articles there are several sentences in a different type of print. Efficient readers get a general idea about the article by reading this material, which is sometimes called an **abstract**.
   Read the abstract below the title of the magazine article on page 117. Answer the following questions.

   1. Is migration something new?
   2. Does migration occur in all parts of the world?
   3. Do people always migrate because they want to?
   4. Is all migration legal?
   5. Is all migration permanent?
   6. What is the most common reason for migration?

Focus for the First Reading

Read the questions before you read the selection. You should be able to answer them after you finish the first reading.

1. How do receiving countries feel about foreign workers?
2. Does the author believe that migration for purposes of work will continue?

Migration All Over the World

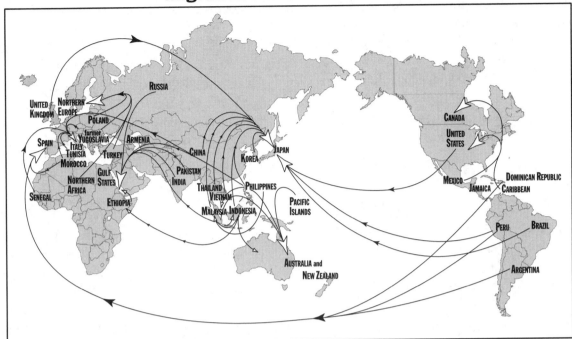

About 70 million people now work or live in foreign countries.

Outflow of Asian Migrant Workers 1990–1991			
Philippines	530,600	China	73,900
Pakistan	128,300	Thailand	63,500
Bangladesh	125,500	Korea	55,800
Indonesia	105,500	Sri Lanka	53,800

Source: *World Population Monitoring 1993*, New York: United Nations, 1996, p. 206.

Millions of Workers on the Move

by **Peter Stalker**

Throughout[1] history and throughout the world, men and women have had to reconcile themselves to[2] migration, to leaving their homelands to make a new start in a foreign country. A quick look at the map illustrates the extent and importance of migration today. Legal or illegal, temporary, seasonal or permanent, migration for employment is one of the most common features of the world of work.

1   Peruvian labourers in Japan. Russian scientists in Israel. Sri Lankan housemaids in Singapore. Around 70 million people now work or live in foreign countries.

There are also millions of refugees, people who are forced from their homelands by natural disaster or military conflict. And the numbers are rising[3]: one million people

---

[1] **throughout**   during all time, in all places
[2] **reconcile themselves to**   accept an unpleasant situation
[3] **rising**   going up

emigrate permanently each year, while another million seek political asylum.[4]

2   Most migrant workers are forced to go to other countries by low wages and unemployment, or they are simply attracted by better opportunities elsewhere. One or two people migrate at first, but then others follow from the same community, establishing complex chains of migration linking poor countries to rich countries: Brazil to Japan, Turkey to Germany, Iran to Sweden.

3   Not all international migration is from developing to industrialized countries. There is also migration between developing countries[5]: Colombians to Venezuela, Malians to Côte d'Ivoire. And many countries, like Malaysia and Nigeria, are both senders and receivers of migrants.

4   Migration for some workers is a short-term solution: a two-year contract in the Gulf to save the money for a new house or to buy some land. Others travel seasonally, like the Poles who pick fruit in Germany or France. But millions would like permanent residence, maybe even citizenship,[6] in a new country.

5   The receiving countries say they want fewer immigrants, but it is not certain that they can substantially reduce the numbers, especially where borders are "porous."[7] First, because there are still plenty of the dirty, dangerous and difficult jobs which only immigrants are willing to do.[8] And second, because the numbers seeking work will continue to grow: 38 million people enter the labor force in developing countries each year, joining the 700 million or so who are already unemployed. At all levels, from skilled engineers and high-level managers to bricklayers and housemaids, there will probably be many workers seeking opportunities around the globe for many years to come.

---

[4] **political asylum**   protection people seek in another country when they leave their native country for political reasons

[5] **developing countries**   largely agricultural countries with relatively little industry

[6] **citizenship**   the legal right of being a member or citizen of a particular country

[7] **where borders are "porous"**   where people can easily cross the official line between countries

[8] **are willing to do**   agree to do

 Comprehension Check

A. First Reading

*Mark the statements **T** (true) or **F** (false). Be prepared to show evidence in the selection that supports your answers.*

1.   T   F   Receiving countries do not always welcome immigrants.

2.   T   F   The author thinks that in the future there will be less migration for purposes of work.

B. Second Reading

Read the selection again. Then answer the questions. Be prepared to find evidence in the selection that supports your answers.

1.   Paragraph 1 states several reasons people migrate. One reason is to find work. What are three other reasons?

2. What economic conditions at home force people to look for work in other countries?

3. What are some countries that people migrate to?

4. Not all migration is for permanent residence. What are examples of non-permanent migration?

5. Why can't receiving countries always control the number of immigrants who enter the country?

6. What are two reasons that migration for work will continue?

 Vocabulary

 A. Vocabulary Building

Find a word or expression in the selection that means the same as the words or expressions below.

1. work or job (abstract) _____
2. people forced to leave home (¶ 1) _____
3. earthquakes, floods, or hurricanes (¶ 1) _____
4. war (¶ 1) _____
5. increasing; getting larger (¶ 1) _____
6. look for (¶ 1) _____
7. payment for work (¶ 2) _____
8. in another place (¶ 2) _____
9. connecting (¶ 2) _____
10. a lower number of (¶ 5) _____
11. decrease; make smaller (¶ 5) _____
12. a lot of (¶ 5) _____

 B. Word Analysis

Related Words

The suffix *-ment* changes a verb to a noun. For example, *employ* (v) / *employment* (n).

The past participle of a verb can function as an adjective. For example, a person who has a job is an *employed* person.

The prefix *un-* reverses the meaning of a word. For example, *employment* means the state of having a job; *unemployment* means the state of not having a job.

Verb	Adjective	Noun
employ	employed	employment
	unemployed	unemployment

1 *Complete the sentences with the appropriate words from the box on page 119.*

1. People need to find _____ in order to support their families.

2. When they are _____, there is pressure for them to migrate to other countries to look for work.

The suffix *-ly* changes an adjective to an adverb.

Adjective	Adverb
permanent	permanently
temporary	temporarily
seasonal	seasonally

---

2 *Complete the sentences with the appropriate words from the box above.*

1. Many immigrants want to stay in their new country; they want to migrate _____.

2. Many others migrate for only a few years; their migration is _____.

3. When people go to another country to work every summer, for example, we call that _____ migration.

C. Vocabulary Review

Complete the following statements about the reading selection with the correct word or expression from the list below. Use each word or expression only once.

border	employment	natural disasters	refugees
developing	immigrants	plenty of	rise
elsewhere	migrate	political asylum	wages

1. Many people _____ to other countries to seek better economic opportunities.

2. Often migrants go from _____ countries where there are few opportunities for _____ to industrialized countries where there are _____ jobs.

3. When _____ are low and unemployment is high, people are forced to look for work _____.

4. But not all people migrate to find work. Some seek _____ in a foreign country because their ideas are different from their government's ideas.

5. Other migrants are _____, people who leave their homeland to escape war or _____.

6. Even though receiving countries do not always welcome _____, the numbers will probably continue to _____.

7. It is difficult to control every place of entry along the _____ of a country, and opportunities in industrialized countries will always attract immigrants.

Sharing Your Thoughts

1. Talk about some people you know who have left their homelands. In Before Reading, on page 116, you made a list of the reasons these people migrated. Now consider the following questions.
   a. What risks did they have to take to leave?
   b. Did they leave permanently or temporarily?
   c. What problems, if any, did they have finding work?
   d. What kind of work did they do in the foreign country?
   e. Were they happy in the foreign country?
   f. How did people in the foreign country treat them?

2. What are some of the differences between (1) migrating seasonally or temporarily and (2) going to another country permanently? Consider, for example, the required legal documents, the need to adjust to life in the foreign country, the way people in the foreign country treat temporary versus permanent immigrants.

 Text Analysis

A. Grammar-Meaning Connection: Understanding Passive Sentences

In most sentences in English, the agent (doer of the action) comes first. These are active sentences.

<u>Polish workers</u> pick fruit in France and Germany.
  (agent)

Sometimes the agent or doer comes after the word *by* at the end of the sentence or does not appear at all. These are passive sentences. Verbs in passive sentences are formed with the verb *be* plus a past participle.

In France and Germany fruit *is picked* by <u>Polish workers</u>.
                                                    (agent)

Sometimes immigrants *are not treated* well. (no agent)

The agent is not always a person.

Sometimes the fruit *is picked* by <u>machine</u>
                                    (agent)

Read the following passive sentences. Notice the verb forms **are forced** *and* **are attracted.** *Notice the use of the word* **by**. *Then answer the question below each sentence.*

1. . . . people . . . are forced from their homelands by natural disaster or military conflict. (¶ 1)
    What forces people to leave their homelands?

2. Most migrant workers are forced to go to other countries by low wages and unemployment . . . (¶ 2)
    What forces migrant workers to go to other countries?

3. (People are) attracted by better opportunities elsewhere. (¶ 2)
    What attracts people to other countries?

B. Analyzing Complex Sentences

When a sentence is long and difficult, sometimes we can understand it better if we break it into simple sentences with only one idea in each sentence. Sometimes it also helps to change the order of the parts.

Look at the first sentence in the abstract:

Throughout history and throughout the world, men and women have had to reconcile themselves to migration, to leaving their homelands to make a new start in a foreign country.

This sentence has four ideas:

Men and women have had to reconcile themselves to migration.

They have had to leave their homelands to make a new start in a foreign country.

They have migrated throughout history.

They have migrated throughout the world.

Read the long sentences. Then complete each of the shorter sentences, adding only one idea from the longer sentence.

1. One or two people migrate at first, but then others follow from the same community, establishing complex chains of migration linking poor countries to rich . . . (¶ 2)

    One or two people _____

    Others follow _____

    All these people establish _____

    These chains of migration link _____

2. The receiving countries say they want fewer immigrants, but it is not certain that they can substantially reduce the numbers, especially where borders are "porous." (¶ 5)

    The receiving countries _____

    It is not certain _____

    Reducing the numbers is especially difficult where _____

Writing Task

1. Write a paragraph that begins with the sentence below. Use information from Selection One and the map on page 117 to support this statement.

    Many people migrate for purposes of work.

2. If you have left your country, write a paragraph about your experience. Use these questions as a guide.

    Why did you leave?
    What things were you happy about?
    What things were you nervous or sad about?
    How do you feel now?

    You might start your sentences with phrases such as:

    My family decided to . . .
    In some ways I looked forward to this . . .
    On the other hand, I felt nervous (or sad) because . . .
    Now . . .

3. If you have not left your country, write about a change in your life such as changing schools, changing jobs, or moving from one place to another within your country. Use these questions as a guide.

What was the change?
Why did you make this change?
What was good about it?
What was bad about it?
How do you feel about it now?

Selection Two

⬤ Before Reading

This selection is from the personal story of Mark Grottel as told to Al Santoli for his book, *New Americans*. Mark Grottel is a Russian Jew who came to New York with his wife and daughter in 1979. Jews were finally permitted to leave the former Soviet Union in the 1970s, and many left to escape anti-Semitism, or hatred of Jews. Most of them went to Israel, Canada, Australia, and the United States. Mr. Grottel was a physics professor in Leningrad, but after he migrated he worked in a nuclear-engineering firm in New York because he could not get a job as a professor.

Discussion

When you don't know the customs of a new place, it is natural to continue to do things in the ways you already know. However, if customs are different, this can cause problems—sometimes serious, sometimes amusing.

Share stories with your classmates about a time when not knowing the local customs caused a problem. Think of social situations, work situations, school situations.

Previewing

Read the first paragraph of this selection. Answer these questions.

1. Who is telling the story?
2. Where does the story take place?
3. Do you think it will be amusing or serious?

Focus for the First Reading

Read these questions before you read the selection. You should be able to answer them after you finish the first reading.

1. Why didn't Mark pay attention to the people in his office?
2. What mistake did he make?

Smile

by Mark Grottel as told to Al Santoli

1   I have to tell you my favorite story about America. It was maybe one month after I began working at my first job in New York, at an engineering firm. Every day I sat at my desk, concentrating very hard. I was very serious. The problem was that I couldn't speak English and I was trying to learn new skills. My co-workers would pass back and forth[1] in front of my desk. But I was concentrating so heavily that I didn't pay attention to them.

2   One day a group of people came to the office. They just stood there looking at me. I didn't pay attention to them. One of these guys cried out very loud, "SMILE."

[1] **back and forth**   in one direction and then in the opposite direction

3   At first I didn't realize that he was talking to me. I looked up and saw everybody looking at me. He repeated, "SMILE."

4   My supervisor said to him, "Sir, this man just came from Russia. He has a problem with English." The man said, "Okay. He cannot talk. But, still, he can smile."

5   I understood what they were saying. So I started to smile. And everybody started to smile. When the group of men left the office, I was told that the man was a vice-president of our company.

6   I always think about this incident and laugh. Because in Russia, if you smile during working hours, your boss will say, "You are not working. You are just wasting time." When a supervisor comes into the work area, suddenly everybody becomes very serious. Here it is just the opposite. The vice-president couldn't understand why I was so serious. He was trying to cheer me up.

7   For the first time, I understood that in this country everybody has to smile.

Comprehension Check

A. First Reading

*Mark the statements **T** (true) or **F** (false). Be prepared to show evidence in the selection that supports your answers.*

1.   T   F   Mark was very serious in the office.

2.   T   F   His behavior was appropriate for an office in the United States.

B. Second Reading

1   *Read the selection again. Sort the statements into two categories according to the view expressed in the reading—those that apply to customs in offices in Russia (mark these **R**) and those that apply to customs in offices in the United States (mark these **US**).*

___ **a.** You can be friendly and smile and do a lot of work at the same time.

___ **b.** Employees are supposed to be serious while they are working.

___ **c.** It is OK not to pay attention to co-workers and supervisors.

___ **d.** If employees are not serious, supervisors think they are not working.

___ **e.** Everybody is supposed to be friendly in the workplace.

2   *Answer the questions. Be prepared to show evidence in the selection that supports your answers.*

1. Who visited the office on this day?

2. What excuse did one of Mark's co-workers make for him?

3. How did the visitor respond?

 Vocabulary

 A. Vocabulary Building

Look at the underlined words or expressions in the sentences on the left. Find them in the selection. Then match them with the correct meaning on the right.

___ **1.** Every day I sat at my desk, <u>concentrating</u> very hard. (¶ 1)

a. abilities that you develop through practice

___ **2.** I was very <u>serious</u>. (¶ 1)

b. people who work with you

___ **3.** . . . I was trying to learn new <u>skills</u>. (¶ 1)

c. unsmiling; not joking

___ **4.** My <u>co-workers</u> would pass back and forth in front of my desk. (¶ 1)

d. make me happy

___ **5.** . . . I didn't <u>pay attention to</u> them. (¶ 1)

e. using your time inefficiently

___ **6.** . . . I didn't <u>realize</u> that he was talking to me. (¶ 3)

f. carefully listen to or watch

___ **7.** . . . your <u>boss</u> will say, "You are not working." (¶ 6)

g. supervisor; superior in a workplace

___ **8.** "You are just <u>wasting time</u>." (¶ 6)

h. thinking very carefully

___ **9.** He was trying to <u>cheer me up</u>. (¶ 6)

i. understand; know

 B. Using a Dictionary

A word can have more than one meaning. Indicate which meaning in the dictionary entry below best defines the underlined word as it is used in the sentence.

> **just**[1] /dʒʌst/ *adv* **1** exactly: *My brother looks just like my dad.* **2** only: *I just play the piano for fun.* | *It happened just a few weeks ago.* | *Can you wait five minutes? I just have to iron this.* (=it's the last thing I have to do) **3** if something has just happened, it happened only a short time before: *I just got back from Marilyn's house.*

1. They <u>just</u> stood there . . . (¶ 2)   Definition _____

2. Sir, this man <u>just</u> came from Russia. (¶ 4)   Definition _____

3. You are <u>just</u> wasting time. (¶ 6)   Definition _____

4. Here it is <u>just</u> the opposite. (¶ 6)   Definition _____

C. Vocabulary Review

Complete the following statements about the reading selection with the correct word or expression from the list below. Use each word or expression only once.

bosses	**just**	**realized**	**skills**
concentrating	**pay attention**	**serious**	**wasting time**

1. At the time of this incident, Mark Grottel, a Russian immigrant to the United States, had _____ started his new job in New York.

2. He had a very _____ attitude about his work, and he was worried about learning new _____.

3. One day visitors came into the office while he was _____ very hard on his work. Mark didn't _____ to them. One of the visitors, the vice-president of the company, didn't understand why Mark was so serious. He told him to smile.

4. When Mark finally _____ what they were saying, he started to smile.

5. Mark thought this incident was funny because in Russia if workers smile, _____ think they are not working and that they are just _____.

Sharing Your Thoughts

1. Which adjectives do you think describe the way Mark felt when he began working in the engineering firm? Why do you think he felt that way? Find evidence in the selection that supports your answers.

angry	nervous
confused	optimistic
disappointed	scared
embarrassed	serious
foolish	sure of himself
happy-go-lucky	under pressure

2. Discuss office rules in your culture. If you do not have experience working in an office, ask someone from your country who has worked in an office. Consider the following:

   a. How are you supposed to address co-workers and supervisors? Is it correct to use titles (Mr., Miss, Mrs., Ms.) or first names?

   b. Is it appropriate to be friendly with co-workers and supervisors? Do employees socialize? Are there office parties?

   c. What are the rules about breaks during work hours?

   d. What is the correct way to dress?

   e. What are the rules about being on time?

   f. What are the rules about missing work for particular reasons?

3. In which of the following situations, in your culture, would you expect people to smile? In which situations would you expect people to be serious?

   a job interview

   a meeting between a parent and a teacher

   a wedding

   a funeral

   a school graduation

   a conversation between a store employee and a customer

   a conversation with an employee in a government office

4. Look at the list and discuss the kinds of problems workers might have in a foreign country. You might want to consider if agricultural workers, factory workers, and professional workers such as doctors and engineers all have the same problems.

   language

   relationships with bosses

   relationships with co-workers

   transportation

   filling out forms (bureaucracy)

   legal issues (visas)

   unemployment

   discrimination

Text Analysis

Grammar-Meaning Connection: Using *can* / *can't* and *could* / *couldn't*

Use *could* / *couldn't* to describe ability / inability in the past.

EXAMPLE: Mark *could speak* Russian, but he *couldn't speak* English.

Use *can* / *can't* to describe ability / inability in the present.

EXAMPLE: The vice-president says that Mark *can smile* even if he *can't speak* English.

1. Practice using *could* / *couldn't* and *can* / *can't* to express past and present ability. Talk about things you *could* or *couldn't* do when you were younger and things you *can* or *can't* do now. Consider skills such as playing a musical instrument, riding a bicycle, or cooking.

   EXAMPLE: When I was younger, I couldn't speak English, but now I can speak it pretty well. I still can't understand everything in English, but I'm doing better.

2. Think about the kindergarten children and the college students that Robert Fulghum describes in Unit Three, Selection Four. What are some of the things kindergarten children can do? What are some of the things college students could do when they were younger, but now say they can't do?

Writing Task

1. Mark Grottel is describing an incident that happened to him, so he uses the pronoun *I*. Imagine you are Mark's friend or co-worker. Tell another person about the incident. Use the pronoun *he* to refer to Mark. You might begin like this:

   There was a Russian immigrant who worked in our office. When he started to work there . . .

2. In this selection Mark Grottel did not understand how to act in a new situation. Many times immigrants or visitors to another culture do not understand things they see. Read the following example.

   I am a teacher from the United States who lived and worked in Poland for a year. When I was there, I noticed lines of people waiting patiently outside of stores, but the stores were not very crowded[1] inside. This is exactly the opposite of what I expected. In the United States stores are crowded inside, and there are lines at the check-out counter, but you never see lines outside. At first I couldn't understand what was going on. Then I noticed that no one went into the store without a basket. There were a limited number of baskets, and when someone left the store

---

[1]*crowded* = full of people

another person went in. I finally realized that in one system you wait in line to get out, and in the other you wait in line to get in.

Write about a situation like this in which you did not know how to act or in which you observed something that you did not at first understand. Use these questions as a guide.

Where did the incident take place?
What were you doing or what did you observe?
How was this different from what you expected?
What was it that you did not understand?

Selection Three

Before Reading

This selection is also from Al Santoli's book, *New Americans*. Trong Nguyen tells about his experience as a leader of the Vietnamese refugee community in Chicago. He came to Chicago in 1976, the year after the Vietnam War ended. Many other refugees from the former South Vietnam also left at that time. They wanted to escape life under the Communist government that was in control after the war.

Discussion

You have read and talked about different reasons immigrants leave their homelands. Whatever the reason for migrating, immigrants often make important contributions to their new country. Think about groups of immigrants that you are familiar with (the Cubans in Florida, perhaps), individual immigrants that you know, or famous immigrants such as Albert Einstein (a mathematician and physicist who migrated from Germany to Switzerland and later to the United States) or Madeleine Albright (the first female Secretary of State of the United States who was an immigrant from the former Czechoslovakia).

Talk about the contributions they have made in their place of work, in their community, to their adopted country, or to the world.

Previewing

Preview this selection by reading all of the first paragraph, the first sentence of each of the other paragraphs, and all of the last paragraph.
This selection is about:
a. restaurants in a Vietnamese neighborhood
b. a change in a neighborhood

Focus for the First Reading

Read these questions before you read the selection. You should be able to answer them after you finish the first reading.

1. Why didn't Chinese owners want to rent to Vietnamese people?

2. How did Trong convince the Chinese to rent to the Vietnamese?

3. What did the Uptown neighborhood become well known for?

Uptown

by Trong Nguyen as told to Al Santoli

1   The business strip on Argyle Street was a disaster area. Around sixty percent of the buildings were owned by a Chinese association, Hip Sing, which had a vision in the late 1960s of turning the area into a new Chinatown. But they had little

success, because of crime and the depressed environment. Still, the Vietnamese thought that maybe it could be a good place to start our business area.

2   We asked the Hip Sing to rent us some abandoned storefronts. They said, "No, you're not Chinese. This is the New Chinatown." But I began to work closely with a Chinese manager of one of the buildings. I said, "If you can help us, we can all benefit. There aren't that many Chinese living in the area. If you let the Vietnamese rent spaces, this area can be developed. And I can place new refugees in apartment buildings that the Hip Sing owns, that have a low occupancy rate. They will shop here on Argyle and the area will grow and develop." He agreed.

3   I didn't know anything about business in America; I could only advise refugees on social issues. But we were able to provide a translation service so they could obtain business permits. The neighborhood began to grow.

4   Nearly all the businesses owned by refugees were started by families pooling their money together or borrowing from friends. The first places were restaurants and small supermarkets. As more refugees moved into the neighborhood and new businesses were springing up, the gangs,[1] the drug addicts, and the winos[2] had fewer and fewer abandoned buildings to hang out in.[3] And as the neighborhood began to come back to life, the police sent more security. But in the alleys and side streets[4] it was still something else.

5   Argyle Street became a kind of a beachhead[5] where people could have a semblance of ordinary life, and it has become an international area. There are more than fifty Vietnamese family-owned businesses on the strip. There are also stores owned by Khmer, Lao, Chinese, Ethiopians, a Jewish kosher butcher,[6] two Hispanic grocers, a black record shop, and an American bar. There are Japanese, Thai, Indian, and Mexican restaurants in the area. And a McDonald's.

6   I remember in 1978–79, when I worked with American sponsors[7] from the suburbs, if I said, "Why don't you come to Uptown to work with the refugees?" they would say, "No way, it's too dangerous." Now people from many areas like to come to Argyle Street to shop, and enjoy coming to community activities like the annual Argyle Street Festival or Lunar New Year Celebration.

7   The Vietnamese restaurants do a lot of their business from tourists on weekends. Many don't earn a lot, but they survive by family manpower. For example, Mr. and Mrs. Phan, who own the Nha Tang Restaurant, had a simple dream. They came here as boat people[8] in 1979, worked in a factory to save enough to make a $700 lease payment on a small storefront to open a twelve-table restaurant. His wife is a very good cook, and they charge low prices. Since they opened in 1981, they

[1] **gangs**   groups of young people who cause trouble, fight, commit crimes
[2] **winos**   drunks; people who drink cheap wine and live on the street
[3] **hang out in**   spend time in
[4] **alleys and side streest**   not main streets or avenues
[5] **beachhead**   military term that means "starting point"; a strong position from which to advance further

[6] **kosher butcher**   meat store; meat sold there has to be killed and processed according to Jewish dietary laws

[7] **sponsors**   people or organizations that help refugees get started in their new country

[8] **boat people**   Vietnamese refugees who left their country by boat after the Vietnam War

stay open seven days a week from 9:00 A.M. until 10:00 P.M. They earn enough to keep the family well fed and have a little profit left over for saving.

8   The most famous place in the neighborhood is the Mekong Restaurant, on the corner of Argyle and Broadway, which attracts many people from the suburbs and other states. The owner, Mr. Lam Ton, worked with the U.S. State Department in Vietnam.

9   The first year his restaurant opened, in 1983, Lam Ton lost money. The neighborhood's reputation was still very rough. But, all of a sudden, his business turned around after some Chicago newspaper people wrote very favorably about the restaurant. The Mekong brought Uptown into the limelight,[9] especially in 1985, when a lot of media attention was given to the tenth anniversary of the fall of Saigon.

[9] **limelight**   attention from the public

10   Newspeople saw a lot of new stores with posterboards written in Vietnamese. They wrote stories emphasizing how the refugees revitalized Uptown and turned the slum area[10] into a more beautiful place. They began calling Argyle Street "Little Saigon."

[10]**slum area**   poor area of a city

Comprehension Check

A. First Reading

*Mark the statements **T** (true) or **F** (false). Be prepared to show evidence in the selection that supports your answers.*

1. T   F   The Chinese didn't want to rent to the Vietnamese because they wanted to build a mall in the area.

2. T   F   Trong convinced them to rent to the Vietnamese by telling them that everyone would benefit.

3. T   F   Vietnamese restaurants brought good publicity to the neighborhood.

B. Second Reading

1   *Read the selection again. Sort the words and expressions into two categories—those that describe Uptown before the Vietnamese transformed it (mark these **B**) and those that describe Uptown after the Vietnamese transformed it (mark these **A**).*

_____ abandoned storefronts   _____ more community activities

_____ dangerous   _____ new stores

_____ depressed environment   _____ revitalized

_____ drug addicts, gangs, and winos   _____ rough reputation

_____	family-owned businesses	_____	safer
_____	favorable newspaper reviews	_____	slum area
_____	international area	_____	variety of ethnic restaurants
_____	low occupancy rate	_____	visitors and tourists

2 *Answer the questions. Be prepared to show evidence from the selection that supports your answers.*

1. How did the Vietnamese get the money to start their businesses?
2. What kinds of businesses did they start?
3. What did Argyle Street become known for?

Vocabulary

 ## A. Vocabulary Building

Look at the underlined words or expressions in the sentences below. Find them in the selection. Then choose the correct meaning for the context.

1. . . . Hip Sing . . . had a vision in the late 1960s of <u>turning</u> the area <u>into</u> a new Chinatown. (¶ 1)
   a. changing to
   b. moving to

2. But <u>they had little success</u> . . . (¶ 1)
   a. they had some success
   b. they didn't have much success

3. . . . because of crime and <u>the depressed environment</u>. (¶ 1)
   a. bad economic conditions
   b. good economic conditions

4. If you can help us, we can all <u>benefit</u>. (¶ 2)
   a. do well
   b. do poorly

5. And I can place new refugees in apartment buildings that the Hip Sing owns, that <u>have a low occupancy rate</u>. (¶ 2)
   a. are almost full
   b. are not very full

6. They will shop here on Argyle and the area will grow and <u>develop</u>. (¶ 2)
   a. increase in size
   b. do better economically

7. Nearly all the businesses . . . were started by families <u>pooling their money together</u> . . . (¶ 4)
   a. putting their money together
   b. putting their money in the bank

8. . . . or <u>borrowing</u> from friends. (¶ 4)

   a. giving away money

   b. taking money temporarily

9. Many don't <u>earn</u> a lot, but they survive by family manpower. (¶ 7)

   a. save money

   b. make money

10. . . . Mr. and Mrs. Phan . . . worked in a factory to save enough to make a $700 <u>lease</u> payment on a storefront to open a twelve-table restaurant. (¶ 7)

    a. rental contract

    b. employment contract

11. . . . <u>they charge low prices</u>. (¶ 7)

    a. the restaurant is expensive

    b. the restaurant is not very expensive

12. They earn enough to keep the family well fed and have a little <u>profit</u> left over for saving. (¶ 7)

    a. money made from a business

    b. money used to start a business

13. The first year . . . Lam Ton <u>lost money</u>. (¶ 9)

    a. earned more money than he spent

    b. spent more money than he earned

14. But, all of a sudden, his business <u>turned around</u> . . . (¶ 9)

    a. began to do well

    b. got worse

15. They wrote stories emphasizing how the refugees <u>revitalized Uptown</u> and turned the slum area into a more beautiful place. (¶ 10)

    a. made Uptown come to life again

    b. destroyed Uptown

 ## B. Compound Words

> A word made up of two or more whole words is called a **compound word**. Some are connected with hyphens (*twelve-table restaurant*). Others are written as one word (*beachhead; limelight*).

Find the compound word in the selection that means the same as the phrases below.

1. an area of a city where there are many Chinese residents and many Chinese businesses (¶ 1)   _____

2. a store at the front part of a
building on the street level (¶ 2)

_____

3. a store that sells primarily food (¶ 4)

_____

4. businesses owned by a family (¶ 5)

_____

5. workers or employees (¶ 7)

_____

6. a paper that reports the news (¶ 9)

_____

7. people whose work is getting news
to the public (¶ 10)

_____

8. boards with information posted
on them (¶ 10)

_____

C. Vocabulary Review

*Complete the following statements about the reading selection with the correct
word or expression from the list below. Use each word or expression only once.*

benefited	**newspapers**	**slum**
borrowed	**profit**	**supermarkets**
family-owned	**revitalized**	**turned it into**

1. A group of Vietnamese refugees _____ a depressed area in
   Chicago; they _____ a successful neighborhood now known
   as "Little Saigon."

2. Vietnamese families pooled their money or _____ from
   friends to start _____ businesses.

3. Restaurants and small _____ began to appear along the
   business strip.

4. The Vietnamese worked hard and their businesses began to make a
   _____.

5. When good reviews of the restaurants in the area appeared in the
   _____, tourists and other visitors came to Argyle Street.

6. The hard work of a group of immigrants changed a dangerous Chicago
   _____ into a good neighborhood, and all the citizens of
   Chicago _____ from their contribution.

Sharing Your Thoughts

1. Mr. and Mrs. Phan (¶ 7) are a good example of successful businesspeople. Why were they successful? First, list what the Phans did that made them successful. Second, list other things that make a business successful, for example, treating customers nicely.

2. In Before Reading you talked about contributions immigrants make to their new country. The immigrants in this selection changed a bad neighborhood into a good one. List the characteristics of a good neighborhood.

3. Selection One (¶ 2) referred to groups of migrants from the same community settling in the same places in their new country—the Vietnamese in Chicago, for instance. What are some of the advantages and disadvantages of doing this?

Text Analysis

A. Chronological Order

> The most basic way to describe a process such as turning a neighborhood around is to put the steps of the process in the order in which they happened. This is called **chronological order**.

The first sentence of a paragraph is provided below. Number the remaining sentences 1 through 5 to show the chronological order of the events.

Establishing a strong and safe neighborhood on Argyle Street was a long process.

___ **a.** He helped the Vietnamese get business permits.

___ **b.** Trong first got the Chinese landlords to rent property in a slum area to Vietnamese people by convincing the Chinese that everyone would benefit.

___ **c.** Finally, the media began to pay attention to the neighborhood, which they called "Little Saigon," and it became well known.

___ **d.** When they started their businesses, the criminals began to leave.

___ **e.** Once the neighborhood began to turn around, other ethnic groups started businesses on Argyle Street.

B. Grammar-Meaning Connection: Noun Modifiers

In English, nouns can be modified by both adjectives and other nouns. **Noun modifiers** always go before the nouns they modify. For example, an area for businesses is a *business area*. Both *business* and *area* are nouns; *business* modifies *area*.

Try to figure out the nouns and noun modifiers for each of the phrases below. Then scan the appropriate paragraph in the selection to check your answers.

1. an area that looks as if a disaster occurred there (¶ 1) _____
2. buildings that have apartments (¶ 2) _____
3. the rate of occupancy in a building (¶ 2) _____
4. a service that does translation (¶ 3) _____
5. permits for starting businesses (¶ 3) _____
6. people who are addicted to drugs (¶ 4) _____
7. streets to the side or off the main streets (¶ 4) _____
8. a shop that sells records (¶ 5) _____
9. activities that are planned by and for a community (¶ 6) _____
10. people that left their country in boats (¶ 7) _____
11. people that work for newspapers (¶ 9) _____
12. attention from the media or media people (¶ 9) _____
13. an area of a city that has slums (¶ 10) _____

Writing Task

1. Write two paragraphs contrasting the neighborhood before and after its transformation. You might want to start your paragraphs like this:

   Before the Vietnamese came to Uptown it was . . .
   After they had been there a while, it . . .

2. Imagine you are a restaurant reviewer for a Chicago newspaper. You eat at a small, family-run Vietnamese restaurant in "Little Saigon" and talk to the owner. You like the restaurant and decide to write a review for the paper. In your review, be sure to include the following information: the location of the restaurant, something about its physical appearance, the food, and the service.

Selection Four

Before Reading

William Saroyan (1908–1981) was the son of immigrants who migrated from Armenia to California. Many Armenians left their homeland between 1894 and 1916 so they would not be killed by Turks. Most of them went to Russia, Western Europe, the Middle East, or the United States.

Discussion

Talk with your classmates about what makes you happy or sad in the place you live.
> Do you like where you live?
> What might make immigrants happy in a new country?
> What might make them homesick?
> In addition to moving from one country to another, is it especially difficult for peasants—people from rural or farm areas—to leave their homes?

Previewing

Read the first paragraph of the story. List details about Sarkis and his life in Armenia. Based on the information in this paragraph, how do you think he will adjust to life in America?

Focus for the First Reading

This story is divided into two parts. On the first reading, try to follow what happens to Sarkis Khatchadourian after he leaves his hometown, Gultik, in 1908.

After you read Part 1 (¶ 1–17), you should be able to answer these questions.

1. Where does he arrive?

2. Where does he go next?

3. What kind of work does he do?

Before you read Part 2 (¶ 18–34), answer these questions.

1. Why is Sarkis going to California?

2. Do you think he will be happier there?

After you read Part 2 (¶ 18–34), you should be able to answer these questions.

1. What kind of work does Sarkis do in his new home?

2. Is he happy there?

The Peasant

by William Saroyan

Part 1

1   There was a man by the name of Sarkis who came to America from the village of Gultik, in Armenia, in 1908 when he was not yet thirty years of age. He was a big peasant with thick heavy hair and a large black moustache. He weighed about two hundred pounds but wasn't fat, and had an unusually melancholy¹ expression. In Gultik he hadn't been very important—no one in Gultik had been very important—but he had gotten along² very well and had had many friends: Armenians, Kurds, Turks, Arabs, Jews, Greeks, Bulgarians, and men of many other tribes and nations. He had spoken in Armenian, Kurdish, Turkish, and Arabic with these people of Asia Minor, and when he had left Gultik he had left many friends behind him.

2   He reached New York in May, in 1908.

3   It was a very bewildering place and there was no one to talk to. There were very few people in New York in 1908 who could speak so much as three words of Armenian, Kurdish, Turkish, or Arabic. It was very lonely.

4   He went up to Lynn, Massachusetts, and got a job in a shoe factory and began to learn a little English.

5   It was very hard work, especially for a big man. It wasn't work that a man did with his legs and shoulders and trunk,³ it was exasperating work,⁴ with the fingers and with some of the muscles of the arm. And with the eye.

6   He worked in the shoe factory a year and his loneliness grew and grew. There were a number of Armenian families in Lynn, but he didn't like them. They weren't like the people of Gultik.

7   An Armenian from California came to Lynn and one evening Sarkis Khatchadourian met this man in a coffee house and drank *rakki*⁵ with him and the man told Sarkis about California.

8   It is Armenia again, the man said. Sunshine, vines, meadows, olive trees, fig trees, brooks, cows.

9   Cows, my countryman? the peasant cried. Did you say cows?

10   Hundreds of them, the man said.

11   My God, the peasant said. Cows.

12   And work? he said. What is the nature of the work?

13   Farm work, the man said.

14   My God, the peasant said. In the sun, he mused.⁶ My beloved countryman, he cried, are there many of our people in California? That is the question.

15   There are many, said the man.

¹ **melancholy**   sad

² **had gotten along**   had been successful enough

³ **trunk**   torso; main part of the human body

⁴ **exasperating work**   work that bothers him, upsets him, frustrates him

⁵ *rakki*   alcoholic drink

⁶ **mused**   imagined; thought

16   My God, the peasant said. Then I shall go to California.

17   And he did.

Before you read Part 2 (¶ 18–34), answer these questions.

1. Why is Sarkis going to California?

2. Do you think he will be happier there?

Part 2

18   He reached California in August, just in time to pick grapes. It was better work than working in a shoe factory, but it had its bad points too. The workers were mostly Mexicans and Japanese. Strange people. He wanted to talk, but nobody could understand him so he had to work and not talk.

19   The work was to cut a bunch of grapes at the stem and place it on a timber tray which remained under the sun, and the grapes, drying, became raisins. After the grapes had been dried on one side two workers went down a row, lifting a tray and turning the grapes over on to another tray, so that the sun would dry the other side.

20   It was not pleasant to do this work with a Mexican, a man one could not talk to.

21   It was very mournful to turn trays hour after hour with a Mexican.

22   He did this work all summer, and in the winter he plowed the earth[7] and pruned the vines,[8] and on Sundays he went to the city, to an Armenian coffee house on Mariposa Street where he drank *rakki* and coffee and played *scambile* and *tavli*[9] and talked with his countrymen. They were all new people, men he had met in California.

23   One Sunday a man came to this coffee house while the peasant was there, and this man was Arshag Dombalian, who was from Gultik. Arshag Dombalian had known Sarkis Khatchadourian in the old country. In the old country they had spoken to one another. It was very pleasant for Sarkis to meet this man from Gultik in America.

24   They shook hands solemnly, and almost cried.

25   Ahkh, brother Sarkis, Arshag Dombalian said, how are you?

26   I am well, brother Arshag, Sarkis said mournfully. I am well indeed. How are you?

27   Ahkh, I am very well, my beloved brother, said Arshag. And how do you like America, my friend from Gultik?

28   Ahkh, America, said Sarkis. How do I like it? What shall I say? Go; come; and with men known and unknown turn trays. That is all. Go, come; go, come; known, unknown; and turn trays. Who are they? How should we know, my brother? We have never seen them before. What nation are they of? What tongue[10] do they speak? Who can tell?

[7] **plowed the earth**   turned the earth to prepare it for planting

[8] **pruned the vines**   cut the vines so they would grow better

[9] *scambile, tavli*   Armenian games

[10] **tongue**   language

29   Sarkis Khatchadourian took a wife the year after he reached California. This girl bore him a son the following year. He worked hard and saved three hundred dollars and made a down payment[11] on a ten-acre vineyard. He was now a farmer in his own right.[12] He owned horses, a cow, he had a house, a good wife, and a son.

30   One became two, two became three, three became four: days, months, years, and children. It was all very good indeed: he would not say it was not good, but he did not know. He was prospering. As he earned money, he bought more land, plowed, planted, pruned, irrigated, harvested. His vineyard of ten acres grew until it was a vineyard of thirty, then forty, then fifty.

31   And he put up a new house, with electricity; he bought a phonograph; he bought an automobile; he took his wife and his children to the city for ice cream; soda water; he took them into moving-picture theatres. The years went by. His first son graduated from high school and the peasant sat in the auditorium of the school and saw the boy get his diploma and his eyes filled with tears. It was all fine. He knew it was all splendid. His first son married an Armenian girl born in California and the boy bought a small vineyard of his own and at the wedding there was real Armenian and Turkish and Kurdish music and singing and dancing. Fine, fine. His second son not only graduated from high school, he went to Berkeley and graduated from college. It was splendid.

32   It was all marvelous. The change he had seen in life and in the world, right before his very eyes. The telephone. The automobile. The tractor. Carpet sweepers. Vacuum cleaners. Washing machines. Electric refrigerators. The radio. His sons and daughters speaking English, writing English, learning many things. It was a great age, a great time.

33   Still it was sad. He did not know. In Gultik it was fine too. One knew the man one spoke to. Arab, Arab; Kurd, Kurd; Turk, Turk; one knew. One knew the face, the eye, the nose, the very smell. It was home. One talked and knew who one was talking to; but in America what was it? He could never forget what it was in America.

34   Sometimes important Armenians, professional men, visited him. Sometimes, sipping coffee, they said, Well, countryman, how do you like America? And always he looked mournfully into the face of the man he knew, into the eyes he knew, and he said, What do I know? Go, come; and with men known and unknown turn trays.

[11] **down payment**   first (partial) payment on something expensive
[12] **in his own right**   as an independent person; not working for another person

Comprehension Check

A. First Reading

Fill in the blanks with an appropriate word or phrase.

PART 1

Sarkis arrived in _____ in 1908, but he didn't stay there. He went
(1)

to _____, where he worked in a _____, but he was not
(2)   (3)

happy there and decided to go to California.

PART 2

When he arrived in California, he got a job picking _____. Life was
(4)

better there, but he was still _____.
(5)

B. Second Reading

*Read the selection again. Then mark the statements **T** (true) or **F** (false). Be
prepared to show evidence in the selection that supports your answers.*

1. T   F   In California, Sarkis didn't like working with Mexicans and
            Japanese because he couldn't communicate with them.

2. T   F   Sarkis's success and possessions made him happy.

3. T   F   Sarkis finally returned to his homeland.

Vocabulary

A. Vocabulary Building

*Three of the words in each row are similar in meaning, at least for this context.
Each of them could complete the sentence without changing its original meaning.
Underline the three words that are similar. Use a dictionary if necessary.*

1. Sarkis came to America from the _____ of Gultik, in Armenia. (¶ 1)
    a. village   **b.** small town   **c.** big city   **d.** community

2. (He) had an unusually _____ expression. (¶ 1)
    a. sad   **b.** pleasant   **c.** mournful   **d.** melancholy

3. (He) had many friends: Armenians, Kurds, Turks, Arabs, Jews, Greeks, Bulgarians, and men of many other _____. (¶ 1)

   a. political parties   **b.** ethnic groups   **c.** tribes   **d.** nations

4. He _____ New York in May, in 1908. (¶ 2)

   a. arrived in   **b.** got to   **c.** contacted   **d.** reached

5. It (New York) was a very _____ place, and there was no one to talk to. (¶ 3)

   a. wonderful   **b.** confusing   **c.** bewildering   **d.** puzzling

6. There were very few people in New York in 1908 who could speak so much as three words of Armenian, Kurdish, Turkish, or Arabic. It was very _____. (¶ 3)

   a. friendless   **b.** lonely   **c.** solitary   **d.** friendly

7. He was _____. As he earned money, he bought more land . . . (¶ 30)

   a. doing well   **b.** prospering   **c.** succeeding   **d.** protesting

8. It was all _____. (¶ 31, 32)

   a. fine   **b.** complex   **c.** splendid   **d.** marvelous

B. Vocabulary Review

Complete the following statements about the reading selection with the correct word or expression from the list below. Use each word or expression only once.

bewildering	**marvelous**	**prospered**	**village**
loneliness	**melancholy**	**reached**	

1. Sarkis Khatchadourian, a peasant from Armenia, always had a

   _____ expression on his face.

2. He _____ New York in 1908 and found the city a

   _____ place, very different from his little _____

   in Armenia.

3. He lived in Lynn, Massachusetts, for a while. Even though there were

   Armenians there, his _____ grew.

4. He went to California, where there were more Armenians and where he

   could do farm work. Things went well for him, and he _____.

   He was able to give his children all the _____ things of

   modern life, but, sadly, he never completely adapted to his new country and

   always felt homesick.

Sharing Your Thoughts

1. On your first reading of this story, did you predict that Sarkis would be happy in California? On what basis did you make your prediction? Was your prediction correct?

2. Why do you think that Sarkis was always mournful and melancholy in the United States—even though he socialized with Armenians and was prosperous? What was it he could never forget in America? (¶ 33)

3. What are some of the differences between migrating alone, as Sarkis did, versus migrating as a family?

4. What did you learn about Sarkis's children? How are they similar to or different from him? Which son do you think he might feel closer to? Why?

5. Saroyan said that he wrote this story to remember "the great, slow, difficult, expensive, and almost always painful journey from the old world to the new." Which adjective or adjectives in this statement (*slow, difficult, expensive, painful*) does the story illustrate best? Is this experience typical for most immigrants? Share stories about other immigrants that you know or have read about in Units One through Four. Does Saroyan's view of migration describe their experiences?

Text Analysis

Characterization

> The people in a story are the **characters**. Sarkis is clearly the most important, or main, character in this story. Most of the details in the story help paint a picture of him. We learn about Sarkis mostly from Saroyan's words about him, but sometimes we learn about Sarkis through the things he says in the story.

Each of the following statements tells something about Sarkis's character. Choose adjectives or phrases from the list below to describe Sarkis's character according to each statement. Use other adjectives if you want. Be prepared to explain your choices. Numbers 1 and 2 have been done as examples.

cheerful	not cheerful
easily bored	can tolerate repetitive work
flexible	inflexible
needs to be with Armenians	likes to meet new people
open-minded	closed-minded
likes to work outdoors	likes to work indoors; sedentary
sociable; talkative	unsociable; not talkative
sophisticated	unsophisticated; simple

DETAILS IN SAROYAN'S WORDS:

1. He . . . had an unusually melancholy expression. (¶ 1) _not cheerful_

2. In Gultik . . . he had gotten along very well and had had many friends . . .
   (¶ 1) _sociable (in Armenia)_

3. It (New York) was a very bewildering place and there was no one to talk to.
   (¶ 3) _____

4. There were a number of Armenian families in Lynn, but he didn't like them.
   They weren't like the people of Gultik. (¶ 6) _____

5. It was not pleasant to do this work with a Mexican, a man one could not talk
   to. (¶ 20) _____

6. . . . on Sundays he went to . . . an Armenian coffee house . . . (¶ 22)
   _____

DETAILS IN SARKIS'S WORDS:

7. Cows, my countryman? . . . Did you say cows? . . . In the sun . . . My beloved
   countryman, are there many of our people in California? (¶ 9–14)
   _____

8. Ahkh, America . . . How do I like it? What shall I say? Go; come; and with
   men known and unknown turn trays. (¶ 28) _____

Writing Task

1. Write a paragraph describing Sarkis's character. Choose the adjectives and
   details from the Text Analysis exercise that you consider most important.

2. Imagine you are Sarkis Khatchadourian, a sixty-year-old prosperous farmer
   who grows grapes in California in the late 1930s or early 1940s. Write a
   letter to a friend in Gultik who is thinking about migrating to California.
   What would you tell him about your life? What advice would you give him?

3. If you are an immigrant, write two or three paragraphs comparing and
   contrasting your experience to that of Sarkis. Make a Venn diagram to help
   organize your ideas before you start writing. Think about your arrival in
   your new country, work, places you have lived, language difficulties,
   emotions, and feelings toward people you have met. You might begin like
   this:

   > My experience as an immigrant is quite similar to / different from
   > Sarkis's.

   You may find some of these phrases helpful: *however, in contrast, on the
   other hand, like Sarkis, unlike Sarkis.*

Selection Five

Before Reading

Pat Mora is the daughter of Mexican immigrants to the United States. She grew up in El Paso, Texas, on the border between Mexico and the United States, very much between two worlds. "Elena" is from a volume of poems called *Chants*.

Discussion
Think about immigrant families that you know or have read about. List differences between the lives of immigrant parents and those of their children. Consider language, education, social life, problems.
How do you think the parents feel about these differences? How do these differences affect family life?

Focus for the First Reading
The first line of this poem expresses Elena's problem. The rest of the poem divides into two parts.

1. Where does the first part take place?
2. Where does the second part take place?
3. What is Elena thinking about in the first part?
4. What is she thinking about in the second part?

Elena

by Pat Mora

1 My Spanish isn't enough.
    I remember how I'd smile
    listening to my little ones,
    understanding every word they'd say,
5 their jokes, their songs, their plots.[1]
    Vamos a pedirle dulces a mamá. Vamos.[2]
    But that was in Mexico.
    Now my children go to American high schools.
    They speak English. At night they sit around
10 the kitchen table, and laugh with one another.
    I stand by the stove and feel dumb,[3] alone.
    I bought a book to learn English.
    My husband frowned,[4] drank more beer.
    My oldest said, "*Mamá*, he doesn't want you

[1] **plots** secret plans

[2] ***Vamos a pedirle dulces a mamá. Vamos.*** Spanish for "Let's go ask mom for candy. Come on."

[3] **dumb** two meanings: (1) unable to speak; (2) stupid

[4] **frowned** made a disapproving, unhappy facial expression

15 to be smarter than he is." I'm forty,
   embarrassed[5] at mispronouncing words,
   embarrassed at the laughter of my children,
   the grocer, the mailman. Sometimes I take
   my English book and lock myself in the bathoom,
20 say the thick words softly,
   for if I stop trying, I will be deaf[6]
   when my children need my help.

[5] **embarrassed**   ashamed or nervous, especially in front of other people

[6] **deaf**   unable to hear

Comprehension Check

A. First Reading

Fill in the blanks with an appropriate word or phrase.

Elena thinks about her life and her relationship with her children first in

_____, where everyone speaks _____. Now she and her
     (1)   (2)

family live in _____, where everyone speaks _____. Elena
                 (3)   (4)

is _____ about her language problem and the way it affects her
    (5)

relationship with her children.

B. Second Reading

1 *Read the poem again. Then answer the questions. Be prepared to find evidence in the poem that supports your answers.*

  1. What happy memory does Elena have of Mexico?
  2. What do Elena's children do at home in the evening now? How does she feel about this?
  3. How does she try to resolve her problem with English?
  4. What does Elena fear about the future?

2 *Decide whether the statements below are reasonable (**R**) or unreasonable (**U**) inferences. Circle your answers. Give the evidence in the selection that supports your answers.*

  1. R U   Elena's children are probably happy in the United States.
  2. R U   Elena feels closer to her children now than when they were younger.
  3. R U   Elena's husband has probably learned English well.

4. R U Living in the United States is probably helping the relationship between Elena and her husband.

5. R U Elena locks herself in the bathroom so no one can laugh at or criticize her.

6. R U Elena was probably happier in Mexico than in the United States.

Sharing Your Thoughts

1. Do you think people really laugh at Elena's English, or is this her imagination? Explain.

2. How do you think Elena's children feel about their mother?

3. Can you relate to Elena's feelings about learning English? Explain.

4. What aspects of the immigrant experience, other than language, separate parents from children?

5. Do you have similar or different reactions to Sarkis and Elena? Explain.

6. What similarities and differences do you find between this poem and the poem in Unit One, "To a Daughter Leaving Home" by Linda Pastan?

Writing Task

1. With a partner, imagine that one of you is Elena and the other is one of her children, her husband, or a female friend who is also an immigrant from Mexico. Write a conversation between them. What would Elena tell the other person? How would this person respond? Have each person speak at least three times.

2. In a group or as a class, write all the words associated with your feelings about learning English. Try to use some of them to write your own poem or a paragraph. You might start the same way Elena did:

My <u>(the name of your first language)</u> isn't enough.

A Final Look

Discussion

1. Work with a partner, in a small group, or as a whole class. Drawing on all five selections in this unit, discuss the focus questions on page 115.

2. Discuss the lines from the poem by Nagesh Rao on page 115. Do you think the immigrants in Selections Two through Five would understand what the poet feels? What about their children? Do you understand what he feels?

3. Finding similarities and differences, or comparing and contrasting, is an important academic skill. Fill in as much information as you can in the chart below. Then use the information to talk about the similarities and differences among these immigrants.

	Mark	Trong	Sarkis	Elena
Why did they leave their country?				
How much education or work experience did each have?				
How did this affect their experience in their new country?				
How well did they adjust to their new life?				
What characteristics helped them or made it difficult for them to adjust to their new life?				

4. Talk about the ways migration changes a person's life. List the sacrifices (things immigrants have to give up) and the benefits (things they gain) from migrating to another country. Are the sacrifices and benefits the same for adults and children?

5. Talk about the advantages and disadvantages of becoming like the people in the new country or maintaining the language and culture of your homeland.

Unit Project

Migration is not a new phenomenon. As a class, list the migrations you can think of. Consider migrations from different time periods, such as the examples below:

Prehistoric migrations:	Asians crossing the Bering Strait into North America
Colonization:	the French in eastern Canada; the Spanish and Portuguese in South America; Europeans in Africa
Migrations of the nineteenth and twentieth centuries:	Japanese to Brazil and Peru; Jews leaving Europe at the time of World War II to escape the Nazis

Work in a group of three or four students. Each group will research one migration.

Step 1 *Refer to encyclopedias, history books, references such as* The Cambridge Survey of World Migration *(Robin Cohen, ed., Cambridge University Press, 1997), which is about migrations from the sixteenth through the twentieth centuries. Try to answer the following questions:*

When did the group migrate?

Where did they come from and where did they go?

Why did they migrate?

What contributions did they make in their new home?

Did they migrate permanently, or did they return home?

What effect did the migration have on world history?

Step 2 *Write a report that includes answers to the questions.*

Step 3 *Compare your group's findings with the findings of the other groups. What similarities among the different migrations do you find? Do groups of people tend to migrate for the same reasons throughout history, or are the reasons changing?*

UNIT 5

Health: The Mind-Body Connection

It is part of the cure to wish to be
cured.
— Seneca (2,000 years ago)

FOCUS

➤ How can your mind affect your health?

➤ How can a person contribute to his or her
own health?

➤ What is the role of doctors in treating the
whole person, both mind and body?

Selection One

Before Reading

This selection is a research review. This type of academic writing summarizes what scholars and researchers have learned about a specific area of study. The studies in this review support the idea that there is a relationship between one's mental state and one's physical state or health.

Discussion

1. *Talk with your classmates about stressful situations that cause you to feel nervous, scared, or embarrassed. List examples in the chart below.*

Nervous	Scared	Embarrassed
before an important exam		

2. *Talk about how your body reacts in these situations.*
   Think about your heart, skin, stomach, etc. The fact that your emotions cause changes in your body shows that there is a connection between your mental state and physical state.

3. *Talk about what you already know about the following:*

   - what might happen if your response to nervousness or fear lasted a long time

   - how your body works to keep you healthy through your immune system

   - how your mental attitude could affect the way your body fights illness

Previewing
Read the first two paragraphs, the headings, and the first sentence under each heading to be sure you understand what immunosuppression *and* immunoenhancement *mean; the definitions of these important terms are given just after the headings.*

Focus for the First Reading
Read these questions before you read the selection. You should be able to answer them after you finish the first reading.

1. There are two main sections in this research review. What does the first group of studies show?

2. What does the second group of studies show?

The Mind-Body Connection

1   Every day our bodies are exposed to harmful organisms[1] and substances[2] that can cause us to get sick. Fortunately, we have immune systems which usually protect us from these harmful substances and keep us healthy.

2   Sometimes our immune systems seem to work better than others. What conditions could influence the way an immune system works? In other words, what could make an immune system work less efficiently, and what could make it work better? The research reported below may have some of the answers.

Immunosuppression

3   When an immune system is working less efficiently than it should, we call that *immunosuppression.*

4   Seaward (1997, p. 43) cites several studies that demonstrate the relationship between emotional stress[3] and immunosuppression. He cites a study by Launderslanger et al. (1983), for example, which found that when rats received electric shocks to their feet that they could not control, their bodies' immune function decreased significantly. The researchers concluded that a helpless-hopeless attitude, caused by an inability to control the shocks, can lead to illness.

5   Similar immunosuppression occurs in humans. Seaward (1997, p. 43) cites a study done at Ohio State University (Kiecolt-Glaser et al., 1984) in which the researchers found a lower number of lymphocytes[4] in medical students during the first day of exams than before and after exam periods.

6   Individuals who have recently lost their spouse suffer immunosuppression. Bergel (1996) cites Bartrop et al. (1977), who examined the effect of bereavement[5] on lymphocyte function of 26 recently widowed subjects and found significantly lowered T-cell function.

7   These studies support the idea that for both humans and animals there is a relationship between immune system functioning and emotional-mental state.

Immunoenhancement

8   In the same way that stress and a helpless-hopeless mental attitude can suppress the immune system, other conditions can make it work better; this is called *immunoenhancement.*

9   Chopra (1989, p. 33) describes one accidental and very surprising finding in a study of heart disease done at Ohio State University in the 1970s. In this study researchers fed a high cholesterol diet[6] to rabbits in order to duplicate the effect of a high cholesterol diet in humans. The expected atherosclerosis[7] appeared in all the groups except one, which mysteriously had 60% fewer symptoms.[8] Nothing about the rabbits could explain this difference until the researchers discovered that the student who fed this particular group of rabbits held each one lovingly before he fed it. It was very surprising, indeed,[9] that this affection alone helped the rabbits

---

[1] **organisms** living things

[2] **substances** physical matter; solids or liquids with particular qualities

[3] **stress** continuous feelings of worry caused by difficulties in your life that stop you from relaxing

[4] **lymphocytes** special white blood cells, including T-cells and B-cells, that destroy harmful organisms

[5] **bereavement** state of sorrow when spouse or loved one dies

[6] **high cholesterol diet** food that contains fatty substances that can contribute to heart disease

[7] **atherosclerosis** condition that develops when arteries are partially closed by deposits that slow the circulation of the blood

[8] **symptoms** physical indications that show you may have a particular disease

[9] **indeed** a word used to emphasize a statement

overcome the normally harmful effect of the diet. In repeat experiments, the researchers, Nerem et al. (1980), confirmed these results: the rabbits in the experimental groups who got 30 minutes of love and attention before their morning feeding and 5-minute visits during the day had significantly lower levels of atherosclerosis than the animals in the control groups.

10   There is also research on the health benefits of social support for humans. One of the most often cited studies is Berkman and Syme (1979). They studied the social contacts of almost 5000 adults between the ages of 30 and 69, and related this to mortality rates[10] from 1965–1974. Social contacts included: marriage, contacts with close friends and relatives, church membership, and informal and formal group associations. They found that people who had strong social connections had the lowest mortality rates. The social connections that had the strongest relationship with low mortality rates were happy marriages and frequent contact with close friends and relatives. The findings were independent of other factors such as health habits and socioeconomic status.

11   Thus social contact and social support seem to be an extremely important factor in health.

Conclusion

12   These findings do not mean that every illness is the result of one's mental and emotional state. Nor do they mean that we can cure any illness by changing our mental or emotional condition. They do mean that our thoughts can affect our health, that there is a connection between mind and body.

Bibliography

Bergel, M. (1996). *From mechanistic to holistic concepts of health: The paradigm shift in Western society.* Unpublished doctoral dissertation, American University, Washington, DC.

Berkman, L. F., & Syme, L. (1979). Social networks, host resistance, and mortality: A nine-year follow-up study of Alameda County residents. *American Journal of Epidemiology, 109* (2), 186–204.

Chopra, D. (1989). *Quantum healing: Exploring the frontiers of mind/body medicine.* New York: Bantam Books.

Nerem, R. M., Levesque, M. J., & Cornhill, J. F. (1980, June 27). Social environment as a factor in diet-induced atherosclerosis. *Science, 208,* 1475–1476.

Seaward, B. L. (1997). *Managing stress: Principles and strategies for health and well being* (2nd ed.) Sudbury, MA: Jones and Bartlett Publishers.

---

[10] **mortality rate**   the number of deaths during a particular period among a particular group of people, for example, the number of deaths per 1,000 people in a particular group

Comprehension Check

A. First Reading

Fill in the blanks with an appropriate word or phrase.

These studies show that there is a relationship between the way our

_____ system functions and our mental state. This effect can
                (1)
work in both a negative and a _____ way. A bad mental state
                                          (2)

can result in decreased functioning of the immune system, known as

_____; a good mental state can result in more efficient
(3)

functioning of the immune system, known as _____.
(4)

B. Second Reading

Read the selection again. The studies described in this review are identified by the author's name and the date of publication. Match each study listed on the left with its main finding on the right.

EXAMPLES OF IMMUNOSUPPRESSION

___ **1.** Launderslanger et al.[1] (1983)

___ **2.** Kiecolt-Glaser et al. (1984)

___ **3.** Bartrop et al. (1977)

MAIN FINDING

a. Recently widowed people had lower immune function.

b. Rabbits on a high cholesterol diet were less likely to develop atherosclerosis if they received affection.

c. When rats felt stress because they couldn't control electric shocks to their feet, they became ill.

EXAMPLES OF IMMUNOENHANCEMENT

___ **4.** Nerem et al. (1980)

___ **5.** Berkman & Syme (1979)

d. People with strong social contacts usually live longer.

e. Students' immune systems functioned less efficiently during stressful times such as exam periods.

_____
[1]*et al.* = and other authors

A. Vocabulary Building

Look at the underlined words or expressions in the sentences below. Find them in the reading. Then choose the correct meaning for the context.

1. Every day our bodies are exposed to <u>harmful</u> organisms and substances that can cause us to get sick. (¶ 1)

   a. good

   b. bad

2. Seaward . . . <u>cites</u> several studies . . . (¶ 4)

   a. does

   b. mentions

3. The researchers concluded that a <u>helpless</u>-hopeless attitude, caused by an inability to control the shocks, can lead to illness. (¶ 4)

   a. without help from others

   b. unable to take care of yourself

4. . . . a helpless-hopeless attitude . . . can <u>lead to</u> illness. (¶ 4)

   a. cause

   b. cure

5. . . . Bartrop et al. (1977) . . . examined the effect of bereavement on lymphocyte function of 26 recently <u>widowed</u> subjects . . . (¶ 6)

   a. left without a spouse when the spouse dies

   b. left in a weak state or condition

6. . . . researchers fed a high cholesterol diet to rabbits in order to <u>duplicate</u> the effect of a high cholesterol diet in humans. (¶ 9)

   a. increase

   b. copy

7. It was very surprising, indeed, that this <u>affection</u> alone helped the rabbits overcome the normally harmful effect of the diet. (¶ 9)

   a. gentle love and caring

   b. lack of attention

8. . . . this affection alone helped the rabbits <u>overcome</u> the normally harmful effect of the diet. (¶ 9)

   a. not be affected by

   b. benefit from

9. The findings were <u>independent of</u> other factors such as health habits and socioeconomic status. (¶ 10)

   a. not influenced by

   b. influenced by

10. . . . factors such as health habits and <u>socioeconomic status</u>. (¶ 10)

    a. social support

    b. social and economic position

B. Vocabulary Building

Some of the specialized vocabulary used in many academic areas is the vocabulary used to describe research. Match the word or expression on the left with its meaning on the right.

___ 1. experimental groups (¶ 9)   **a.** connection or association between two things (one may or may not cause the other)

___ 2. control groups (¶ 9)   **b.** help confirm; help prove

___ 3. factors (¶ 10, 11)   **c.** groups that did not receive special treatment

___ 4. relationship (¶ 4, 10)   **d.** groups that received special treatment

___ 5. significantly (¶ 4, 6, 9)   **e.** decided something based on all the information about it

___ 6. concluded (¶ 4)   **f.** with a high level of certainty based on statistical tests

___ 7. support (v) (¶ 7)   **g.** things that influence or cause a situation

C. Vocabulary Review

Complete the following statements about the reading selection with the correct word or expression from the list below. Use each word or expression only once.

affection	immunosuppression	overcome	support
concluded	lead to	relationship	widowed
factor	mortality rate		

1. Many studies _____ the idea that there is a

   _____ between our immune systems and our mental state.

2. A recently _____ person, for example, may experience a

   decrease in the functioning of the immune system, called

   _____, because of the extreme stress of losing a spouse.

3. A positive mental state can _____ better functioning of the

   immune system.

4. In a surprising, accidental finding, Ohio State University researchers

   discovered that human contact and _____ were sufficient

   for rabbits to _____ the effects of a diet that can cause

   atherosclerosis.

5. Humans are also healthier when they have strong social support: happily

   married people with close relationships with friends and relatives have a

   lower _____.

6. Many researchers have _____ that our mental state is a

   _____ that affects our health.

Sharing Your Thoughts

1. What, if anything, surprised you about the information in this selection? Which study surprised the researchers? What can happen when scientists get surprising results?

2. Which, if any, of these studies could you relate to personally? For example, have you ever gotten sick during exam periods? Talk about other examples you know of that support the idea of a relationship between mental attitude and health.

3. Talk with your classmates about changes in a person's life that can cause stress. Add to the list below, and discuss where the stress comes from.

MAJOR LIFE CHANGES	POSSIBLE CAUSES OF THE STRESS
a. losing your job	You're afraid you won't have enough money.
	You're under pressure to look for a new job.
	You may have low self-esteem; you feel maybe your work wasn't good enough.
b. migration to a foreign country	
c. retirement (stopping work at about age sixty-five	
d. _____	
e. _____	

 **Text Analysis**

Bibliography and Citations

In academic writing, writers tell readers where their information comes from for two reasons: first, to give credit to the author or researcher, and second, to enable the reader to locate the source. They give this information in two places: in **citations** in the text, and in the **Bibliography** or **References** at the end of the text.

Citations

In a citation, the writer includes the author's name, the date of publication, and the page number(s) if relevant.

Examples:

a. In repeat experiments . . . Nerem et al. (1980) confirmed these results.

b. Seaward (1997, p. 43) cites several studies that demonstrate the relationship between emotional stress and immunosuppression.

With the author's name and date of publication, you can locate complete information about the source in the bibliography.

Bibliography

In the bibliography, the writer includes slightly different information, depending on whether the source is a book or an article.

For books: author(s). (year of publication). title. city: publisher.

Example:

Seaward, B. L. (1997). *Managing stress: Principles and strategies for health and well being* (2nd ed.). Sudbury, MA: Jones and Bartlett Publishers.

For articles: author(s). (date). title of the article. title of the magazine or journal, volume number (issue number), pages.

Example:

Berkman, L. F., & Syme, L. (1979). Social networks, host resistance, and mortality: A nine-year follow-up study of Alameda County residents. *American Journal of Epidemiology 109* (2), 186–204.

Examine the citations and bibliography in Selection One. Answer these questions.

1. What information is included in both the citation and the bibliography?

2. Finding the bibliographic information for a source is a two-step process when one researcher cites the research of another. Where would you find the bibliographic information for these studies?

   a. Launderslanger et al.

   b. Kiecolt-Glaser et al.

   c. Bartrop et al.

3. There are three other sources that are cited directly. Which two are journal articles and which is a book?

Writing Task

1. Write about a person you know or have heard about that supports the idea that there is a connection between mind and body. Use these questions as a guide.

   Who was sick?
   What were his or her symptoms?
   What was the person's mental state?
   What makes you think there was a connection between the person's mental attitude and his or her health?

2. Select a research article in your academic field that you are already familiar with. Write a short summary of the research. Use these questions as a guide. Be sure to cite the source correctly in your summary (author's name, date of publication) and give complete bibliographic information at the end.

   Who did the research?
   What did they study?
   Who were the subjects?
   What data did they collect? or What was the treatment in the experimental group?
   What were the findings of the study?

Selection Two

Before Reading

This selection is from the book *Minding the Body, Mending the Mind* by Joan Borysenko. Dr. Borysenko has a doctorate in anatomy and cellular biology. She has worked with Dr. Herbert Benson, who coined the term "the relaxation response." They both consider the relaxation response, which lowers blood pressure and reduces stress, an important part of how people can overcome negative mental states and enjoy better health.

Discussion

In Selection One you learned that there is a connection between various types of stress and physical health. The author of Selection Two says that although we don't get sick every time we are under stress, stress is clearly a factor that contributes to illness (Borysenko, 1987, p.16).

Talk with your classmates. How does your body feel when you are stressed? What do you do to reduce stress?

Previewing

Read the boldfaced sentences after numbers 1–8 in the selection. These sentences are:

a. statements about meditation

b. instructions for meditation

Focus for the First Reading

Read these questions before you read the selection. You should be able to answer them after you finish the first reading.

1. How should you relax the different parts of your body when you meditate?

2. What should you focus on?

3. What will you find difficult at first?

The Process of Meditation

by Joan Borysenko

1 **1. Choose a quiet spot where you will not be disturbed by other people or by the telephone.** This extends to animals as well. Inevitably, if you have a dog or a cat, it will find a way into your lap, so arrange to put it in another room.

2 **2. Sit in a comfortable position,** with back straight and arms and legs uncrossed, unless you choose to sit cross-legged on a floor cushion.

3 **3. Close your eyes.** This makes it easier to concentrate.

4 **4. Relax your muscles sequentially from head to feet.** This step helps to break the connection between stressful thoughts and a tense body. For now, just become aware of each part of your body in succession, letting go as much as you can with the out breath. Take a second now just to take a deep breath in. Let it

go. Notice how your body relaxes as you let go. This is the good old sigh of relief.[1] The pull of gravity[2] is always present, encouraging us to let go, but if there is no awareness of being uptight, there can't be any letting go. Notice your shoulders right now. Is there any room to let them down more, cooperating with gravity and your own out breath? Every out breath is an opportunity to let go.

5 Starting with your forehead, become aware of tension as you breathe in. Let go of any obvious tension as you breathe out. Go through the rest of your body in this way, proceeding down through your eyes, jaws, neck, shoulders, arms, hands, chest, upper back, middle back and midriff, lower back, belly, pelvis, buttocks, thighs, calves, and feet.[3] This need only take a minute or two.

6 **5. Become aware of your breathing, noticing how the breath goes in and out, without trying to control it in any way.** You are breathing all the time, aware of it or not. For the purpose of meditation, *let the breath happen by itself.* You may notice that your breathing gets slower and shallower as the meditation progresses. That's due to the physiological effects of the relaxation response, the fact that your body requires less oxygen because your metabolism[4] has slowed down.

7 **6. Repeat your focus word silently in time to your breathing.** Choose a word or phrase to repeat just on the out breath. You can simply repeat *one* on each out breath, or choose a phrase that is broken up, part on the in breath and part on the out breath.

8 **7. Don't worry about how you are doing.** As soon as you start to worry about whether you are doing it right, you have

shifted from meditation to anxiety. Without doubt, you will do this a lot at first; it's just the habit of the mind to question and criticize our own performance. If you notice that tendency, try labeling it *judging*, then let go, coming back to the breath and the focus, which are your anchors.[5]

9 The most common experience and complaint about meditation is "I can't stop my mind from wandering."[6] That's fine. Don't try. Just practice bringing it back to concentration on the breath and focus whenever you notice its wanderings. The awareness you develop in meditation will begin to carry over into life, affording you much more choice in how you respond and restoring your ability to enjoy life.

10 **8. Practice at least once a day for ten to twenty minutes.** The preferred times are early morning, after a shower and exercise if you do it, but before breakfast, or before dinner. The only times to avoid are when you're tired, simply because meditation is a concentration exercise and, if you're tired, you'll fall asleep, and just after a heavy meal, since the process of digestion makes people sluggish.[7] Remember that practice is indispensable to progress at anything. Your goal is to sit and do the meditation. Even if it seems that the only thing you're doing is chasing after your mind to tie it down again, remarkably the relaxation response is still most likely occurring. Long before patients* think they know "how to do it," they begin to notice that they are generally feeling more peaceful and their symptoms are beginning to improve. Of course, it does get easier and more deeply peaceful after repeated practice.

*Dr. Borysenko worked with patients at the Mind/Body Clinic at New England Deaconess Hospital.

---

[1] **sigh of relief**   slow out breath, or exhalation, to show feeling of comfort
[2] **gravity**   force that makes objects fall to the ground; force that pulls toward the center of the earth
[3] **(body parts)**   For body parts, see pictures on page 194.
[4] **metabolism**   chemical processes in your body that change food into energy

[5] **anchors**   weights that keep something firmly in place, as an anchor keeps a ship in place
[6] **wandering**   moving; no longer paying attention
[7] **sluggish**   working or reacting more slowly than normal

Comprehension Check

A. First Reading

Check the statements that are in agreement with Borysenko's instructions for meditation.

___ **1.** Lie on your back, close your eyes, and relax your whole body all at once.

___ **2.** Pay attention to your breathing, and repeat the word or phrase you have chosen each time you exhale (breathe out).

___ **3.** It is normal for your mind to wander; just practice bringing it back to concentration as you focus on breathing.

B. Second Reading

Read the selection again. Then answer the questions. Be prepared to show evidence in the selection to support your answers.

1. How can you avoid being disturbed while you meditate?

2. Draw stick figures of the two positions for meditation described in paragraph 2.

3. Why does your breathing get slower during meditation?

4. What should you do during meditation if your mind wanders?

5. When should you meditate?

6. How will you feel as a result of meditation?

Vocabulary

A. Vocabulary Building

Three of the words in each row are similar in meaning, at least for this context. Each of them could complete the sentence without changing its original meaning. Underline the three words that are similar. Use a dictionary if necessary.

1. Choose a quiet spot where you will not be _____. (¶ 1)

    a. interrupted   **b.** bothered   **c.** evaluated   **d.** disturbed

2. Relax your muscles _____ from head to feet. (¶ 4)

    a. sequentially   **b.** comfortably   **c.** in succession   **d.** in order

3. . . . but if there is no _____ of being uptight, there can't be any letting go. (¶ 4)

    a. realization   **b.** awareness   **c.** consciousness   **d.** expression

4. As soon as you start to worry about whether you are doing it right, you have _____ from meditation to anxiety. (¶ 8)

    a. moved   **b.** shifted   **c.** progressed   **d.** changed

5. The awareness you develop in meditation will begin to carry over into life, . . . _____ your ability to enjoy life. (¶ 9)

    a. reducing   **b.** restoring   **c.** returning   **d.** bringing back

6. Remember that practice is _____ to progress at anything. (¶ 10)

    a. necessary   **b.** essential   **c.** normal   **d.** indispensable

7. Even if it seems that the only thing you're doing is chasing after your mind . . . , _____ the relaxation response is still most likely occurring. (¶ 10)

    a. logically   **b.** amazingly   **c.** surprisingly   **d.** remarkably

8. Of course, it does get easier and more deeply _____ after repeated practice. (¶ 10)

    a. restful   **b.** helpful   **c.** relaxing   **d.** peaceful

B. Distinguishing Grammatical Function: Nouns, Verbs, Adjectives

The grammatical category or part of speech of words is often marked by suffixes. Three common noun suffixes you have seen are *-tion*, *-sion*, and *-ness*. Sometimes one suffix can mark two different parts of speech. For example, verb base + *-ing* is a verb when it follows a form of *be.*

I *am walking.*

They *were crying.*

verb base + *-ing* without an auxiliary can function as a noun.

Walking is good exercise.

Sometimes in English verbs become nouns (or nouns become verbs) with no change in form. You have to decide if the word is a verb or a noun by noticing how it is used in the sentence.

VERB	NOUN	ADJECTIVE
meditate	medita*tion*	
concentrate	concentra*tion*	
relax	relaxa*tion*	
	ten*sion*	tense
	aware*ness*	aware
let go	lett*ing* go	
breathe	breath*ing* (also breath*)	
wander	wander*ing*	
practice	practice	
anchor	anchor	
focus	focus	

*breath (n) = air itself that comes in and goes out

*breathing (n) = process of inhaling and exhaling

1 *Complete each of the sentences with the correct form of the word.*

1. aware / awareness

   a. Become _____ of each part of your body.

   b. If you have no _____ of being tense, you cannot relax.

2. tense / tension

   a. Let go of any obvious _____ as you breathe out.

   b. As you relax your muscles, you will break the connection between stressful thoughts and a _____ body.

3. breath / breathe / breathing

   a. Become aware of your _____.

   b. Take a deep _____.

   c. Repeat the word *one* as you _____out.

4. let go / letting go

   a. If there is no awareness of being uptight, there can't be any _____.

   b. Notice how your body relaxes as you _____.

5. wander / wandering

   a. The most common complaint about meditation is, "I can't stop my mind from _____."

   b. Our minds _____ easily, but just come back calmly to your focus.

2 *Decide if the underlined word is functioning as a noun (**N**) or a verb (**V**) in the sentences below. Circle your answers.*

1. N V a. <u>Practice</u> at least once a day.

   N V b. <u>Practice</u> is indispensable.

2. N V a. Breath and the focus are your <u>anchors</u>.

   N V b. Concentration <u>anchors</u> your thoughts

3. N V a. When you meditate you <u>focus</u> on your breathing.

   N V b. Come back to the breath and the <u>focus</u>.

C. Vocabulary Review

Complete the following statements about the reading selection with the correct word or expression from the list below. Use each word or expression only once.

aware	**let go**	**restore**
breathe	**metabolism**	**tension**
focus	**practice**	**wanders**

1. Meditation is a restful activity that helps you to clear your mind and reduce

   _____ in your body. It does this by slowing down your

   _____ and lowering your blood pressure and heart rate.

2. You must become _____ of each part of your body in

   succession from your forehead down to your feet.

3. Your goal is to _____ of the uptight feeling as you exhale or

   _____ out.

4. If your mind _____, don't worry, but try to bring it back and

   _____ on your breathing.

5. Remember that successful meditation requires _____. It will

   get easier and could _____ your ability to enjoy life.

Sharing Your Thoughts

1. Look at the different uses of the phrase *let go* in Step 4 in Selection Two. What do you think the author means? Does she always mean the same thing? What could you be letting go of?

2. There are many ways to relax and reduce stress. Look at the list below, and share your thoughts with your classmates. Add to the list. Then talk about the advantages and disadvantages of each way.

   play a musical instrument or sing

   laugh (watch funny movies)

   write in a journal

   draw or paint

   spend time with a pet

   _____

   _____

   _____

   _____

3. Does your culture or your religion have a form of meditation or a practice, such as prayer, that has a similar effect? If so, do people associate this with stress reduction and better health?

4. At home, follow Borysenko's instructions for meditation. Then talk in class about what happened and how you felt.

Text Analysis

Grammar-Meaning Connection: Imperatives

> English sentences must have an expressed subject.
>
> *Meditation* is one way to help you relax.
>
> *It* is not the only way.
>
> The one exception is **imperative** sentences—sentences that give instructions or orders. In this case, the subject *you* is understood.
>
> (You) Choose a quiet spot.
>
> (You) Don't worry about how you are doing.

The eight steps in "The Process of Meditation" are imperatives. List other imperatives you find in the text.

Writing Task

1. Write a paragraph describing your experience at trying to meditate. Use these questions as a guide.

   Where and when did you try to meditate?
   What did you do?
   How did you feel while you were trying to meditate? After you meditated?
   Why do you think you were or were not successful?

2. Write about how you like to reduce stress and tension. Use these questions as a guide.

   What do you do?
   How often do you do it?
   How does it make you feel?
   Why do you like this form of relaxation?

Selection Three

Before Reading

This selection is from Norman Cousins's book *Head First—The Biology of Hope*. Cousins, a magazine editor for many years, had ankylosing spondylitis, a rare and usually incurable disease. He believed one of the reasons for illness was stress and negative emotions, so in cooperation with his doctor, he designed a therapy which included watching old comic movies in order to turn a negative mental state into a positive one.

Discussion

Just before telling the story you will read in this selection, Cousins stated, "We live at a time when progress in overcoming illness is equated with pills." What do you think Cousins meant? What was he saying about doctors and patients? Is the situation the same or different today? Explain. What other ways of treating illness do you know about?

Previewing

Read the first paragraph. Answer the questions.

1. In his lectures to medical students, what three things did Dean Mellinkoff emphasize?

    a. the need to _____

    b. the need for _____

    c. the need for _____

2. What will Cousins write about?

    a. the use of technology for diagnosing what is wrong with a patient

    b. an example of the importance of effective communication with a patient

Focus for the First Reading

Read these questions before you read the selection. You should be able to answer them after you finish the first reading.

1. Who is the patient, and what is wrong with him?

2. Do the doctors expect him to get better?

3. What did Dean Mellinkoff do that turned this patient's condition around?

More than Medicine

by Norman Cousins

1   In his lectures to medical students, Dean Mellinkoff gave the greatest emphasis to the need to avoid the quick fix,[1] for disciplined and creative attention to what the patient was saying, and for using their own judgment at least as much as technology in arriving at a diagnosis. I saw a good example of this

---

[1] **quick fix**   a fast and easy cure or remedy

one day when the dean[2] invited me to join him on medical rounds.[3]

2   We met with residents and interns[4] for the purpose of discussing interesting and instructive cases that had come to the UCLA[5] hospital. The specific case at hand concerned a Guatemalan male, age thirty-four, diagnosed as suffering from a combination of tuberculosis[6] and inflammation[7] of the liver. The patient had unremitting fever[8] and was not responding to treatment. Additional diagnostic tests were scheduled, but not much hope was held for his survival.

3   Dean Mellinkoff inquired about the patient's diet and learned that the nutritional level was very low because the man had no desire to eat. Consequently, the patient was receiving intravenous supplementation.[9]

4   After asking several more questions about the patient's medical history and general background, Dr. Mellinkoff asked to see the patient. When he came to the patient's room with the staff members, it was learned that he had been taken in a wheelchair downstairs for X-rays.

5   "I just hope they gave him a specific time appointment for the X-rays," the dean said. "He's in no condition to have to wait on line, even if he is in a wheelchair. Let's go downstairs and see how he is."

6   As the dean feared, the Guatemalan, wan and thin, was huddled under a blanket in his wheelchair in the hallway, outside the X-ray room. If the dean was displeased by the reality of his foreboding that the patient would have to wait, he gave no sign of it. He approached the patient and, in Spanish, introduced himself and, very gently, asked how he felt.

7   The patient, obviously flattered by the presence of the dean, smiled and said everything was all right. Then the dean asked if he was able to eat his meals.

8   The patient mumbled something to the effect that he was not hungry.

9   "Are you getting food you like?"

10   The patient said nothing but his expression indicated that he found it awkward to answer the question.

11   "Do you get the kind of food you have at home?"

12   An ever-so-slight shake of the head indicated the answer was negative.

13   The dean put his hand on the man's shoulder and his voice was very soft.

14   "If you had food that you liked, would you eat it?"

15   "Sí, sí," he said.

16   The change in the appearance and mood of the patient couldn't have been more striking.[10] The exchange with the dean was reassuring and therapeutic.

17   The dean looked over at the interns and residents. Nothing was said but it was easy to tell that a message was being sent and was also being received.

18   Back in the conference room the dean asked why the Guatemalan wasn't getting food he could eat.

19   One of the residents ventured that "we all know how tough it is to get the kitchen to make exceptions."

20   "Suppose," the dean countered, "you felt a certain medication was absolutely necessary but that our pharmacy didn't carry[11] it, would you accept defeat or would you come down as hard as possible to insist the pharmacy meet your request?"

21   "Probably the latter,"[12] the resident said.

---

[2] **dean**   head of a college or faculty; as used here, head of the medical school
[3] **medical rounds**   visits to patients in the hospital
[4] **residents and interns**   doctors in late stage of training, after graduation from medical school
[5] **UCLA**   University of California at Los Angeles
[6] **tuberculosis**   a disease of the lungs
[7] **inflammation**   swelling and soreness
[8] **fever**   body temperature above normal
[9] **intravenous supplementation**   additional nourishment given directly into a vein

---

[10] **couldn't have been more striking**   was very noticeable
[11] **carry**   have for sale; keep in stock
[12] **latter**   the second thing mentioned ("insist the pharmacy meet your request")

22   "Very well," the dean replied. "You might want to try the same approach to the kitchen. It won't be easy but if you want more troops[13] on your side, I'm available. Meanwhile, let's get some nourishment inside this chap[14] as fast as possible, and stay with it. Incidentally, there must be someone among you who can speak Spanish. If we want to make real progress, we're going to need effective communication."

23   Three weeks later, Dean Mellinkoff informed me that the Guatemalan had left the hospital under his own power. He had responded beautifully to treatment. He was gaining weight. The disease in both lungs and liver had receded, the fever had disappeared, and the prospects were good.

24   I rejoiced in the news but also recognized that there might have been an entirely different result if the dean had not intervened. The lesson to be learned was that there was much more to effective treatment than medication, and that good communication and reassurance were vital parts of any strategy for recovery.

---

[13]**troops**   soldiers; fighters
[14]**chap**   guy; fellow; man (British)

 **Comprehension Check**

A. First Reading

*Mark the statements **T** (true) or **F** (false). Be prepared to show evidence in the selection that supports your answers.*

1.   T   F   The patient has cancer.

2.   T   F   The doctors expect him to get better.

3.   T   F   Dean Mellinkoff made the patient feel more comfortable when he spoke to him in Spanish.

4.   T   F   Dean Mellinkoff found out that the patient was not eating, but that he would eat Guatemalan food.

5.   T   F   The patient got better because Dean Mellinkoff suggested a change in medication.

B. Second Reading

Read the selection again. Then answer the questions. Be prepared to show evidence in the selection that supports your answers.

1. When Dean Mellinkoff went to the patient's room and learned that he was downstairs for X-rays . . .

    a.   he was angry because he hadn't ordered an X-ray.

    b.   he was worried that the patient was too sick to have to wait.

    c.   he was upset because he wanted to take the patient to the X-ray room himself.

2. Dean Mellinkoff's conversation with the patient was . . .

  a. awkward. The patient was uncomfortable with the doctor.

  b. reassuring. The patient cheered up.

  c. not effective. The patient didn't understand English.

3. Dean Mellinkoff convinced the residents and interns to get the right food for the patient by . . .

  a. asking them what they would do if the pharmacy would not cooperate.

  b. giving them a lecture on the importance of nutrition.

  c. saying that it would be easy to deal with the kitchen.

4. What are the signs that the patient was getting better?

5. Find the sentence that summarizes the lesson that Dean Mellinkoff teaches.

Vocabulary

A. Vocabulary Building

Look at the underlined words or expressions in the sentences on the left. Find them in the selection. Then match them with the correct meaning on the right.

Match 1–7 with a–g.

___ 1. . . . the need to <u>avoid</u> the quick fix . . . (¶ 1)

___ 2. . . . using their own judgment . . . in arriving at a <u>diagnosis</u>. (¶ 1)

___ 3. The patient . . . was <u>not getting better</u>. (¶ 2)

___ 4. not much hope . . . for his <u>survival</u>. (¶ 2)

___ 5. . . . the <u>nutritional level</u> was very low . . . (¶ 3)

___ 6. . . . he found it <u>awkward</u> to answer the question. (¶ 10)

___ 7. The exchange with the dean was <u>reassuring</u> . . . (¶ 16)

a. uncomfortable; embarrassing

b. the method for curing the patient was not working

c. quantity of nutrients

d. not use something; not do something (intentionally)

e. comforting; made the patient feel less worried

f. decision as to what illness a person has

g. continuing to live

*Match **8–15** with **h–o**.*

___ **8.** . . . we all know how <u>tough</u> it is to get the kitchen to make exceptions. (¶ 19)

h. taken a role; come between the patient and the residents and interns

___ **9.** . . . would you accept defeat or . . . <u>insist</u> the pharmacy meet your request? (¶ 20)

i. chances of future success

___**10.** You might want to try the same <u>approach</u> to the kitchen. (¶ 22)

j. very important; necessary

___**11.** Meanwhile, let's get some <u>nourishment</u> inside this chap . . . (¶ 22)

k. demand; require

___**12.** The disease . . . <u>had receded</u> . . . (¶ 23)

l. food needed to be healthy

___**13.** . . . the <u>prospects</u> were good. (¶ 23)

m. hard; difficult

___**14.** . . . if the dean had not <u>intervened</u>. (¶ 24)

n. was going away; was disappearing

___**15.** . . . good communication and reassurance were <u>vital</u> . . . for recovery. (¶ 24)

o. way of doing something

B. Paraphrasing and Skipping Non-essential Vocabulary

*Read each sentence, skipping the crossed-out words. Then choose the sentence (**a** or **b**) that has the closest meaning. If you can choose the correct answer, the crossed-out words are not essential. If you can't, the crossed-out words are essential to understanding the sentence, and there may be an important word you need to look up in a dictionary.*

1. The patient had ~~unremitting~~ fever and was not responding to treatment. (¶ 2)
   a. The patient's body temperature was normal, and he was getting better.
   b. The patient's body temperature was above normal, and he was not getting better.

2. Additional diagnostic tests ~~were scheduled,~~ but not much hope ~~was held~~ for his survival. (¶ 2)
   a. The doctors thought the patient would probably not get better.
   b. The doctors thought the patient would get better.

3. As the dean feared, the Guatemalan, ~~wan~~ and thin, was ~~huddled~~ under a blanket in his wheelchair . . . (¶ 6)
   a. The patient looked OK.
   b. The patient looked weak.

4. If the dean was displeased ~~by the reality of his foreboding that the patient would have to wait,~~ he gave no sign of it. (¶ 6)
   a. The dean showed his feelings.
   b. The dean didn't show his feelings.

5. The patient, ~~obviously flattered by the presence of the dean,~~ smiled and said everything was all right. (¶ 7)
   a. The patient said he was fine.
   b. The patient said he wasn't feeling well.

6. ~~An ever so slight shake of~~ the head indicated the answer was negative. (¶ 12)
   a. The patient didn't respond.
   b. The patient's answer was no.

7. . . . would you accept ~~defeat~~ or . . . ~~come down as hard as possible to~~ insist the pharmacy meet your request? (¶ 20)
   a. The dean is asking, "Would you do nothing or fight the pharmacy?"
   b. The dean is asking, "Would you forget about the medicine or would you change the prescription?"

8. . . . good communication and reassurance were vital ~~parts of any strategy~~ for recovery. (¶ 24)
   a. Good communication and reassurance were not important for getting better.
   b. Good communication and reassurance were important for getting better.

C. Vocabulary Review

Complete the following statements about the reading selection with the correct word or expression from the list below. Use each word or expression only once.

approach	**diagnosis**	**nourishment**	**tough**
avoid	**insist**	**reassuring**	**vital**

1. Some doctors consider only physical symptoms in making a _____ and prescribing a treatment. But this incident shows that this is not enough; doctors have to treat the whole person.

2. Dean Mellinkoff knew what questions to ask and how to communicate with the Guatemalan man. His manner was very _____, and the man seemed happier right away.

3. The doctor knew the man was not eating and needed _____.

4. One resident said it was too _____ to get the kitchen in the hospital to prepare special food for a patient.

5. Dean Mellinkoff believed things like diet were as important as medication. He showed the residents and interns that it was wrong to _____ dealing with the kitchen. He convinced them that they must _____ that the kitchen do what they asked.

6. He also knew that good communication between patient and doctor was _____ for the patient's recovery. His _____ was successful in this case.

Sharing Your Thoughts

1. Which adjectives do you think describe the way the Guatemalan patient felt in the hospital? Why do you think he felt that way? Show evidence in the selection that supports your opinion.

   afraid

   angry

   confused

   embarrassed

   nervous

   optimistic

   uncomfortable

   weak and hungry

2. When doctors treat the whole person, mind and body, they are practicing holistic medicine. In addition, "a holistic approach to medicine and health care includes understanding and treating people in the context of their culture, their family, and their community" (Hastings, A., et al., 1980, p. 16). In what ways did Dr. Mellinkoff follow the principles of holistic medicine?

3. Based on what you learned in this selection and your personal experience, what are the important ingredients in the doctor-patient relationship? What, if anything, does this have to do with the mind-body connection?

Text Analysis

Paragraph Focus

Match each paragraph or set of paragraphs with its contribution to the whole piece of writing.

___¶ 1	**a.** the dean's conversation with the patient
___¶ 2–3	**b.** the discussion and decision between Mellinkoff and students about the patient's care
___¶ 4–5	**c.** background information about the case
___¶ 6–17	**d.** the author's reaction and comment
___¶ 18–22	**e.** the results of the treatment
___¶ 23	**f.** what Dean Mellinkoff wants to teach
___¶ 24	**g.** locating the patient in the hospital

Writing Task

1. Summarize this selection using your own words. Use these questions as a guide. You may want to begin with this sentence:

   Norman Cousins gave a good example of a doctor treating the whole person.

   > Who was the doctor? Who was he teaching?
   > Who was the patient? What was wrong with him?
   > Was he getting better? Why or why not?
   > What did Dean Mellinkoff do?
   > What were the results?

2. Write about a medical service in your community. Describe the service. Tell what is good about it or what needs to be improved.

Selection Four

Before Reading

O. Henry is the pen name of William Sidney Porter (1862–1910). For the last eight years of his life he lived and wrote in New York City, near Greenwich Village, an old part of the city where this story takes place. The rents on apartments in Greenwich Village were low, so many artists who had very little money lived there.

Discussion

Talk with your classmates. Why do you think that some people who get sick don't want to get well? What kind of thoughts come into their minds? How do they show that they don't want to survive?

Previewing

Read the title and the first two paragraphs of the story. Answer these questions.

1. Who are the characters?

2. Where are they from?

3. Who is sick?

4. What do you think might happen in this story?

Focus for the First Reading

This story is divided into two parts. After you read Part I (¶ 1–25), you should be able to answer these questions.

1. What is Johnsy's attitude toward her health? What is she doing that demonstrates this attitude?

2. How does Sue react to Johnsy's attitude? What does she try to do?

Before you read Part 2, answer this question.

Do you think Johnsy is going to get better or not? Explain.

Greenwich Village in New York City

After you read Part 2 (¶ 26–49), you should be able to answer these questions.

1. Who is Behrman and what is his relationship to Johnsy and Sue?
2. What was the weather like for two nights in a row?
3. What did you expect to happen?
4. When does Johnsy's attitude change? Why does it change?

The Last Leaf

by O. Henry

Part 1

1   Sue and Johnsy had their studio at the top of a three-story brick building in Greenwich Village. "Johnsy" was a nickname for Joanna. She was from California, Sue from Maine. They had met in a restaurant on Eighth Street, found that they had similar taste in art, food, and other things, and decided to share a studio.

2   That was in May. In November there was an epidemic of pneumonia[1] in New York. Johnsy, accustomed to the warm weather of California, was a victim. She lay there, scarcely moving, on her painted iron bed, looking through the small window at the blank wall of the next brick house.

3   One morning the busy doctor invited Sue into the hallway.

4   "She has one chance in—let us say ten," he said. "And that chance is for her to want to live. This way people have of thinking they are going to die makes all the medicine in the world look ridiculous. Your friend has decided that she is not going to get well. Does she have anything on her mind?"

5   "She—she wanted to paint the Bay of Naples some day," said Sue.

6   "Paint?—bosh! Does she have anything on her mind that is worth thinking about twice—a man, for instance?"

7   "A man?" said Sue. "Is a man worth—but no, doctor; there is nothing of the kind."

8   "Well, it is the weakness, then," said the doctor. "I will do all that I can. But whenever a patient begins to count the carriages in her funeral[2] procession, I subtract 50 per cent from the curative power of medicines. If you can get her to ask about the new winter styles, I will promise you a one-in-five chance for her, instead of one in ten."

9   After the doctor left, Sue went into the workroom and cried. Then she went into Johnsy's room with her drawing board, whistling[3] a happy tune.

[1] **epidemic of pneumonia** time when many people in the same area had pneumonia, a disease of the lungs

[2] **funeral** ceremony for burying a dead person

[3] **whistling** making a musical sound by blowing air out through your lips

10   Johnsy lay, scarcely moving, with her face toward the window. Sue stopped whistling, thinking she was asleep.

11   Sue began a drawing for a magazine story. As she was working, she heard a low sound, several times repeated. She went quickly to the bedside.

12   Johnsy's eyes were open wide. She was looking out the window and counting—counting backward.

13   "Twelve," she said, and a little later "eleven"; and then "ten," and "nine"; and then "eight" and "seven," almost together.

14   Sue looked out the window. What was there to count? There was only a bare yard and the blank side of the brick house twenty feet away. An old, old ivy vine[4] climbed halfway up the brick wall. The cold wind had blown its leaves from the vine until its almost bare branches clung to the old bricks.

15   "What is it, dear?" asked Sue.

16   "Six," said Johnsy, in almost a whisper. "They're falling faster now. Three days ago there were almost a hundred. It made my head ache to count them. But now it's easy. There goes another one. There are only five left now."

17   "Five what, dear? Tell your Sudie."

18   "Leaves. On the ivy vine. When the last one falls I must go, too. I've known that for three days. Didn't the doctor tell you?"

19   "Oh, I never heard of such nonsense," said Sue. "What do old ivy leaves have to do with your getting well? And you used to love that vine, so, you naughty girl. Don't be silly. Why, the doctor told me this morning that your chances for getting well real soon were—let's see exactly what he said—he said the chances were ten to one! That's almost as good a chance as we have in New York when we ride on the street cars or walk past a new building. Try to have some soup now, and let me finish this drawing so I can sell it and buy port wine for you and pork chops for me."

20   "You don't have to buy any more wine," said Johnsy, looking out the window. "There goes another. No, I don't want any soup. That leaves just four. I want to see the last one fall before it gets dark. Then I'll go, too."

21   "Johnsy, dear," said Sue, "will you promise me to keep your eyes closed, and not look out the window until I am finished working? I must deliver these drawings tomorrow. I need the light, or I would pull the shade down."

22   "Couldn't you draw in the other room?"

23   "I'd rather be here by you," said Sue. "Besides, I don't want you to keep looking at those silly ivy leaves."

24   "Tell me as soon as you finish," said Johnsy, closing her eyes, "because I want to see the last one fall. I'm tired of waiting. I'm tired of thinking. I want to let go of everything, and go down, down, just like one of those poor, tired leaves."

25   "Try to sleep," said Sue. "I must call Behrman up to be my model for the old hermit miner. I'll only be gone a minute."

[4] **ivy vine**   a plant with dark green leaves that often grows on walls

Before you read part 2, answer this question.
Do you think Johnsy is going to get better or not? Explain.

Part 2

26   Old Behrman was a painter who lived below them. He was more than sixty and had a long, gray beard. Behrman was a failure in art. For forty years he was always about to paint a masterpiece,[5] but had never yet begun it. He earned a little money by serving as a model for young artists in the colony who could not pay the price of a professional model. He drank too much gin and still talked about his coming masterpiece. For the rest he was a fierce little old man who criticized softness in anyone, and he regarded himself as the protector of the two young artists in the studio above.

27   Sue found Behrman smelling of gin in his apartment below. In one corner was a blank canvas on an easel[6] that had been waiting there for twenty-five years to receive the first line of the masterpiece. She told him about Johnsy's crazy idea and how she feared that Johnsy, light and fragile as a leaf herself, would float away when her slight hold on the world grew weaker.

28   Old Behrman shouted his contempt for such an idiotic idea.

29   "Vass!" he cried. "Is dere people in de world mit der foolishness to die because leafs dey drop off from a vine? No, I will not pose as a model for you. Vy do you allow dot silly business to come in der brain of her? Ach, dot poor little Miss Yohnsy."

30   "She is very sick and weak," said Sue, "and the fever has made her think strange and morbid[7] thoughts. Very well, Mr. Behrman, if you do not want to pose for me, you don't have to. But I think you are a horrid old man."

31   "You are just like a woman!" yelled Behrman. "Who said I will not pose? I come mit you. Gott! dis is not any place in which one so goot as Miss Yohnsy shall lie sick. Some day I will paint a masterpiece, and ve shall all go away. Gott! yes."

32   Johnsy was sleeping when they went upstairs. Sue pulled the shade down and she and Behrman went into the other room. They looked out the window fearfully at the ivy vine. Then they looked at each other for a moment without speaking. A cold rain mixed with snow was falling.

33   The next morning Sue found Johnsy with wide-open eyes staring at the shade.

34   "Put it up; I want to see," she ordered in a whisper.

35   Sue obeyed.

36   But, lo! After the rain and strong wind throughout the night, there stood out against the brick wall one ivy leaf. It was the last on the vine, still dark green near its stem, yellow at the edges. It hung there bravely from a branch some twenty feet above the ground.

37   "It is the last one," said Johnsy. "I thought it would surely fall during the night. I heard the wind. It will fall today, and I shall die at the same time."

[5] **masterpiece**   a work of art that is of the highest quality compared to others of its kind

[6] **blank canvas on an easel**

[7] **morbid**   related to death

38   "Dear, dear!" said Sue, "think of me if you won't think of yourself. What would I do?"

39   But Johnsy did not answer. As the day wore on, they could see the lone ivy leaf clinging to its stem against the wall. And then, as night came it got windy again and the rain continued to fall.

40   When it was light enough, Johnsy ordered Sue to raise the shade.

41   The ivy leaf was still there.

42   Johnsy lay for a long time looking at it. And then she called Sue, who was stirring soup on the gas stove.

43   "I've been a bad girl, Sudie," said Johnsy. "Something has made that last leaf stay there to show me how bad I was. It is a sin[8] to want to die. You may bring me a little soup now, and some milk with a little port wine in it, and—no; bring me a hand mirror first, and then put some pillows around me, and I will sit up and watch you cook."

44   An hour later she said:

45   "Sudie, some day I hope to paint the Bay of Naples."

46   The doctor came in the afternoon, and Sue went into the hallway as he left.

47   "Even chances,"[9] said the doctor, taking Sue's thin hand in his. "With good nursing you'll win. And now I must see another case downstairs. Behrman his name is—some kind of artist, I believe. Pneumonia too. He is an old, weak man. There is no hope for him; but he goes to the hospital today to be made more comfortable."

48   The next day the doctor said to Sue: "She's out of danger. You've won. Nutrition and care now—that's all."

49   And that afternoon Sue came to the bed where Johnsy lay. "I have something to tell you, white mouse," she said. "Mr. Behrman died of pneumonia today in the hospital. He was sick only two days. The janitor found him on the morning of the first day in his room downstairs. His shoes and clothing were wet through and icy cold. They couldn't imagine where he had been on such an awful night. And then they found a lantern,[10] still lighted, and a ladder, and some brushes, and a palette[11] with green and yellow colors mixed on it, and—look out the window, dear, at the last ivy leaf on the wall. Didn't you wonder why it never moved when the wind blew? Ah, darling, it's Behrman's masterpiece—he painted it there the night that the last leaf fell."

[8] **sin** something that is against religious laws

[9] **even chances** a 50 percent chance (50-50)

[10]**lantern**

[11]**brushes and palette**

Comprehension Check

A. First Reading

1 *Complete the sentences about Part 1 with an appropriate word or phrase.*

Johnsy has pneumonia. She has a _____ attitude about her illness
(1)

and has decided that she will _____ when the last leaf of an ivy vine
(2)

on the wall opposite her window falls. She is _____ backward as each
(3)

leaf falls. Sue tells Johnsy she is being _____. Sue is really very
(4)

worried, but she tries to seem _____ in front of Johnsy.
(5)

2 *Mark the statements about Part 2 **T** (true) or **F** (false). Be prepared to show evidence in the story that supports your answers.*

1. T F Behrman is a successful artist.

2. T F He is angry when Sue tells him what Johnsy is doing.

3. T F When the wind stops, Johnsy sees that there is still a leaf on the ivy vine, and she decides to get well.

B. Second Reading

Before you read the selection again, read items 1–6 so you will know what information to look for.

1. List things Johnsy says that show her negative attitude about getting well.
2. List things Sue says and does to cheer Johnsy up and change her mental attitude.
3. List details that show what the doctor believes.
4. List details that show what Behrman is like.
5. Why does Johnsy's attitude change?
6. How does Behrman get sick? What happens to him?

Vocabulary

 A. Vocabulary Building

Look at the underlined words or expressions in the sentences below. Find them in the selection. Then choose the correct meaning for the context.

PART 1

1. She lay there, <u>scarcely moving</u>, on her painted iron bed . . . (¶ 2, 10)
   a. moving a lot
   b. moving very little

2. She has one <u>chance</u> in . . . ten. (¶ 4)
   a. possibility
   b. desire

3. This way people have of thinking they are going to die makes all the medicine in the world look <u>ridiculous</u>. (¶ 4)
   a. reasonable
   b. stupid

4. Does she have anything on her mind that is <u>worth thinking about twice</u> . . . ? (¶ 6)
   a. unimportant
   b. important

5. There was only a <u>bare</u> yard and the blank side of the brick house twenty feet away. (¶ 14)
   a. full
   b. empty

6. The cold wind had blown its leaves from the vine until its almost bare branches <u>clung to</u> the old bricks. (¶ 14)
   a. held on to
   b. let go of

7. "Six," said Johnsy, in almost a <u>whisper</u>. (¶ 16)
   a. loud voice
   b. soft voice

8. Oh, I never heard of such <u>nonsense</u> . . . (¶ 19)
   a. a stupid idea
   b. blindness

9. Don't be <u>silly</u>. (¶ 19)
   a. stupid
   b. playful

10. I must call Behrman up to be my <u>model</u> for the old hermit miner. (¶ 25)
    a. a perfect example of something
    b. the person an artist copies

PART 2

11. . . . Johnsy . . . would float away when her <u>slight</u> hold on the world grew weaker. (¶ 27)
    a. strong
    b. minimal or weak

12. . . . Sue found Johnsy with wide-open eyes <u>staring at</u> the shade. (¶ 33)
    a. looking at something without moving her eyes
    b. thinking seriously about something

13. They couldn't imagine where he had been on such an <u>awful</u> night. (¶ 49)
    a. wonderful
    b. very bad

14. Didn't you <u>wonder</u> why it never moved when the wind blew? (¶ 49)
    a. ask yourself
    b. forget

B. Vocabulary Review

Complete the following statements about the reading selection with the correct word or expression from the list below. Use each word or expression only once.

bare	**masterpiece**	**ridiculous**	**slight**
chance	**pneumonia**	**sin**	**worth**

1. Johnsy and Sue were two young artists in New York in the early 1900s. Johnsy had _____ and was very weak indeed.

2. The doctor was pessimistic and told Sue that her friend had about one _____ in ten to recover. The only thing that could help would be for Johnsy to want to live.

3. Even with the support of Sue, who tried to cheer her up, Johnsy felt there was nothing _____ living for.

4. She decided that she would die when the last leaf fell off the almost _____ branches of the ivy vine, which Sue thought was _____.

5. With all the wind, rain, and snow, it seemed certain that all the leaves would fall and that Johnsy too would let go of her _____ hold on life.

SELECTION FOUR   **185**

6. After two nights of bad weather, there was still one leaf on the vine. Johnsy's attitude changed. She said it was a _____ to want to die, and she started to get better.

7. Behrman died of pneumonia after painting his _____: a single green and yellow ivy leaf.

Sharing Your Thoughts

1. In what ways is Johnsy similar to or different from the Guatemalan patient in Selection Three?
2. Although the story gives little or no information about Johnsy's reasons for wanting to die, what do you think they could be?
3. Johnsy says it is a sin to want to die. What do you think she means?
4. What is your opinion of Behrman? Do you think he was a hero?
5. What, if any, relationship do you see between this story and Selection One? Consider mental attitude and social support.
6. In your opinion, is this a happy or sad story? Explain.

Text Analysis

Surprise Endings

O. Henry is famous for the surprise endings of many of his stories. Why is the ending of this story a surprise?

List details that lead a reader to think that the last leaf certainly would fall and therefore Johnsy would die.

It's winter _____

_____

_____

_____

When did you realize that the last leaf was not a real leaf? When do you think Johnsy realized this? Looking back, were there clues earlier in the story that Behrman painted the leaf?

Writing Task

1. Seneca's words on page 153 are relevant to this story. Write a paragraph showing how this story supports Seneca's statement. Think about what the doctor said, and think about Johnsy's behavior. You may want to begin like this:

   > Two thousand years ago Seneca said, "It is part of the cure to wish to be cured." Johnsy, one of the main characters in "The Last Leaf," . . .

2. Write a paragraph describing the effect the surprise ending of this story had on you. Consider what you talked about in Text Analysis.

Selection Five

Before Reading

"Manuel García" is a song by North American folk singer and song writer David Roth. It tells a true story about a Puerto Rican man from Milwaukee, Wisconsin, who was diagnosed with stomach cancer at the age of thirty-nine.

Discussion

Do you know anyone who has had cancer? How did this person's family and friends help him or her deal with the illness? What medical treatment did the person receive?

Cancer patients are often given chemotherapy; they take strong drugs to kill the cancerous cells in their bodies. What are some secondary, or side, effects of chemotherapy treatment?

Cancer patients often lose hope. They feel lonely, scared, and isolated from others. What would you do to help a person with cancer feel better?

Focus for the First Reading

Read these questions before you read the song lyrics. You should be able to answer them after you finish the first reading.

1. What do we know about Manuel García before he got sick?

2. What did the doctors tell him about his illness and his choices for treatment?

3. How did the treatment affect him?

4. How did his friends and relatives show their love and support for him?

Manuel García

by David Roth

1 Manuel García, a proud youthful father
   Was known on his block as a hard-working man.
   With a wife and a family, a job and a future
   He had everything going according to plan.

2 One day Manuel García, complaining of stomach pains
   Went to the clinic to find the cause.
   His body was found to have cancerous tissue
   Ignoring[1] the order of natural laws.

¹ **ignoring**   not paying attention to

3   So Manuel García of Milwaukee County
    Checked into the medical complex in town.
    Suddenly seeing his thirty-nine years
    Like the sand in an hourglass[2] plummeting down.

[2] **hourglass**

4   "What are my choices?" cried Manuel García.
    "You've basically two," was the doctor's decree.[3]
    "Your cancer untreated will quickly be fatal,[4]
    But treatment is painful with no guarantees . . ."

[3] **decree**   official statement

[4] **fatal**   resulting in death

5   And so it began, Manuel's personal odyssey[5]—
    Long sleepless nights in a chemical daze[6]
    With echoes of footsteps down long lonely corridors[7]
    Tolling his minutes and hours away.[8]

[5] **odyssey**   very long trip

[6] **daze**   unclear mental state

[7] **corridors**   hallways; halls

[8] **tolling his minutes and hours away** marking the passing of time or his life

6   With the knowledge that something inside was consuming him
    Manuel García was filled with despair.[9]
    He'd already lost forty pounds to the cancer,
    And now to the drugs he was losing his hair.

[9] **despair**   a hopeless feeling; extreme unhappiness

7   After nine weeks in treatment the doctor came calling.
    Said "Manuel, we've done about all we can do.
    Your cancer could go either way at this juncture;[10]
    It's out of our hands and it's now up to you."[11]

[10] **at this juncture**   at this point in time

[11] **it's up to you**   you are responsible

8   Manuel looked in the mirror, a sad frightened stranger[12]
    So pale, so wrinkled, so lonely, so scared.
    Diseased, isolated, and feeling unlovable—
    One hundred twenty-six pounds and no hair.

[12] **stranger**   a person you don't know

9   He dreamed of his Carmen at sixty without him,
    His four little children not having their dad,
    Of Thursday night card games at Julio's,
    And everything else he'd not done that he wished that he had.

10 Awakened from sleep on the day of his discharge[13]
    By shuffling feet going all around his bed,
    Manuel opened his eyes and thought he was still dreaming—
    His wife, and four friends with no hair on their heads.

[13] **the day of his discharge**   the day he was leaving the hospital

11 He blinked and he looked again, not quite believing
    The four shiny heads all lined up side by side.
    And still to that point not a word had been spoken,
    But soon they were laughing so hard that they cried.

(continued on page 190)

12 And the hospital hallways were ringing with voices.
    "*Patrón*,[14] we did this for you," said his friends.
    And they wheeled him out to the car they had borrowed.
    "*Amigo, estamos contigo ves...*"[15]

13 So Manuel returned to his neighborhood
    Dropped off in front of his two-bedroom flat.[16]
    And the block seemed unusually deserted[17] for Sunday;
    He drew a deep breath[18] and adjusted his hat.

14 But before he could enter, the front door flew open.
    Manuel was surrounded with faces he knew—
    Fifty-odd loved ones and friends of the family
    With clean-shaven heads and the words "We love you!"

15 And so Manuel García, a person with cancer,
    A father, a husband, a neighbor, a friend,
    With a lump in his throat[19] said "I'm not one for speeches,
    But here I have something that needs to be said.

16 "I felt so alone with my baldness and cancer.
    Now you stand beside me, thank Heaven above
    For giving me strength that I need may God bless you,
    And long may we live with the meaning of love.

17 "For giving me strength that I need may God bless you,
    And long may we live with the meaning of love."

[14] ***Patrón***   Hey, man (a form of address that shows friendship; from Spanish)

[15] ***Amigo, estamos contigo ves...***   Friend, we're with you, see . . .

[16] **flat**   apartment that is on one floor of a house
[17] **deserted**   empty and quiet
[18] **drew a deep breath**   breathed in deeply

[19] **lump in his throat**   feeling in the throat when you are going to cry

Comprehension Check

A. First Reading

*Mark the statements **T** (true) or **F** (false). Be prepared to show evidence in the selection that supports your answers.*

1. T F Manuel García was single and unemployed when he got sick.

2. T F The doctors operated on Manuel García to remove the tumor.

3. T F Manuel García lost his hair and a lot of weight.

4. T F About fifty friends and relatives shaved their heads so he would not feel alone.

B. Second Reading

Read the song again, concentrating on the stanzas listed below on the left. They show something about Manuel García's mental state. Match each one with the appropriate sentence on the right.

___ Stanza 1

___ Stanza 3

___ Stanza 6

___ Stanza 8

___ Stanza 9

___ Stanza 11

___ Stanza 15

___ Stanza 16

a. When Manuel sees the bald heads of his friends, they all start laughing.

b. Manuel saw himself as sick, unlovable, skinny, bald, and alone.

c. Manuel feels very emotional, but he wants to tell his friends something.

d. He tells them that he appreciates their support and feels that their love has given him the strength he needs.

e. He lost a lot of weight, he lost his hair, and he felt extremely sad.

f. He went to the hospital feeling afraid that this was the end of his life.

g. Everything in Manuel's life was going well.

h. Manuel thinks about what he will lose if he dies.

Sharing Your Thoughts

1. Continue to trace Manuel García's mental state on the graph below from his positive mental state in Stanza 1 through his treatment to the end of the song. Different students will have slightly different graphs. Compare your graph with a classmate's, and talk about any differences in your interpretation of his feelings.

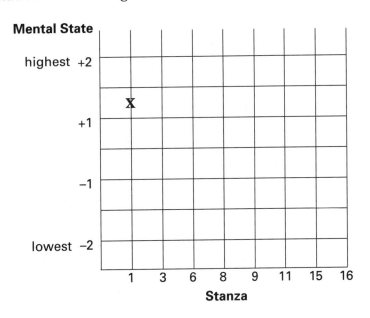

2. Why do you think Manuel's family and friends chose to show their support by shaving their heads? What does it tell you about his family and friends?

3. Talk about similarities and differences among Manuel García, Johnsy, and the Guatemalan patient. Who or what is responsible for changing their mental attitudes?

Writing Task

The inspiring, true story of Manuel García appeared in various newspapers.

1. Work with a classmate. Student A is a newspaper reporter; Student B is Manual García. Student A writes five or six possible interview questions to ask Manuel García. Role play the interview. Student A may have to modify some of the questions, depending on Student B's answers. Write out the conversation.

2. Imagine you are a newspaper reporter. Write a newspaper article telling Manuel García's story.

A Final Look

Discussion

1. Work with a classmate, in a small group, or as a whole class. Drawing on all five selections in this unit, discuss the focus questions and quote on page 153.

2. We often hear people comment about psychosomatic illness, meaning that the illness is caused by a person's mental attitude. The word *psychosomatic* comes from Greek (*psycho* = mind; *soma* = body). Discuss the following quote from the book *Getting Well Again* (Simonton et al., 1978, p. 29).

   "Just as one can be psychosomatically ill, so one who is ill can move in the other direction and become psychosomatically healthy."

   How does it summarize the main idea of this unit?
   What kinds of things could a person do to be "psychosomatically healthy"?

3. Sometimes a patient is not happy if a doctor won't prescribe some medication. At other times even though the medication may not help, some doctors prescribe it anyway if they know it can't hurt the patient. What could a doctor's reasons be? What kind of results could this lead to?

4. If you are planning to be a doctor, what, if anything, in this unit made you see the profession differently?

5. In his book *Quantum Healing*, Deepak Chopra said, "Everyone's body knows how to heal a cut, yet apparently only a few people have bodies that know how to cure cancer" (p. 41). What do you think he means by this?

There are many ways people can relax, reduce stress, lower blood pressure and heart rate, and enhance the functioning of their immune systems. You already practiced with one set of instructions for meditation by Joan Borysenko. The same author has other exercises in a chapter of her book called "Breaking the Anxiety Cycle." Here is an exercise that can be done anywhere.

THE BACK RELAXER

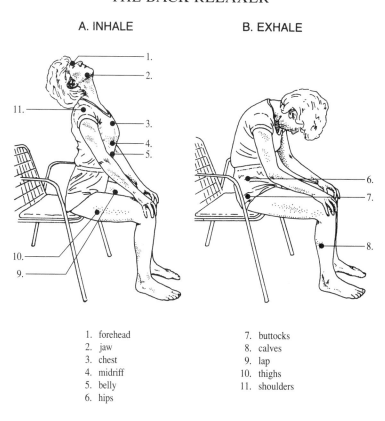

1. forehead
2. jaw
3. chest
4. midriff
5. belly
6. hips

7. buttocks
8. calves
9. lap
10. thighs
11. shoulders

Move to the edge of your chair. With eyes closed so that you can pay closer attention to inner sensations, notice how your back feels. On the next breath, arch backward (A), stretching your spine only as far as feels comfortable. Exhale and round your back (B), rolling your shoulders forward and letting go. Repeat three times, keeping full attention on breathing, stretching, and letting go (long pause).

Look at the pictures for the *back relaxer*, and read the instructions on how to do the exercise. Write eight to ten imperative sentences based on Dr. Borysenko's instructions. Some of your instructions will be exactly the same as hers. You will have to change others slightly to make them imperative sentences. You may want to add other instructions that will help your classmates do the exercise correctly. (Use the body parts identified above. If you need more help, check a dictionary.)

If possible, tape-record your version of the instructions three times, with pauses between each repetition. You may want to record the instructions with relaxing music in the background. If you do not have a tape recorder, read the instructions to a classmate who will do the exercise.

6 Computers: Changing the Way We Live

> *Technology and human purpose work best when combined in support of a common human goal.*
> — Michael Dertouzos

FOCUS

➤ What are some of the ways computers and telecommunications are changing our lives?

➤ What is a network of computers?

➤ What are some potential benefits of this new technology?

➤ What are some potential problems and dangers of this new technology?

Selection One

Before Reading

This selection is an adapted excerpt from *The Wired Neighborhood* by Stephen Doheny-Farina. He is a university professor interested in the effects of new technology on social organization and community.

Discussion

Look at the picture on page 197 of computers around the world connected by fiber optic cable.

The world of computers is known as the virtual world, as opposed to the physical world we are so familiar with. The world of connected computers is often called cyberspace. With this new technology, people can stay at home and telecommute to work or school.

Talk with your classmates about what equipment you would need to do this and what it would be like to work or study from home.

Previewing

Read paragraph 1 and the first sentence of paragraph 2. Answer these questions.

1. People can telecommute to

   a. work

   b. school

   c. both

2. This selection will be about telecommuting to

   a. work

   b. school

Focus for the First Reading

Read these questions before you read the selection. You should be able to answer them after you finish the first reading.

1. What is Peg Fagen's profession?

2. Where does she live and work?

3. Why is this convenient for her?

Telecommuting

by **Stephen Doheny-Farina**

1   One of the most powerful attractions of the net[1] is that it will take us back home. It will enable us to telecommute to work and will create ultra-accessible virtual schools. It will allow us to spend more time with our families and stay closer to our communities. As work becomes increasingly knowledge based,[2] workers become knowledge manipulators.[3] Work involving knowledge—whether on the job or in school—is the kind of work that can be done on the net. Radio and television brought entertainment home, and now telecommuting seems to deliver our work and school there, too.

2   Peg Fagen, for example, lives in Massachusetts and works for a company in New York. She is an environmental[4] engineer, and in her home office she has all the necessary items to do her work: dedicated phone and fax line,[5] computer and modem,[6] e-mail and file-transfer connectivity,[7] copier and so on.[8] A babysitter takes care of her preschool-age children while Peg works, largely uninterrupted, in her office. Peg is one of

---

[1] **the net**   the Internet, a worldwide network of computers
[2] **knowledge based**   involving the handling of information
[3] **manipulators**   handlers; movers
[4] **environmental**   relating to the air, land, and water
[5] **dedicated phone and fax line**   specifically for the computer (separate from the home phone line)
[6] **modem**   separate machine (or part of the computer) which sends and receives digital information from the phone line and stores it in a computer
[7] **e-mail and file-transfer connectivity**   software programs that handle the sending of communications
[8] **and so on**   etc.

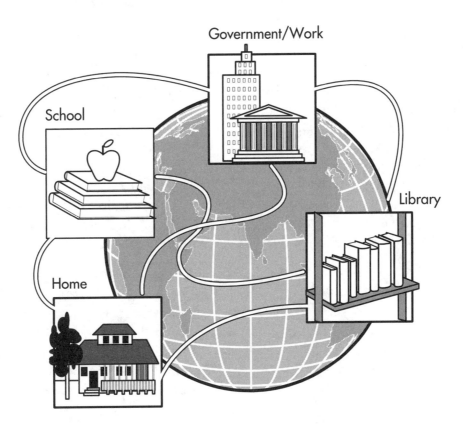

those people whose expertise and net connections enable them to do valuable, high-skilled, and challenging work from their homes or mobile[9] offices.

3   Peg began working at the New York office of the firm in 1989. Less than two years later she and her husband moved to Massachusetts so that he could take a job there. With that move and the hope of starting a family, Peg asked her employers if she could begin telecommuting. At that time the company was small and most employees worked with the owners in a close-knit group; therefore the company's managers knew the quality of Peg's work and were aware of her value to the company. They agreed to let her try it, and seven years later she is still telecommuting each day.

4   Peg was the first employee in the firm to telecommute. A number of others have requested a similar arrangement, but only a few of those requests have been approved. As Peg herself recognizes, much of the work of the firm requires that its employees be at the office dealing with co-workers and clients. Most of her work, however, involves analyzing and reporting on environmental pollution[10] data.

5   She has disciplined herself not to mix work around the house with her engineering work. When she goes into her office, she is at work. When the sitter leaves or when the children awaken, she is at home. If the day's work is not completed when the sitter leaves, then she returns to her office after the children have been put to bed. In addition to her ability to manage her time productively, one of the keys to her success, she says, is her relationship with one manager at the firm's office. Because she had worked for that person before she started telecommuting, the manager understands what Peg does best, and can send appropriate work her way. Peg recognizes that it is difficult to develop a solid working relationship long-distance with someone she has never met. As a result, she visits the office every few months to see both new and old employees.

6   Peg's one disadvantage as a telecommuter involves her progress within the company. Co-workers with similar education, on-the-job experience, and time with the company have moved up the company's management ladder faster than Peg. She believes that although she can work as a technical analyst from home, she cannot so easily manage others remotely. While she might give up telecommuting after her children are all in school full-time, Peg is thankful that her arrangement has enabled her to stay current in a highly technical field that changes rapidly. If she had taken five or six years off to raise children, she would have been out of touch with the science and technology of the field.

7   Peg is certainly not alone in her method of employment. More and more workers are doing all or most of their work from wherever their electronic connectivity allows. The issue is no longer the feasibility[11] of telecommuting but the quality of life that net-infused[12] work will create.

---

[9] **mobile**   movable; portable
[10] **pollution**   dangerous additions to air, land, and water

[11] **feasibility**   ability to do it
[12] **net-infused**   using the Internet often

Comprehension Check

A. First Reading

Fill in the blanks with an appropriate word or phrase.

Peg Fagen is an environmental _____ (1) . She works for a

company in _____ (2) , but she lives in _____ (3) ,

several hundred miles away. Telecommuting is convenient for her because she

lives _____ (4) from her company's office and has

_____ (5) children.

B. Second Reading

1 *Read the selection again. Mark the statements **T** (true) or **F** (false). Be prepared to show evidence in the selection that supports your answers.*

1. T   F   Peg started telecommuting because her husband took a job outside New York.

2. T   F   Peg's company allowed her to start telecommuting because her work was valuable to the company.

3. T   F   The company doesn't approve all requests for telecommuting because the necessary hardware is too expensive.

4. T   F   Peg doesn't see any disadvantages to telecommuting.

5. T   F   Telecommuting has allowed Peg to stay up-to-date in her field.

2 *Check the reasons mentioned in the selection that make it possible for Peg to be a productive worker from home.*

___ **1.** She doesn't mix work and family.

___ **2.** She has a good working relationship with her manager.

___ **3.** She visits the office every few months.

___ **4.** Her husband helps her with housework.

___ **5.** She has a home office with the equipment she needs.

___ **6.** Her job involves working with information which can be sent electronically.

___ **7.** Her kids are in school most of the day.

Vocabulary

A. Vocabulary Building

Find a word or expression in the selection that means the same as the words or expressions below.

1. make it possible for (¶ 1)   _____

2. very easy to use (¶ 1)   _____

3. permit; let (¶ 1)   _____

4. knew about; were conscious of (¶ 3)   _____

5. plan; agreement (¶ 4)   _____

6. accepted; given the OK (¶ 4)   _____

7. working with (¶ 4)   _____

8. customers; people you provide a service to (¶ 4)   _____

9. combine (¶ 5)   _____

10. organize (¶ 5)   _____

11. principal reasons for (¶ 5)   _____

12. from far away (¶ 5)   _____

13. up-to-date (¶ 6)   _____

14. not in contact (¶ 6)   _____

15. question; matter; point (¶ 7)   _____

B. Distinguishing Grammatical Function: Nouns and Verbs

*Decide if the underlined word is functioning as a noun (**N**) or a verb (**V**) in the sentences below. Circle your answers.*

1. N V **a.** In her home office she has all the necessary items to do her <u>work</u>.

   N V **b.** Peg <u>works</u>, largely uninterrupted, in her office.

2. N V **a.** Less than two years later she and her husband <u>moved</u> to Massachusetts.

   N V **b.** With that <u>move</u> and the hope of starting a family, Peg asked her employers if she could begin telecommuting.

3. N V **a.** With that move and the <u>hope</u> of starting a family, Peg asked her employers if she could begin telecommuting.

   N V **b.** Peg and her husband <u>hoped</u> to start a family.

4. N V **a.** The company managers were aware of her <u>value</u> to the company.

   N V **b.** The managers <u>value</u> her work.

5. N V **a.** A number of others have <u>requested</u> a similar arrangement,

   N V **b.** but only a few of those <u>requests</u> have been approved.

6. N V **a.** She has <u>disciplined</u> herself not to mix work around the house with her engineering work.

   N V **b.** She has self-<u>discipline</u>.

7. N V **a.** She has disciplined herself not to <u>mix</u> work around the house with her engineering work.

   N V **b.** Peg's arrangement is a good <u>mix</u> of work and family life.

8. N V **a.** Her one disadvantage as a telecommuter involves her <u>progress</u> within the company.

   N V **b.** She can't <u>progress</u> as fast as people who work in the office.

9. N V **a.** Co-workers with similar education and on-the-job <u>experience</u>, have moved up faster than Peg.

   N V **b.** Peg <u>experiences</u> some problems with telecommuting.

C. Vocabulary Review

Complete the following statements about the reading selection with the correct word or expression from the list below. Use each word or expression only once.

allows	**current**	**mix**
approved	**dealing with**	**progress**
arrangement	**manage**	**remotely**

1. Telecommuting can be a very convenient _____ for many people.

2. Peg Fagen is glad her company _____ her request to telecommute, but they cannot let all employees telecommute because some must be in the office _____ co-workers and clients.

3. Peg is a successful telecommuter because she has learned to _____ her time productively; she doesn't _____ work around the house with her engineering work.

4. Peg says telecommuting does have disadvantages. For one, her co-workers who are in the office daily can _____ faster in the company than she can. Peg also mentions that managing other workers _____ is not easy.

5. Perhaps when her children are in school, she will stop telecommuting, but she is thankful that telecommuting _____ her to continue working, stay _____ in a highly technical field, and have a family.

Sharing Your Thoughts

1. Discuss whether each job listed below (1) can be done principally by telecommuting, (2) can be done partially by telecommuting, or (3) cannot be done telecommuting.

   accountant

   actor

   disk jockey

   editor

   electrician

   lawyer

   nurse

   psychologist

   sales representative of a company

   teacher

   waitress

2. Imagine you are trying to decide whether to accept a job offer that requires you to telecommute to work. List the pros and cons that you have to consider. For example,

PROS	**Cons**
save money on gasoline	lack of social contact
_____	_____
_____	_____
_____	_____

3. Telecommuting also has advantages and disadvantages for a company. How do you think telecommuting would affect the factors listed below?

   hiring (finding the right employees)

   employee productivity (how much work employees do)

   employee morale (how satisfied employees are)

   operating costs (office space, energy, landscaping, security, equipment)

   maintenance (keeping equipment in working condition)

4. What, if any, benefits and costs do you think there might be for society as a whole? For example, consider traffic and pollution.

5. Do you know anyone who telecommutes to work or school? How do they like it?

Text Analysis

A. Extended Example

In Unit Three you saw how an extended example clarified the definition of personal style. In this selection, the extended example of Peg Fagen's experience as a telecommuter allows the writer to provide detailed content about different aspects of telecommuting.

Match paragraphs 2–6 with the content of the paragraph on the right.

¶ 1 Introduction

¶ 2 _____   **a.** disadvantages and advantages of telecommuting, for both the company and Fagen

¶ 3 _____   **b.** what makes it possible for Fagen to telecommute

¶ 4 _____   **c.** how some jobs within the company allow for telecommuting but others do not

¶ 5 _____   **d.** how Fagen got started telecommuting and why

¶ 6 _____   **e.** details about Fagen's work arrangement

¶ 7 Conclusion

B. New Words in a Language

Languages are constantly changing. New words come into a language as we need them. One way we create new words is by shortening longer words. What do you think is the long form of each of the words below?

> **EXAMPLE:** *fax* is the first part of *facsimile* (which means "copy")

A fax machine sends electronic instructions to make a copy of a document on another fax machine.

the Net   _____

copier   _____

e-mail   _____

phone   _____

Writing Task

1. Write a paragraph about why you think telecommuting to work or school is something you would or would not like to do.

2. Write about a home-based business you might start. It could be a serious business—for example, a translating business. Or you could come up with a fun idea such as a business where people can rent virtual exercise equipment. Explain the services you would provide and how you would use telecommunications in that business.

Selection Two

Before Reading

This selection is adapted from *What Will Be* by Michael Dertouzos, head of the Massachusetts Institute of Technology Laboratory for Computer Science. In this book, he discusses how information technology will change all aspects of our lives. Dertouzos says that the reality he describes in this selection is only ten or twenty years in the future.

Discussion

Talk with your classmates about how the electronic transfer of information from one place in the world to another can be used in medical situations. In what situations might this be very useful? For example, in a small town there are often no specialists, so a family doctor might use telecommunications to consult a specialist. What types of information might be sent?

Previewing

Scan paragraph 1. Find answers to these questions.

1. Where are the husband and wife?

2. Who is sick?

3. What are the person's symptoms?

Focus for the First Reading

Read these questions before you read the selection. You should be able to answer them after you finish the first reading.

1. How serious is the man's health problem?

2. Where were the doctors who treated him?

3. What happens to him at the end of the selection?

A View of the Future

by Michael Dertouzos

1   A husband and wife are on vacation in Ruby Creek, a remote settlement in Alaska. Their accommodations at the hostel,[1] which serves tourists and functions as the meeting place, post office, and general store for the sixty year-round residents, are comfortable. The man has not slept well the past few nights, however, finding it a bit difficult to breathe. Tonight he gets worse rapidly. He feels feverish, can't get enough air, and is scared. His wife calls the lone clerk, who helps the man to an eight-foot-high medical kiosk[2] at one end of the hostel's wide lobby. Meanwhile, the settlement's emergency medical technician, whom the clerk has called, arrives. He's not a doctor but knows basic procedures.

[1] **hostel**   informal kind of hotel

[2] **kiosk**   small booth or stand where things are sold, or a column on which announcements are posted

2   The technician asks the man a few questions as he hooks him to several probes on the kiosk. The machine records the man's pulse,[3] blood pressure, temperature, and respiration rate.[4] The technician inserts the man's medical identification card into a slot, and the kiosk sends the data from the card to the man's primary care physician, who is waking up back in Philadelphia. An alarm sounds on a computer reserved for emergency communications at the physician's home. He finds the data and symptoms disturbing. He transfers the record over a wireless line to Philadelphia General Hospital, where lung specialist Michael Kane can review it. Fortunately, he is available.

3   Using one of the hospital computers, Kane immediately connects to the kiosk. His face and voice appear on the kiosk's small screen. He tells the technician to take an X-ray[5] of the man's lungs.[6] By entering a security code, the technician instructs the safety shield on one side of the kiosk to retract, revealing a small X-ray unit mounted on a robot arm.

4   While the technician maneuvers the unit, the kiosk's computer retrieves Kane's auto-script[7] for handling X-rays.

> *Send chest X-ray to A. Smith at Medlab 1.*
> *Max[8] transport time 2 minutes.*
> *Min[9] security level is telephonic.*
> *Min overall reliability 99.99 percent.[10]*
> *Return reading to M. Kane at Philadelphia General.*

5   By now the X-ray is done and the kiosk, as instructed, sends the image to A. Smith, the hospital's radiologist.[11] Smith examines it and records his interpretation, which will be attached to the image. The three people in Ruby Creek try to relax.

6   Kane rules out his first guess and asks the technician if the kiosk is equipped with a spirometer and a pulse oximeter. It is. The technician instructs the man to blow into the machine and completes the oximeter test. Kane looks at all the data accumulating in front of him with the wisdom of his specialty and fifteen-year practice. He mumbles to himself, "Your respiration rate is high, oxygen saturation[12] is low and dropping, and the forced expiratory volume[13] after 1 second is abnormally low. No doubt about it: Extremely severe asthma."[14]

7   Hearing the diagnosis, the man's wife lets out a sigh of relief and tells the physician of their unspoken fear that it might have been worse. Kane is not about to frighten them, at least right now, that the man might be dead in less than six hours if he does not receive immediate care. Instead he says that the situation is still dangerous and they must move the man immediately to a hospital where he can be watched and, if necessary, intubated.[15] The technician understands more than he lets on. He orders a helicopter to take the man to Fairbanks General Hospital even before Kane stops speaking. Each hour saved is vital, and the Information Marketplace[16] has saved several hours already. On that frightening night, it has saved the man's life as well.

---

[3] **pulse**   beat of your heart pumping blood, usually felt at the wrist

[4] **respiration rate**   how many times a person breathes per minute

[5] **X-ray**   picture showing bones and internal organs

[6] **lungs**   organs for breathing

[7] **auto-script**   instructions

[8] **max**   maximum

[9] **min**   minimum

[10] **reliability 99.9%**   very close to perfect

[11] **radiologist**   medical doctor who interprets X-rays

[12] **oxygen saturation**   amount of oxygen in the blood

[13] **forced expiratory volume**   amount of air a person can push out of his lungs

[14] **asthma**   illness that causes difficulties in breathing

[15] **intubated**   have breathing tubes inserted

[16] **Information Marketplace**   the author prefers this phrase to *Information Highway*, a common name for the Internet

Comprehension Check

A. First Reading

*Mark the statements **T** (true) or **F** (false). Be prepared to show evidence in the selection that supports your answers.*

1. T   F   The man had a heart attack.

2. T   F   The man is in Alaska, but doctors in Philadelphia are consulted.

3. T   F   He has to be flown to Philadelphia.

B. Second Reading

1 *Read the selection again. Then answer the questions. Be prepared to find evidence in the selection that supports your answers.*

1. What kind of medical services are available in Ruby Creek, Alaska?

2. Who is the first person the technician consults long distance?

3. Who does that person consult and why?

4. What tests or procedures does Dr. Kane order the technician to do?

5. What is Kane's diagnosis?

6. How seriously ill is the man?

2 *List the equipment that you know the kiosk has because it was used in this case. Based on this information and using your imagination and general knowledge of medical equipment, draw a picture of this futuristic kiosk as you imagine it. You might want to label certain parts.*

Vocabulary

 A. Vocabulary Building

Look at the underlined words or expressions in the sentences below. Find them in the reading. Then choose the correct meaning for the context.

1. A husband and wife are on vacation in Ruby Creek, a <u>remote</u> settlement in Alaska. (¶ 1)

    a. near

    b. distant

2. <u>Their accommodations</u> at the hostel, . . . are comfortable. (¶ 1)

    a. their room

    b. the lobby

3. The technician asks the man a few questions as he <u>hooks</u> him to several probes on the kiosk. (¶ 2)

   a. connects

   b. cuts

4. The technician <u>inserts</u> the man's medical identification card into a slot . . . (¶ 2)

   a. puts

   b. changes

5. The technician inserts the man's medical identification card into a <u>slot</u> . . . (¶ 2)

   a. big opening

   b. narrow opening

6. He finds the data and symptoms <u>disturbing</u>. (¶ 2)

   a. upsetting, worrisome

   b. unimportant

7. He transfers the <u>record</u> over a wireless line to Philadelphia General Hospital . . . (¶ 2)

   a. disk

   b. information

8. . . . where lung specialist Michael Kane can review it. Fortunately, he is <u>available</u>. (¶ 2)

   a. at the hospital

   b. not at the hospital

9. . . . the technician instructs the safety shield . . . to retract, <u>revealing</u> a small X-ray unit mounted on a robot arm. (¶ 3)

   a. covering

   b. showing

10. While the technician <u>maneuvers</u> the unit, the kiosk's computer retrieves Kane's auto-script for handling X-rays. (¶ 4)

    a. moves into position

    b. turns off

11. . . . the kiosk's computer <u>retrieves</u> Kane's auto-script for handling X-rays. (¶ 4)

    a. records in memory

    b. brings from memory

12. Each hour saved is <u>vital</u>, and the Information Marketplace has saved several hours already. (¶ 7)

    a. full of life and energy

    b. very important

B. Multi-word Expressions

Look at the underlined multi-word expressions in the sentences below. Find them in the selection. Then match them with the correct meaning on the right.

___ 1. Tonight he <u>gets worse</u> rapidly. (¶ 1)

    a. at this time

___ 2. <u>By now</u> the X-ray is done . . . (¶ 5)

    b. shows

___ 3. Kane <u>rules out</u> his first guess . . . (¶ 6)

    c. a breath indicating tension is gone

___ 4. . . . the man's wife <u>lets out</u> a sigh of relief . . . (¶ 7)

    d. doesn't want to

___ 5. . . . the man's wife lets out <u>a sigh of relief</u> . . . (¶ 7)

    e. exhales; breathes out

___ 6. Kane <u>is not about to</u> frighten them . . . (¶ 7)

    f. gets sicker

___ 7. The technician understands more than he <u>lets on</u>. (¶ 7)

    g. eliminates

C. Vocabulary Review

Complete the following statements about the reading selection with the correct word or expression from the list. Use each word or expression only once.

asthma	hooked	record	slot
available	inserted	remote	vital
disturbing	kiosk	ruled out	

1. A husband and wife were staying at a hostel in a _____ settlement in Alaska.

2. The man couldn't breathe well, so his wife took him to the medical _____ in the lobby.

3. Soon the medical technician arrived and _____ the man to the kiosk for basic tests.

4. The technician _____ the man's medical identification card into a _____, and the kiosk sent the test results to the man's doctor in Philadelphia.

5. His doctor found the data and symptoms _____ so he sent the medical _____ to Dr. Michael Kane, a lung specialist at Philadelphia General Hospital.

6. Fortunately Dr. Kane was _____ and ordered an X-ray.

7. From the information on the X-ray, Dr. Kane _____ his first guess and asked for other tests. With the results of the additional tests, he diagnosed "Extremely severe _____."

8. In emergencies like this, saving time is _____, and the speed of telecommunications technology saved the man's life.

Sharing Your Thoughts

1. Talk about some of the effects of telecommunications on the medical profession. When this type of technology is common, will doctors have to be trained differently? Will we need more or fewer doctors? How will it affect the quality of health care?

2. How will this technology affect the doctor-patient relationship?

3. The doctors did not tell the man and his wife the complete truth after they made the diagnosis. Why do you think they did not tell them? Was that right or not?

Text Analysis

Understanding Complex Sentences

It is sometimes easier to understand complex sentences if you break them into simple sentences. Show that you understand these sentences by filling in the blank with a word or words from the original sentence. Number 1 has been done for you.

1. A husband and wife are on vacation in Ruby Creek, a remote settlement in Alaska.

   a. A husband and wife are on vacation in Ruby Creek.

   b. <u>Ruby Creek</u> is a remote settlement in Alaska.

2. Their accommodations at the hostel, which serves tourists and functions as the meeting place, post office, and general store for the sixty year-round residents, are comfortable.

   a. Their accommodations at the hostel are comfortable.

   b. _____ serves tourists and functions as the meeting place, post office, and general store for the sixty year-round residents.

3. The man has not slept well the past few nights, however, finding it a bit difficult to breathe.

   a. The man has not slept well the past few nights.

   b. _____ is finding it a bit difficult to breathe.

4. His wife calls the lone clerk, who helps the man to an eight-foot-high medical kiosk . . .

   a. His wife calls the lone clerk.

   b. _____ helps the man to an eight-foot-high medical kiosk . . .

5. Meanwhile, the settlement's emergency medical technician, whom the clerk has called, arrives.

   a. Meanwhile, the settlement's emergency medical technician arrives.

   b. The clerk has called _____.

6. . . . the kiosk sends the data from the card to the man's primary care physician, who is waking up back in Philadelphia.

   a. . . . the kiosk sends the data from the card to the man's primary care physician.

   b. _____ is waking up back in Philadelphia.

7. Using one of the hospital computers, Kane immediately connects to the kiosk.

   a. Kane immediately connects to the kiosk.

   b. _____ uses one of the hospital computers.

8. By entering a security code, the technician instructs the safety shield on one side of the kiosk to retract . . .

   a. The technician instructs the safety shield on one side of the kiosk to retract . . .

   b. _____ enters a security code.

Writing Task

1. Imagine you are the man's wife. Write a letter to a friend, telling this person about the medical emergency and how telecommunications saved your husband's life.

2. Write about an emergency you experienced when you were away from home. Before you begin to write, make notes of the important details you want to include in telling your story.

Selection Three

 **Before Reading**

The first part of this selection is from a feature article by Laurent Belsie of *The Christian Science Monitor*. The second part is from an editorial column by Debra Saunders of *The San Francisco Chronicle*.

Discussion

Talk with your classmates about how computers are used at all levels of education.

What do students like or dislike about using computers? What benefits do they get from using computers?

Previewing

Read the titles of the two parts of this selection. How will the two parts be different?

Focus for the First Reading

Work with a classmate. One of you will read Part 1 and the other Part 2. Read the questions that correspond to the part of the selection you will read. You should be able to answer them after you finish the first reading.

PART 1: HIGH-TECH TEACHING TOOL

1. How old are the computer users mentioned in this article?

2. How do they like using computers?

3. What do adults who work with them think about using computers with these people?

PART 2: COMPUTERS IN EVERY CLASS? WHY?

1. What is Debra Saunders's opinion about putting computers in every class?

2. What is the problem that many teachers have with using computers as educational tools?

3. What does Saunders think students must be able to do before using computers as educational tools?

PART 1
High-tech Teaching Tool

by **Laurent Belsie** *(The Christian Science Monitor)*

1   It's pretty hard to miss[1] Andrew's enthusiasm.

2   The preschooler punches the computer keyboard. He looks raptly[2] at the computer monitor. Whenever he gets a right answer, he raises both arms above his head in triumph.

3   Cecile is quieter and more accurate. Her task is to put in order four cartoon pictures of a pig making an apple pie. She hits the spacebar of the keyboard until the 1 is beside the picture of the pig picking apples. Then she presses the Enter key. Professor Al, a likable guy on the righthand side of the screen, gives a reassuring nod.[3]

4   Cecile then orders, correctly, pictures of a pig cutting the apples, baking the pie, and eating it. The computer lights up its approval, arcade-style.[4] Professor Al takes a break with his yo-yo.[5]

5   For the preschoolers here at Carnegie Mellon University's day-care center, this is a typical activity. The computer revolution is not waiting to happen for them. It's already here.

6   These children may not be typical. Their parents are university faculty or staff. Still, what is happening here is taking place to one degree or another in schools across the United States, indeed around the world.

7   Ronghua Ouyang, a graduate student who is studying the children and their computers, has found that nearly all the preschoolers at the Carnegie Mellon Children's School learned quickly how to use the machine. In one semester, they went from needing a lot of help from their teachers to almost none. Typical of what's happening in other schools, the children begin to help each other.

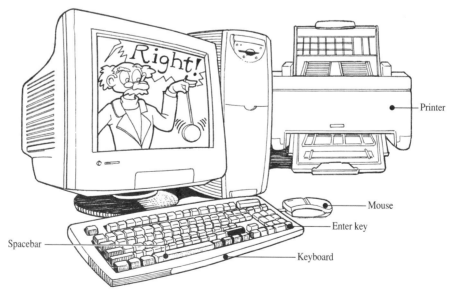

---

[1] **miss**   not see
[2] **raptly**   with concentrated attention
[3] **reassuring nod**   gesture of support, saying yes
[4] **arcade-style**   with lights and sounds like games machines
[5] **yo-yo**   child's toy (see picture on monitor)

8   That's very evident at the Children's School computer lab. Students constantly lean over to see what their classmates are doing. "And they enjoy it," Mr. Ouyang says. As long as children get equal access to a computer at a young age, he says he believes that girls and boys will perform equally well on the machine.

9   The potential[6] changes in education are dramatic. But teachers and researchers are quick to point out that, at the elementary level at least, the changes will be evolutionary rather than revolutionary.[7]

10 "At the younger grades you would expect that human-guided activity is more important than mastery[8] of the machine," parent-volunteer Becky Shapiro says. The teacher-student interaction will remain the primary mode of learning.

11 "We see it as a tool," adds Marsha Poster, director of Carnegie Mellon's child-care center. "We don't see it as an end-all."[9]

12 "We have taken a lot of things from kids' lives," says Ann Taylor, director of the Children's School. "Urban children don't have the trees, the open spaces, and the farm animals that their grandparents grew up with. Maybe the computer—with its ready[10] access to the outside world—will help give some of that back," she says.

---

[6] **potential**   possible
[7] **evolutionary rather than revolutionary**   slow and gradual, rather than quick and sudden
[8] **mastery**   complete learning
[9] **end-all**   end of all problems (complete expression: "the be-all and the end-all")
[10] **ready**   instant; easy to use

PART 2
Computers in Every Class? Why?

by **Debra Saunders** *(The San Francisco Chronicle)*

1   . . . School districts across the country are rushing to purchase computers for their classrooms, even when doing so[11] has required killing a music program (Kittridge Street Elementary School in Los Angeles), turning an art room into a computer lab (that happened in Virginia) or killing vocational classes like shop[12] (as was recommended by Clinton's National Information Infrastructure Advisory Council).

2   I do not mean to suggest that it is wrong for schools to buy computers. I do mean to say that it may not be right. Many teachers aren't trained in using computers as classroom tools. And computers won't help kids who can't read.

3   Computers may not be appropriate in early grades. Some teachers see them as mind-numbing toys with negative effects on young minds akin to[13] those produced by watching too much television—state-of-the-art[14] attention-span killers. Other teachers, however, see computers as tools for motivating students.

4   But does motivation yield[15] great knowledge? The Los Angeles Times recently reported how one local elementary school spent $500,000 and six years in state grant money on computers, but "changes did not register[16] on the school's test scores." That $500,000, used otherwise,[17] might have really helped those kids.

5   Bill Rukeyser, of the non-profit group Learning in the Real World, believes that the big move to spend scarce school dollars on technology is driven[18] not by knowledge, but by faith and fear. Parents are terrified their grown children won't qualify for good

---

[11] **doing so**   doing this; that is, buying computers
[12] **shop**   class to teach carpentry (short form of *workshop*)
[13] **akin to**   like; similar to
[14] **state-of-the-art**   the most recent; with the lastest technology

[15] **yield**   result in
[16] **register**   show
[17] **otherwise**   in another way
[18] **driven**   pushed; caused

jobs if left behind on the information superhighway.[19]

6   Parents ought to fear that their kids can't read. Or that their children will study in college courses what they once studied in high school. Schools have dumbed down[20] because faith-based trends replaced bodies of proven pedagogy.[21] Enough already.

7   The Clinton administration is peddling[22] a one-purchase fix to a years-long slide[23] in academics. Smarten up, folks. Want to give your kids a competitive edge[24] in the learning curve? Try an information medium[25] proven to work, even as it is losing currency.[26] (No modem, no mouse,[27] no Sound Blaster.[28]) It's called a book. Read one, repeat often.

---

[19] **information superhighway**   the Internet
[20] **dumbed down**   lowered the academic level (slang)
[21] **pedagogy**   teaching practices
[22] **peddling**   selling
[23] **slide**   decrease; decline
[24] **competitive edge**   advantage that will help them compete
[25] **medium**   form
[26] **losing currency**   becoming less accepted now; going out of date
[27] **mouse**   remote control with button to press; controls the computer's cursor
[28] **Sound Blaster**   a system that allows a computer to produce sound

Comprehension Check

A. First Reading

Fill in the blanks with an appropriate word or phrase for the part you read. Then ask a classmate the Focus for the First Reading questions for the part you did not read. Your classmate's answers should give you enough information to complete the sentences for that part.

PART 1

This article is about _____ (1) children who use computers at the Carnegie Mellon Children's School. Apparently, the children

_____ (2) using the computers. People who work with them think that the computer is a good _____ (3) to help with learning. They say that the children learn to use the machine _____ (4) .

PART 2

Debra Saunders believes that putting computers in every class may not be

the _____ way to spend education money, at least in
(5)

_____ schools. She mentions two main problems. For teachers,
(6)

the problem is that many of them are not _____ to use
(7)

computers in the classroom. Her concern about students is that many of them

do not _____ well, and that skill is more basic than using a computer.
(8)

B. Second Reading

Now read both parts of this selection. To have an educated opinion on a controversial issue, people need to think about both sides of the issue, both the pros and the cons.

PART 1

1 *Read Part 1 again. Mark the statements **T** (true) or **F** (false). Be prepared to show evidence in the selection that supports your answers.*

1. T F Andrew is an example of a child who enjoys using the computer.

2. T F Mr. Ouyang observed that children learn to use the machines quickly and they help each other learn.

3. T F We can expect that boys will learn to use computers faster than girls.

4. T F According to Shapiro and Poster, elementary school students will soon do all their learning by computer.

2 *People who think that computers are good educational tools often give the following reasons. These reasons are either specifically stated in the article (you can find exact words) or only implied or suggested (you can't find exact words). Mark those that are stated with an **S**, and those that are implied with an **I**. Be prepared to show evidence from the selection that supports your answers.*

___ 1. Children enjoy working with computers.

___ 2. Computer programs for small children present learning in an interesting way.

___ 3. Computer programs are good for teaching thinking skills.

___ 4. Computers lead children to cooperate with each other.

___ 5. Computers might bring the world to the classroom.

PART 2

Check all the statements that Debra Saunders would agree with.

___ **1.** We should not eliminate classes like music, art, and shop just to have computers.

___ **2.** Computers may not be the most important thing for schools to spend their money on, especially in early grades.

___ **3.** To have a competitive edge in the job market, people have to know how to read well.

___ **4.** Schools are requiring more of students now than ever before.

___ **5.** Computers and TV can have a similar effect on the mind.

___ **6.** It's not a good idea to invest money in equipment that teachers don't know how to use.

___ **7.** We need evidence that computers are better than other methods in helping children learn.

___ **8.** Computers are the best learning tool we have now.

 Vocabulary

 A. Vocabulary Building

Find a word or expression in the selection that means the same as the words or expressions below.

PART 1: HIGH-TECH TEACHING TOOL

1. excitement (¶ 1) _____

2. acceptance of the answer; OK (¶ 4) _____

3. similar to most others (¶ 6) _____

4. occurring; going on (2 correct answers) (¶ 6) _____

5. all the time (¶ 8) _____

6. the same opportunities to use (¶ 8) _____

7. mention (¶ 9) _____

8. way; form (¶ 10) _____

9. something to help you work or learn (¶ 11) _____

10. city (adjective) (¶ 12) _____

PART 2: COMPUTERS IN EVERY CLASS? WHY?

11. might (¶ 2) _____

12. things that help you work or learn (¶ 2) _____

13. the right thing (¶ 3) _____

14. making children want to work and learn (¶ 3)
    _____

15. limited; not a lot of (¶ 5)
    _____

16. extremely afraid or scared (¶ 5)
    _____

17. have the necessary training and preparation for (¶ 5)
    _____

18. should (¶ 6)
    _____

19. get smart (¶ 7)
    _____

20. people (¶ 7)
    _____

B. Word Analysis

Find a compound word in the selection that correctly completes the following sentences.

PART 1: HIGH-TECH TEACHING TOOL

1. A child who hasn't started school yet is a _____. (¶ 2)

2. If something is on the side near your right hand, it is on the _____ side. (¶ 3)

3. A center that takes care of children during the day is a _____ center. (¶ 5)

4. When a human being guides an activity, it is a _____ activity. (¶ 10)

5. A parent who works as a volunteer helper is a _____. (¶ 10)

6. Interaction that involves teachers with students is _____ interaction. (¶ 10)

7. A center that takes care of children can be called a _____ center. (¶ 11)

PART 2: COMPUTERS IN EVERY CLASS? WHY?

8. Toys which numb the mind are _____ toys. (¶ 3)

9. Things which kill a person's ability to pay attention for a span (period) of time are _____ killers. (¶ 3)

10. An organization which does not make a profit is a _____ organization. (¶ 5)

11. One purchase that people hope will fix all problems is a _____ fix. (¶ 7)

12. A slide or decline in academics that lasts for years is a _____ slide. (¶ 7)

C. Vocabulary Review

Complete the following statements about the reading selections with the correct word or expression from the list below. Use each word or expression only once.

access	**motivating**	**qualify**	**state-of-the-art**
enthusiasm	**points out**	**scarce**	**tool**

1. In education, computers can be a useful _____, but they are not a solution to all problems.

2. Children clearly enjoy using computers; their _____ is obvious.

3. They learn fast and soon help each other, and if boys and girls have equal _____ to computers, they both learn to use the machine well.

4. Some people think school districts should not spend _____ money on computers.

5. They realize that computers can be _____ for students, but they wonder if schools should spend money on _____ equipment and sacrifice things like art, shop, and music.

6. Debra Saunders _____ that parents should worry about whether or not their kids can read well. It may be true that people have to know how to use computers to _____ for jobs in today's market, but they also have to know how to read and think.

Sharing Your Thoughts

1. Talk about your own experiences, if any, with computers as a tool for learning. List positive ways computers can be used, and mention ways they can be misused.

2. Computers cost a lot of money. How likely do you think it is that only children whose families are educated and wealthy will get access to computers at home and at school? What could happen if the children of the wealthy get much greater access to computers than poorer children? In what places, other than school, could poorer children and young people get access to computers?

3. Refer to the last paragraph of Part 1. Do you think that electronic access to the world of information could replace the farms and open spaces city children don't have? Explain.

4. In Part 2, paragraph 4, Saunders says that the $500,000 that one elementary school spent on computers might have been spent in better ways. What better ways do you think she might have been thinking of?

5. Work in two groups. One side will argue *for* the following proposition. The other side will argue *against* it. Each group should meet to prepare its arguments. As a start, consider ideas from these articles and Unit Three Selection Three.

> **PROPOSITION:** The $100,000 an elementary school has to spend on improving the learning opportunities of its children should be spent on computers.

> **FACTS YOU NEED TO KNOW:** To do this, the music program must be eliminated and the physical education teacher must be reduced to half-time.

 Text Analysis

A. Newspaper Writing

News articles tend to have more and smaller paragraphs than you find in books. Compare the length of the paragraphs in "High-tech Teaching Tool" with the paragraphs in Selections One and Two of this unit. Reread "High-tech Teaching Tool." Which of the first eight paragraphs go together and could be combined? (The quotes in ¶ 10–12 relate to the idea in ¶ 9, but you should not combine 9–12 because it is customary to put quotes in separate paragraphs.)

B. Grammar-Meaning Connection: Using *may*, *might*, and *will*

Reread "Computers in Every Class? Why?" and underline the examples of the helping verbs *may*, *might* and *will* in the article. Which word or words are used when the writer or speaker feels sure of what he or she is saying? Which word or words sound less sure?

Writing Task

1. If you have access to a computer, how do you use it? Write about your typical uses. Organize your comments in some way, for example: most important to least important, most frequent to least frequent, the use you like the most to the one you like the least.

2. Write a response to Debra Saunders's editorial comment in the form of a letter to the editor. You can agree with her position completely, you may find some points that you agree with and some that you don't, or you may disagree with her position completely. When you begin a letter to the editor, you should refer to the article that inspired you to write. Depending on your position, you might want to begin in one of the following ways:

a. I completely agree/disagree with Debra Saunders's position in her editorial, "Computers in Every Class? Why?"

b. Even though I agree that reading is important, I cannot agree with all of Debra Saunders's ideas about computers in education ("Computers in Every Class? Why?").

Selection Four

Before Reading

Isaac Asimov (1920–1992) migrated to the United States from Russia (the former Soviet Union) in 1923. He had a doctorate in physics and is best known for two kinds of writing: science fiction stories and books that explain science to the general public.

Discussion

In Selection Three you read about and discussed the pros and cons of using computers in education. What would education be like if computers were our only educational tool?

Previewing

Read the title and the first paragraph of the story. Answer these questions.

1. When does the story take place?

2. Who are the characters?

3. What, if anything, can you predict from the title?

Focus for the First Reading

Read these questions before you read the selection. You should be able to answer them after you finish the first reading.

1. Where do Tommy and Margie go to school, and who is their teacher?

2. What is their attitude toward their school and teacher?

The Fun They Had

by Isaac Asimov

1   Margie even wrote about it that night in her diary. On the page headed May 17, 2157, she wrote, "Today Tommy found a real book!"

2   It was a very old book. Margie's grandfather once said that when he was a little boy *his* grandfather told him that there was a time when all stories were printed on paper.

3   They turned the pages, which were yellow and crinkly, and it was awfully funny to read words that stood still instead of moving the way they were supposed to—on a screen, you know. And then, when they turned back to the page before, it had the same words on it that it had had when they read it the first time.

4   "Gee,"[1] said Tommy, "what a waste. When you're through with the book, you just throw it away, I guess. Our television

[1] **Gee** Wow!

screen must have had a million books on it and it's good for plenty more. I wouldn't throw *it* away."

5   "Same with mine," said Margie. She was eleven and hadn't seen as many telebooks as Tommy had. He was thirteen.

6   She said, "Where did you find it?"

7   "In my house." He pointed without looking, because he was busy reading. "In the attic."[2]

8   "What's it about?"

9   "School."

10   Margie was scornful.[3] "School? What's there to write about school? I hate school."

11   Margie always hated school, but now she hated it more than ever.[4] The mechanical teacher had been giving her test after test in geography and she had been doing worse and worse until her mother had shaken her head sorrowfully and sent for the County Inspector.

12   He was a round little man with a red face and a whole box of tools with dials and wires. He smiled at Margie and gave her an apple, then took the teacher apart. Margie had hoped he wouldn't know how to put it together again, but he knew how all right, and, after an hour or so, there it was again, large and black and ugly, with a big screen on which all the lessons were shown and the questions were asked. That wasn't so bad. The part Margie hated most was the slot where she had to put homework and test papers. She always had to write them out in a punch code[5] they made her learn when she was six years old, and the mechanical teacher calculated the mark in no time.

13   The Inspector had smiled after he was finished and patted Margie's head. He said to her mother, "It's not the little girl's fault, Mrs. Jones. I think the geography sector[6] was geared a little too quick.[7] Those things happen sometimes. I've slowed it up to an average ten-year level. Actually, the over-all pattern of her progress is quite satisfactory." And he patted Margie's head again.

14   Margie was disappointed. She had been hoping they would take the teacher away altogether. They had once taken Tommy's teacher away for nearly a month because the history sector had blanked out completely.

15   So she said to Tommy, "Why would anyone write about school?"

16   Tommy looked at her with very superior eyes. "Because it's not our kind of school, stupid. This is the old kind of school that they had hundreds and hundreds of years ago." He added loftily, pronouncing the word carefully, "*Centuries* ago."

17   Margie was hurt. "Well, I don't know what kind of school they had all that time ago." She read the book over his shoulder for a while, then said, "Anyway, they had a teacher."

18   "Sure they had a teacher, but it wasn't a *regular* teacher. It was a man."

[2] **attic**   space under the roof of a house usually used to store things

[3] **scornful**   critical; showing disrespect

[4] **ever**   at any time

[5] **punch code**   system for indicating answers by punching holes in the paper; not normal writing

[6] **sector**   section of the computer's memory

[7] **geared a little too quick**   set to go a little too fast

19   "A man? How could a man be a teacher?"

20   "Well, he just told the boys and girls things and gave them homework and asked them questions."

21   "A man isn't smart enough."

22   "Sure he is. My father knows as much as my teacher."

23   "He can't. A man can't know as much as a teacher."

24   "He knows almost as much, I betcha."[8]

[8] **I betcha**   I bet you; I'm sure.

25   Margie wasn't prepared to dispute that. She said, "I wouldn't want a strange man in my house to teach me."

26   Tommy screamed with laughter. "You don't know much, Margie. The teachers didn't live in the house. They had a special building and all the kids went there."

27   "And all the kids learned the same thing?"

28   "Sure, if they were the same age."

29   "But my mother says a teacher has to be adjusted to fit the mind of each boy and girl it teaches and that each kid has to be taught differently."

30   "Just the same they didn't do it that way then. If you don't like it, you don't have to read the book."

31   "I didn't say I didn't like it," Margie said quickly. She wanted to read about those funny schools.

32   They weren't even half-finished when Margie's mother called, "Margie! School!"

33   Margie looked up. "Not yet, Mamma."

34   "Now!" said Mrs. Jones. "And it's probably time for Tommy, too."

35   Margie said to Tommy, "Can I read the book some more with you after school?"

36   "Maybe," he said nonchalantly. He walked away whistling, the dusty old book tucked beneath his arm.

37   Margie went into the schoolroom. It was right next to her bedroom, and the mechanical teacher was on and waiting for her. It was always on at the same time every day except Saturday and Sunday, because her mother said little girls learned better if they learned at regular hours.

38   The screen was lit up, and it said: "Today's arithmetic lesson is on the addition of proper fractions. Please insert yesterday's homework in the proper slot."

39   Margie did so with a sigh. She was thinking about the old schools they had when her grandfather's grandfather was a little boy. All the kids from the whole neighborhood came, laughing and shouting in the schoolyard, sitting together in the schoolroom, going home together at the end of the day. They learned the same things, so they could help one another on the homework and talk about it.

40   And the teachers were people. . . .

41   The mechanical teacher was flashing on the screen: "When we add the fractions ½ and ¼. . . ."

42   Margie was thinking about how the kids must have loved it in the old days. She was thinking about the fun they had.

Comprehension Check

A. First Reading

Fill in the blanks with an appropriate word or phrase.

Margie and Tommy both go to school at _____. Each one
(1)
has a _____ as a teacher. They read all their lessons on a
(2)
computer screen. Until recently, they had never seen a _____.
(3)
Margie, in particular, _____ school and her teacher. She
(4)
thinks that kids in twentieth-century schools had more _____
(5)
than she has, studying at home.

B. Second Reading

1. List differences between schools and teachers of today and schools and
   teachers as Asimov imagined they would be in 2157. The first line of the
   chart has been done as an example.

Today's Schools	Schools in 2157
humans as teachers	computers as teachers

2. List differences between printed books and telebooks.

3. How does the school system work in 2157? Who determines the curriculum?
   Who makes students work? When do they work?

4. Why does Margie hate her school in 2157?

5. Why does Margie think that the schools we have today were better?

Vocabulary

A. Vocabulary Building

Find a word or expression in the selection that means the same as the words or expressions below.

1. strange, different (¶ 3, 31)   _____

2. use of something that isn't efficient (¶ 4)   _____

3. finished (¶ 4)   _____

4. grade in school (¶ 12)   _____

5. insulted (¶ 17)   _____

6. changed in small ways (¶ 29)   _____

7. put in (¶ 38)   _____

8. correct opening (¶ 38)   _____

B. Multi-word Expressions

Look at the underlined multi-word expressions in the sentences on the left. Find them in the selection. Then match them with the correct meaning on the right.

____ **1.** . . . it was awfully funny to read words that <u>stood still</u> . . . (¶ 3)

a. quickly; fast

____ **2.** When you're through with the book, you just <u>throw</u> it <u>away</u>, I guess (¶ 4)

b. separated into pieces; disassembled

____ **3.** . . . her mother . . . <u>sent for</u> the County Inspector. (¶ 11)

c. didn't move

____ **4.** He . . . <u>took</u> the teacher <u>apart</u>. (¶ 12)

d. each other

____ **5.** Margie had hoped he wouldn't know how to <u>put</u> it <u>together</u> again . . . (¶ 12)

e. Margie didn't cause the problem.

____ **6.** . . . the mechanical teacher calculated the mark <u>in no time</u>. (¶ 12)

f. remove; take out of the house

____ **7.** <u>It's not the little girl's fault</u>, Mrs. Jones. (¶ 13)

g. reassemble; join the different parts

____ **8.** She (Margie) had been hoping they would <u>take</u> the teacher <u>away</u> altogether. (¶ 14)

h. asked or ordered someone to come

____ **9.** . . . they could help <u>one another</u> on the homework and talk about it. (¶ 39)

i. put in the garbage

C. Vocabulary Review

Complete the following statements about the reading selection with the correct word or expression from the list below. Use each word or expression only once.

adjusted	**one another**	**take it away**	**through**
funny	**stood still**	**threw away**	

1. Tommy and Margie were accustomed to reading a screen and had never seen a book with pages that _____ until Tommy found one in the attic of his house.

2. Tommy wonders where you would keep millions of old-fashioned books. He supposes that people _____ their books when they were _____ reading them.

3. The book Tommy found was about the schools children went to years earlier. Margie thought it was _____ that there were human teachers in those schools.

4. She and Tommy were accustomed to their computers, which were _____ to fit their abilities.

5. But Margie hated her teacher-computer and wished that the County Inspector would _____.

6. She kept thinking of the twentieth-century schools where children worked together, helped _____, and had a lot of fun.

Sharing Your Thoughts

1. Refer to the list you made for Comprehension Check, Second Reading, exercise 1, page 224. Talk about the pros and cons of today's schools and the schools Asimov imagined for 2157. Think about the pros and cons from the point of view of teachers, children, parents, administrators, the government. Think about cost, facilities, time, supervision.

2. What do you think Robert Fulghum (Unit Three, Selection Four) would think of schools in 2157?

3. If people are educated like Margie and Tommy and telecommute to work after their education is completed, what kind of people might they grow up to be? Which of their seven intelligences (Unit Three, Selection One) will be best developed and which will be least developed?

4. The number of people in a typical college class who read for pleasure and entertainment (who prefer books to movies, for example) is often quite low. What

are some reasons for this? Do you think it is likely that people will enjoy reading books on the screen more than they enjoy reading a book that they can hold?

5. Asimov predicted that books in their old form would disappear. Do you think this is going to happen? Explain.

6. Some children have always been unable to attend regular schools on a regular basis. Who are some of these children? Could long-distance education help them get an education? Explain.

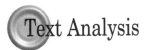Text Analysis

Science Fiction Writing

Science fiction writing extends the present into the future. Science fiction writers start with scientific reality at the time they are writing. Then they imagine how the present reality will develop in the future. Very often they have a social comment to make about the present or the future.

1. Computers were very different when Asimov wrote this story. (See the picture of the old computer on page 195.) Read the information about early computers in the second column of the chart below. Using information from the story, fill in as much of the third column as you can. Use other information in this unit and your own knowledge of computers to fill in the fourth column.

	Early computers (1950–1960s)	Computers as Asimov saw them in 2157	Computers as we know them today
1. size and speed	Computers were enormous and relatively slow.		
2. data entry	Data was entered on cards that had holes punched in them; there were different holes for every symbol.		
3. data display	Data appeared only on paper printouts; there were no monitors.		
4. location	Computers were located in universities and research institutes, not in homes or offices.		
5. availability (how common)	Fewer people used computers, and almost no one saw them.		
6. networks	First networks connected large computers, not PCs.		

2. Compare columns three and four. How much of what we know about computers today did Asimov predict correctly? What didn't he imagine?

3. As mentioned above, science fiction often makes a social comment about the present or the future. What, if any, social comment could Asimov be making in this story?

Writing Task

1. Choose **a** or **b**.

   a. Imagine you are Margie. Write a letter to the County Inspector. Tell him what you think about your school and teacher now that you have read about twentieth-century schools. Mention some changes you would like him to make.

   b. As a person who knows twentieth-century schools, write a letter to Margie telling her some of the pros and cons of the type of school you know.

2. First talk with your classmates about what the world would be like if everyone telecommuted to work and school. How would life be different? Then write about your vision of this future. The number of differences you focus on and the amount of detail you give will determine the number of paragraphs you write.

Selection Five

Before Reading

"The Internet Song" was written by Garrison Keillor and was first sung on his popular Minnesota Public Radio show, "The Prairie Home Companion," in 1996. Keillor is known for his humorous view of life.

Discussion
Talk with your classmates about how personal relationships can develop over the Internet.
What are the pros and cons of meeting people in cyberspace?

Focus for the First Reading
Read these questions before you read the song lyrics. You should be able to answer them after you finish the first reading.

1. Is the singer of the song a beginner with computers or an expert?
2. Is the song serious or humorous?

The Internet Song
by Garrison Keillor

1   Don't know much about the Internet
    Don't know which software[1] to get
    Don't know modems and I don't know ports[2]
    I go online[3] and the screen aborts.[4]

    CHORUS:
    But I do know that I love you
    And I know that if you love me too
    What a wonderful world it would be.

2   I tried to send a message to your house
    Nothing happened when I clicked[5] the mouse[6]
    All I got was just an hourglass[7]
    I press a switch and all my files crashed.[8]

[1] **software**   programs with instructions that tell the computer what to do
[2] **ports**   places to plug other equipment into the computer
[3] **online**   on the Internet
[4] **aborts**   quits (picture disappears)

[5] **clicked**   pressed the button
[6] **mouse**   remote control device for the computer
[7] **hourglass**   shows the computer is working; you have to wait
[8] **crashed**   got lost; failed; closed down

3 Don't know how to access you, darling.
   I'd like to try tonight.
   I'll move my cursor[9] a little closer,
   And give your neck a little gigabyte.[10]

4 Don't know much about the World Wide Web[11]
   The manuals[12] are way beyond my depth
   Don't know much about the protocol[13]
   I click on Help and it's no help at all.

5 So if you and me should interface,[14]
   Let's not do it out in cyberspace.
   Let us actuate[15] a real embrace
   And what a wonderful world it will be.

   (Repeat chorus after verses 2 and 4.)

[9] **cursor**   line on the screen that shows where the next letter or symbol will go
[10] **gigabyte**   bite (literally, a billion sections of computer memory)
[11] **World Wide Web**   the part of the Internet with graphic images
[12] **manuals**   instruction books
[13] **protocol**   instructions for how computers communicate with each other

[14] **interface**   get together; computer word for "communicate between different parts of the system"
[15] **actuate**   put into action

Comprehension Check

A. First Reading

Circle the word that correctly completes the sentence.

1. The singer of this song (knows / doesn't know) computer jargon or vocabulary.

2. The singer is a (beginner / expert) with computers.

3. This is a (serious / humorous) love song.

B. Second Reading

Read the song lyrics again. Then answer the questions. Be prepared to find evidence in the song that supports your answers.

1. What evidence in the song shows that the singer is not very good with computers?

2. How has he tried to contact the person he is interested in? Was he successful?

3. Is he certain of her love?

4. Where does he want to meet her?

Sharing Your Thoughts

1. How do you think these two people met?

2. What might be some of the benefits of a relationship with someone you cannot meet in person right away? What might be some of the difficulties or dangers of this type of relationship?

3. How do you think e-mail and telecommunications will improve the social lives of people? Consider, for example, people in hospitals and older people. What, if any, negative effects might there be?

Writing Task

1. Imagine you have met a new friend on the Internet. You have found out that you live within a day's drive of each other. This person's last e-mail to you suggested that you get together for lunch half-way between your two homes. Write your e-mail response.

2. Even though this song is humorous, Internet communications can be very beneficial for some people, as you discussed in Sharing Your Thoughts, exercise 3. Choose a person you know or a group of people. Write about how e-mail and telecommunications can improve their lives. The number of benefits you focus on and the amount of detail you give will determine the number of paragraphs you write.

A Final Look

Discussion

1. Work with a classmate, in a small group, or as a whole class. Drawing on all five selections in this unit, discuss the focus questions and quote on page 195.

2. Read the following quote.

   "In today's high-tech world of e-mail and microchips, it is easy to forget the importance of human connections in our daily activities. Technology has brought many welcome conveniences to our lives. But it has the potential to create feelings of distance, detachment and isolation among us."

   Hillary Rodham Clinton, *Time*, February 3, 1998

   What is your reaction to Hillary Clinton's statement?

3. Read the following quote.

   "In immersing ourselves in the electronic net, we are ignoring our real, dying communities."

   Stephen Doheny-Farina, *The Wired Neighborhood*

   Do you think Doheny-Farina is right? Are our real communities dying? If he is right, what is taking our attention away from our local communities: people spending too much time on the Net; media focus on world rather than local events; or something else?

   In this unit you have read about ways that computers are changing our lifestyles. What other high-tech inventions are you familiar with, and how are they changing our lives?

Unit Project

Choose Project 1 or Project 2 depending on whether you have access to the Internet.

PROJECT 1

Step 1 *Discuss with your classmates the pros and cons of doing each of the following activities on the Internet rather than in the physical world: shopping, keeping in touch with friends, and reading a newspaper. You may not have experience using the Net, but you can imagine, for example, the difference between buying something in a store versus choosing something you can only see on a computer screen.*

Step 2 *Choose one of the activities you discussed in Step 1. Write about the pros and cons of doing this in the virtual or physical world. Which would you prefer?*

Project 2

Step 1 *If you have access to the Internet, explore an Internet site in order to do one of the following tasks.*

a. *Plan an airline or train trip to a city of your choice. Check the homepages of major airlines. Find one that goes to the city you want to visit, check the schedule, and choose the best flights for you.*

Suggested Internet sites:
FOR AIR TRAVEL: http://www.ual.com
http://www.americanair.com
http://www.delta-air.com
FOR TRAIN TRAVEL: http://www.amtrak.com

b. *Find out if one of the libraries below has a book you want to read.*

http://www.lib.mtu.edu
http://www.brown.edu/Faculties/University__Library/

c. *Find out how you can practice English at the Lingua Center at the University of Illinois in Urbana-Champaign. See Internet site:*

http://www.deil.lang.uiuc.edu

d. *Find information about the Center for Missing and Abused Children, which uses the Internet to help locate missing children. See Internet site:*

http://www.missingkids.org

e. *Find out what you can do at the White House web site at:*

http://www.whitehouse.gov

f. *Find out about one of these world organizations.*

World Conservation Union   http://www.iucn.org
World Health Organization   http://www.who.ch
UNICEF   http://www.unicef.org

Step 2 *Write about your experience on the Internet. Choose one of the following ideas:*

a. Write step-by-step instructions for the process you followed to get to the site you explored.
b. Write about some interesting things you learned at a site you visited.
c. Write about your reaction to the whole experience of using the Internet. Did you find it easy? exciting? frustrating? confusing? Give details of your experience.

Credits

TEXT CREDITS

UNIT 1

1. "My Early Memories"—from *My American Journey,* by Colin Powell with Joseph E. Persico. Copyright © 1995 by Colin L. Powell. Reprinted by permission of Random House, Inc.

2. "Peer Influences on Achievement"—Reprinted with the permission of Simon & Schuster from *Beyond the Classroom* by Laurence Steinberg. Copyright © 1996 by Laurence Steinberg.

3. "It's OK to be Different: Stop Making Fun of My Disability"—From *Newsweek,* 10/24/94, "It's OK to Be Different"/My Turn." All rights reserved. Reprinted by permission.

4. "Two Kinds"—Reprinted by permission of G. P. Putnam's Sons, a division of The Putnam Publishing Group from *The Joy Luck Club,* by Amy Tan. Copyright © 1989 by Amy Tan.

5. "To a Daughter Leaving Home," from *The Imperfect Paradise,* by Linda Pastan. Copyright © 1988 by Linda Pastan. Reprinted by permission of W.W. Norton & Company, Inc.

UNIT 2

1. "Untitled"—"What Do You Care What Other People Think?" from *What Do You Care What Other People Think: Further Adventures of a Curious Character,* by Richard P. Feynman as told to Ralph Leighton. Copyright © 1998 by Gweneth Feynman and Ralph Leighton. Reprinted by permission of W. W. Norton & Company, Inc.

2. Adapted from "Students Think Love Conquers All." Reprinted with permission from USA Today magazine. December 1993. © 1993 by the Society for the Advancement of Education.

3. "Getting Married Young"—Adapted from "They Were Young and in Love," by Cheryl Lavin. © Copyrighted Chicago Tribune Company. All rights reserved. Used with Permission.

4. "Finding a Wife" from *Small Faces,* by Gary Soto. Text copyright © 1986 by Gary Soto. Used with permission of Author and BookStop Literary Agency. All rights reserved.

5. "Sweetheart" by Phil Hey. © 1987 by Simon & Schuster. Reprinted by permission of the author.

UNIT 3

1. "Multiple Intelligences"—Adapted from *Multiple Intelligences in the Classroom,* by Thomas Armstong. Alexandria, VA: Association for Supervision and Curriculum Development. Copyright © 1994 ASCD. Reprinted by permission. All rights reserved.

2. "Styles of Thinking and Learning," by Robert Sternberg. Adapted from *Language Testing,* November 1995. Reprinted by permission of the author.

3. "Windows of Opportunity: What Students Should Study and When"—from "Why Do Schools Flunk Biology," by LynNell Hancock. From Newsweek, Feb.19, 1996, Newsweek, Inc. All rights reserved. Reprinted by permission.

4. "Untitled"—from *Uh-Oh,* by Robert Fulghum. Copyright © 1991 by Robert Fulghum. Reprinted by permission of Villard Books, a division of Random House.

5. "Elizabeth McKenzie" from *Class Dismissed II.* Text copyright 1986 by Mel Glenn. Reprinted by permission of Clarion Books/ Houghton Mifflin Co. All rights reserved.

UNIT 4

1. "Millions of Workers on the Move." Adapted from World of Work, a publication of the International Labour Organization in Geneva, Switzerland.

2. "Smile," from *New Americans: An Oral History,* by Al Santoli. Copyright © 1988 by Al Santoli. Used by permission of Viking Penguin, a division of Penguin Books, USA Inc.

3. "Uptown," from *New Americans: An Oral History,* by Al Santoli. Copyright © 1988 by Al Santoli.Used by permission of Viking Penguin, a division of Penguin Books, USA Inc.

4. "The Peasant," by William Saroyen. Reprinted with the permission of the trustees of Leland Stanford University.

5. "Elena," by Pat Mora is reprinted with permission from the publisher of *Chants* (Houston: Arte Publico Press University of Houston, 1985).

UNIT 5

1. "The Mind-Body Connection." Written by Blau & Gonzalez.

2. "The Process of Meditation"—J. Borysenko, *Minding the Body, Mending the Mind,* pp. 42–46, 71. © 1987 by Joan Borysenko, Ph.D. Reprinted by permission of Addison Wesley Longman.

3. "More Than Medicine"—from *Head First: The Biology of Hope,* by Norman Cousins. Copyright © 1989 by Norman Cousins. Used by permission of Dutton Signet, a division of Penguin Books, USA Inc.

4. "The Last Leaf," by O. Henry (adapted). Public domain.

5. "Manuel Garcia" © 1996 by David Roth/Maythelight Music (ASCAP). Reprinted with permission from the composer.

UNIT 6

1. "Telecommuting"—adapted from Stephen Doheny-Farina, *The Wired Neighborhood,* 1996, Yale University Press. Reprinted with permission from the publisher. All rights reserved.

2. "A View of the Future"—excerpt as submitted and titled from *What Will Be: How the New World of Information Will Change Our Lives,* by Michael Dertouzos. Copyright © 1997 by Michael Dertouzos. Reprinted by permission of HarperCollins Publishers, Inc.

3. From "High-tech Teaching Tool Moves Children Beyond Keyboard Literacy," by Laurent Belsie. Extracted from *The Christian Science Monitor.* © 1991 The Christian Science Publishing Society. All rights reserved.

4. "The Fun They Had," from *Earth Is Room Enough,* by Isaac Asimov. Copyright © 1957 by Isaac Asimov. Used by permission of Doubleday, a division of Bantam Doubleday Dell Publishing Group, Inc.

5. "The Internet Song," by Garrison Keillor. Reprinted by permission of Garrison Keillor. Copyright © 1997 by Garrison Keillor.

WORKS CITED

UNIT 1

Holladay, Ryan. (1994). *What Preteens Want Their Parents to Know*. New York: McCracken Press.

Peck, M. Scott. (1993). *Further Along the Road Not Traveled*. New York: Simon & Schuster.

UNIT 2

Houck, Catherine. (1996, March). "What Makes a Marriage Last." *Reader's Digest*, p. 72.

Sheehy, Gail. (1995). *New Passages*. New York: Random House, p. 52.

UNIT 3

Brim, Gilbert. (1993). *Ambition: How We Manage Success and Failure throughout Our Lives*. New York: Basic Books.

Floyd, Doug. (1995, July). Quotable Quotes. *Reader's Digest*, p. 161.

UNIT 4

Rao, Nagesh. (1997). "I am a door," in *The Edge: The Student E-Journal of Intercultural Relation*. TESOL Matters, December 1995–January 1996. Reprinted by permission of Nagesh Rao.

UNIT 5

Hastings, A., Fadiman, J., and Gordon, J. (Eds). (1980). *The Complete Guide to Holistic Medicine: Health for the Whole Person*. Boulder, CO: Westview Press.

Simonton, O. C., Mathews-Simonton, S., and Creighton, J. L. (1978). *Getting Well Again*. New York: Bantam Books.

UNIT 6

Clinton, Hillary Rodham. (1997, February 3). "Viewpoint: Comfort and Joy." p. 63.

Dertouzos, Michael. (1997). *What Will Be: How the New World of Information Will Change Our Lives*. New York: HarperCollins.

Doheny-Farina, Stephen. (1996). *The Wired Neighborhood*. New Haven: Yale University Press.

Answer Key

This answer key includes answers to objective exercises only. Answers to other exercises may vary.

STUDENT'S INTRODUCTION

COMPREHENSION CHECK

$\underline{5}$ a.
$\underline{3}$ b.
$\underline{1}$ c.
$\underline{2}$ d.
$\underline{4}$ e.

VOCABULARY

Vocabulary Review
1. gradual
2. handle
3. similar
4. expression
5. non-essential
6. look for
7. context
8. guess

TEXT ANALYSIS

in the order in which something is done

UNIT 1

Selection 1

COMPREHENSION CHECK

A. First Reading
1. a
2. c
3. b
4. a

B. Second Reading
1. c
2. e
3. a
4. b
5. d

VOCABULARY

A. Vocabulary Building
¶1
1. c
2. e

3. g
4. f
5. a
6. d
7. b

¶3
8. l
9. j
10. h
11. m
12. i
13. k

¶4
14. o
15. q
16. n
17. p

B. Identifying Non-essential Vocabulary
1. no
2. bad
3. Education was the way up; the way to progress for West Indians.
4. She was a good student.
5. no
6. no

C. Vocabulary Review
1. shock; scolded; cared about
2. athlete
3. an empty lot; disappoint
4. gave up
5. contented

Selection 2

COMPREHENSION CHECK

A. First Reading
1. b
2. c

B. Second Reading
1. T
2. F
3. T
4. T
5. T
6. F

VOCABULARY

A. Vocabulary Building
1. f
2. d
3. g
4. b
5. c
6. h
7. e
8. a

B. Identifying Essential and Non-essential Vocabulary
2. a. E
   b. NE
3. a. E
   b. NE
4. a. NE
   b. E
5. a. E
   b. NE

C. Vocabulary Review
1. whether; behavior
2. findings; influential
3. concerned about; do better
4. peers

TEXT ANALYSIS

A. Topic and Main Idea
1. b
2. c

B. Finding the Writer's Definition
2. used more drugs and alcohol and who had more conduct problems
3. whether students attend class, how much time they spend on homework, how hard they try in school, and the grades they bring home

Selection 3

COMPREHENSION CHECK

A. First Reading
1. F
2. T

B. Second Reading

1

1. F
2. T
3. F
4. T
5. T
6. F

2

1. a, b, c, d
2. b, c, d
3. a, b
4. a, c, d

VOCABULARY

A. Vocabulary Building
1. c
2. b
3. a
4. a
5. b
6. c
7. a

B. Multi-word Expressions

1

1. b
2. a
3. c
4. b
5. b

2

1. putting up with (b)
2. sticking up for (c)
3. found out (a)

C. Vocabulary Review
1. couldn't
2. mean; made fun of
3. ignore; weird
4. stay behind; keep up
5. blamed
6. realized; awkward

TEXT ANALYSIS

A. Topics and Main Ideas in Personal Essays
1. c
2. b

B. Paragraph Topics
¶2 c
¶3 a
¶4 e
¶5–6 b
¶7 d

Selection 4

COMPREHENSION CHECK

A. First Reading
suggested answers
1. prodigy
2. tests
3. hate the tests (angry, feel bad)
4. change

B. Second Reading
1. T
2. T
3. T
4. F
5. F
6. T

VOCABULARY

A. Vocabulary Building
1. e
2. b
3. a
4. f
5. d
6. c

B. Vocabulary Review
1. expectations
2. pictured
3. perfect
4. remarkable
5. disappointed
6. hated
7. willful

Selection 5

COMPREHENSION CHECK

A. First Reading
1. eight years old
2. The parent was teaching the daughter to ride a bicycle.

UNIT 2

Selection 1

COMPREHENSION CHECK

A. First Reading
1. F
2. T
3. T

B. Second Reading
1. F
2. F
3. T
4. T
5. T

VOCABULARY

A. Vocabulary Building
1. a, b, d
2. a, b, c
3. a, c, d
4. a, b, d
5. b, c, d
6. a, c, d
7. b, c, d
8. a, c, d

B. Vocabulary Building
3. b
   words: "go to Barbara's house"
   situation: We know they are going to the movies together, so he must be going to get her.

4. a
   words: "for weeks"
   situation: We know he gave up piano lessons.
5. a
   words: "nice, pretty"
   situation: He's following the rules his mother gave him, so he wouldn't say something mean. He's referring to something specific (her gloves), so the meaning is probably more specific than if he were just making conversation.

C. Vocabulary Review
1. guys; embarrassing
2. advice; supposed to
3. called for
4. cute; sensitive

TEXT ANALYSIS

Using Present Tense in Narratives
suggested answers
   a. He *runs out* onto the rocks.
   b. and *finds* her
   c. He *pushes* her back.

Selection 2

COMPREHENSION CHECK

A. First Reading
1. F
2. T

B. Second Reading
1. Schwebel and Sullivan
2. Ohio State University
3. 238
4. eighteen to thirty-four years old, single
5. a. their beliefs about dysfunctional relationships
   b. 1. casual dating
      2. engagement
      3. after five years of marriage
      4. after fifteen years of marriage
   c. the average American's relationship
6. a
7. b
8. c
9. b

VOCABULARY

A. Vocabulary Building
1. a
2. b
3. b
4. a
5. a
6. b
7. a
8. a
9. b
10. b

B. Word Analysis
1. believe; optimistic
2. expect

3. marriage; success
4. disappointed; successful
5. unrealistic; disappointment

C. Vocabulary Review
1. optimistic
2. believe; honeymoon
3. average
4. disappointment
5. realize; tough; succeed

TEXT ANALYSIS

Making Connections
2. these kinds of expectations
3. the 238 students
4. questionnaire; the second questionnaire
5. the relationships
6. the students' beliefs that their relationships would be much better in the future than those of other couples
7. to realize that marriage can be tough

Selection 3

COMPREHENSION CHECK

A. First Reading
People who were happy that they married young: Charles, Alicia, Robert
People who regretted that they married young: Carol, Lisa, Sarah

B. Second Reading
1. F
2. F
3. T
4. F
5. F
6. T
7. F

suggested answers

| Advantages: | more time together (Charles); safety in monogamy (Robert) |
| Disadvantages: | bad marriage is hard to get out of (Lisa); lose time for yourself (Sarah) |

VOCABULARY

A. Vocabulary Building
1. a
2. b
3. b
4. b
5. a
6. a
7. b
8. a
9. a
10. b
11. a

B. Using a Dictionary
1. V, #2
2. V, #3
3. #1
4. V, #1

C. Vocabulary Review
1. turn out; commitment
2. immature; rush
3. wonderful; support
4. satisfied; better off

TEXT ANALYSIS

Evaluating Inferences
suggested answers for evidence
2. R
   Seven years later she wants to go to college, but he is satisfied.
3. R
   She had a life plan and did not think she would get married young, but her plans "went out the window" and she does not regret it.
4. U
   They argue over bills; divorce is too expensive for them.
5. U
   He says that his single co-workers do not have positive things to say about the people they meet there ("slimy guys" and "psycho women").

Selection 4

COMPREHENSION CHECK

A. First Reading
1. F
2. T

VOCABULARY

A. Vocabulary Building
1. c
2. e
3. f
4. b
5. d
6. g
7. i
8. a
9. j
10. h

B. Identifying Non-essential Vocabulary
1. a dime and five pennies; in the ashtray
2. sunflower seeds; a plate
3. a chair, plants, old newspapers
4. sandwiches, milk; walnuts
5. at a thrift shop; lamps, couches
6. on the table
7. on her neck

C. Vocabulary Review
1. pick
2. cracking; snack
3. bragged
4. courtship; chance

TEXT ANALYSIS

A. Grammar-Meaning Connection
1. no
2. no

3. Carolyn
4. no
5. a

Selection 5

COMPREHENSION CHECK

A. First Reading
1. letter
2. seventeen
3. twenty-three

UNIT 3

Selection 1

COMPREHENSION CHECK

A. First Reading

1. e
2. c
3. g
4. b
5. f
6. a
7. d

2

b

B. Second Reading
1. F
2. F
3. T
4. F
5. T
6. F
7. T
8. T

VOCABULARY

A. Vocabulary Building
1. c
2. b
3. e
4. a
5. d
6. h
7. f
8. j
9. g
10. i

B. Word Analysis

1

suggested answers
1. flight between two nations
2. travel between planets

3. feeding sick people by putting liquid nutrients directly into a vein
4. problems between races
5. a highway that crosses two or more states so you can travel between states on it
6. sports competition within a school; teams from the same school compete

1. a. express b. expression
2. a. perceive b. perception
3. a. transformation b. transform

1. discrimination a. discrimination b. discriminate
2. intend a. intend b. intention
3. limit a. limit b. limitation
4. motivate a. motivation b. motivates
5. production a. production b. produce

1. *-er:* computer programmer, hunter, dancer, composer, performer
2. *-or:* orator, editor, interior decorator, inventor, actor, sculptor
3. *-ian:* politician, mathematician, statistician, logician
4. *-ist:* journalist, scientist, artist

C. Vocabulary Review
1. theory
2. logical
3. reason
4. accurately
5. express
6. performers
7. Interpersonal; moods
8. limitations; self-esteem

TEXT ANALYSIS

Brief Examples
1. occupations
   They are appropriate because they require the intelligence being defined.
2. parentheses

Selection 2

COMPREHENSION CHECK

A. First Reading
1. contracts lawyer; carrying out other people's instructions
2. research scientist; thinking for himself
3. psychotherapist; evaluating people and their problems

B. Second Reading
1. e
2. c
3. f
4. a
5. d
6. g
7. b

VOCABULARY

A. Vocabulary Building
1. d
2. j
3. h
4. g
5. b
6. i
7. f
8. c
9. a
10. e

B. Multi-word Expressions
2. come up with; a
3. draw up; b
4. fall into; a
5. came into his own; a
6. in charge of; a
7. at a dead end; b

C. Vocabulary Review
1. styles
2. model; at a loss
3. guide
4. came into his own
5. come up with
6. evaluate
7. compatible

Selection 3

COMPREHENSION CHECK

A. First Reading
1. b, c
2. c

B. Second Reading

1. c
2. d
3. e
4. a
5. f
6. b

2 *suggested answers*

¶1
1. Researchers at the University of California, Irvine.
2. the power of music
3. preschoolers
4. two groups: one group took piano lessons and sang daily; the other did not.
5. eight months
6. Subjects in the music group scored 80 percent higher in spatial intelligence.

¶3
1. William Greenough; University of Illinois, Urbana-Champaign
2. the effect of exercise on the brain
3. rats

4. three groups: one group did nothing, one group exercised on a treadmill, one group ran an obstacle course.
5. Not mentioned
6. The two groups of active rats grew more brain cells than the inactive ones.

VOCABULARY

A. Vocabulary Building
1. observing
2. visualize
3. enhance
4. budget
5. nutrients
6. confirmed
7. significant
8. implication
9. retained
10. retrieve
11. optimum
12. determined

B. Vocabulary Building
1. b
2. a
3. b
4. a
5. a
6. b
7. a
8. a
9. b
10. a
11. b

C. Vocabulary Review
1. budgets
2. trains
3. nutrients; complex
4. lecture; retain
5. confirms; windows of opportunity

TEXT ANALYSIS

Sources of Information
1. researchers at the University of California, Irvine
2. Gordon Shaw (University of California, Irvine)
3. National Commission on Music Education
4. no source
5. William Greenough, University of Illinois, Urbana-Champaign
6. Robert Sylwester, University of Oregon
7. Harry Chugani, Wayne State University, Children's Hospital
8. Harry Chugani
9. Harry Chugani

Selection 4

COMPREHENSION CHECK

A. First Reading
1. b
2. c

B. Second Reading
2. K, C, K, K, C, C   K, K, C, K, C, K,

VOCABULARY

A. Vocabulary Building

1. f	8. n
2. a	9. l
3. g	10. m
4. b	11. j
5. c	12. k
6. e	13. i
7. d	14. h

B. Vocabulary Review
1. apparent; self-image
2. embarrassed
3. eager; stuff
4. make up
5. majoring in
6. confident; went wrong

TEXT ANALYSIS

A. Using Exact Words
answers will vary
1. They are positive about their abilities.
   Sure! Of Course! No problem. Sure, why not?
   Yes! We're learning that stuff now.
2. They see no limitations.
   Anything! Why not (now)? Any kind!
3. They are imaginative and creative.
   How big you want it? We make them up.

B. Contrast
¶ 1 c
¶ 2–6 d
¶ 7–8 b
¶ 9–10 a

Selection 5

COMPREHENSION CHECK

A. First Reading
1. play
2. class
3. desk
4. drawer

UNIT 4

Selection 1

COMPREHENSION CHECK

A. First Reading
1. T
2. F

VOCABULARY

A. Vocabulary Building
1. employment
2. refugees

3. natural disasters
4. military conflict
5. rising
6. seek
7. wages
8. elsewhere
9. linking
10. fewer
11. reduce
12. plenty of

B. Word Analysis

1. employment
2. unemployed

1. permanently
2. temporary
3. seasonal

C. Vocabulary Review
1. migrate
2. developing; employment; plenty of
3. wages; elsewhere
4. political asylum
5. refugees; natural disasters
6. immigrants; rise
7. border

TEXT ANALYSIS

A. Grammar-Meaning Connection:
Understanding Passive Sentences
1. natural disaster or military conflict
2. low wages and unemployment
3. better opportunities elsewhere

B. Analyzing Complex Sentences
1. . . . migrate at first
   . . . from the same community
   . . . complex chains of migration
   . . . poor countries to rich
2. . . . say they want fewer immigrants
   . . . that they can substantially reduce the numbers
   . . . borders are porous

Selection 2

COMPREHENSION CHECK

A. First Reading
1. T
2. F

B. Second Reading

a. US
b. R
c. R
d. R
e. US

VOCABULARY

A. Vocabulary Building
1. h
2. c
3. a
4. b
5. f
6. i
7. g
8. e
9. d

B. Using a Dictionary
1. Definition 2
2. Definition 3
3. Definition 2
4. Definition 1

C. Vocabulary Review
1. just
2. serious; skills
3. concentrating; pay attention
4. realized
5. bosses; wasting time

Selection 3

COMPREHENSION CHECK

A. First Reading
1. F
2. T
3. T

B. Second Reading

B, B, B, B, A, A, A, B,
A, A, A, B, A, B, A, A

VOCABULARY

A. Vocabulary Building
1. a
2. b
3. a
4. a
5. b
6. b
7. a
8. b
9. b
10. a
11. b
12. a
13. b
14. a
15. a

B. Compound Words
1. Chinatown
2. storefront
3. supermarket
4. family-owned businesses
5. manpower
6. newspaper
7. newspeople
8. posterboards

C. Vocabulary Review
1. revitalized; turned it into
2. borrowed; family-owned
3. supermarkets
4. profit
5. newspapers
6. slum; benefited

TEXT ANALYSIS

A. Chronological Order
a. 2
b. 1
c. 5
d. 3
e. 4

B. Grammar-Meaning Connection: Noun Modifiers
1. disaster area
2. apartment buildings
3. occupancy rate
4. translation service
5. business permits
6. drug addicts
7. side streets
8. record shop
9. community activities
10. boat people
11. newspaper people
12. media attention
13. slum area

Selection 4

COMPREHENSION CHECK

A. First Reading
suggested answers
1. New York
2. Massachusetts
3. shoe factory
4. grapes
5. mournful (melancholy, not very happy)

B. Second Reading
1. T
2. F
3. F

VOCABULARY

A. Vocabulary Building
1. a, b, d
2. a, c, d
3. b, c, d
4. a, b, d
5. b, c, d
6. a, b, c
7. a, b, c
8. a, c, d

B. Vocabulary Review
1. melancholy
2. reached; bewildering; village
3. loneliness
4. prospered; marvelous

TEXT ANALYSIS

suggested answers
3. unsociable; not talkative; unsophisticated; simple
4. inflexible; needs to be with Armenians (but not just any Armenians)
5. unsociable; not talkative; closed-minded
6. needs to be with Armenians
7. likes to work outdoors; needs to be with Armenians
8. easily bored

Selection 5

COMPREHENSION CHECK

A. First Reading
suggested answers
1. Mexico
2. Spanish
3. the United States
4. English
5. embarrassed (worried, insecure)

B. Second Reading

1. R
2. U
3. U
4. U
5. R
6. R

UNIT 5

Selection 1

COMPREHENSION CHECK

A. First Reading
suggested answers
1. immune
2. positive
3. immunosuppression
4. immunoenhancement

B. Second Reading
1. c
2. e
3. a
4. b
5. d

VOCABULARY

A. Vocabulary Building
1. b
2. b
3. b
4. a
5. a
6. b
7. a

8. a
9. a
10. b

B. Vocabulary Building
1. d
2. c
3. g
4. a
5. f
6. e
7. b

C. Vocabulary Review
1. support; relationship
2. widowed; immunosuppression
3. lead to
4. affection; overcome
5. mortality rate
6. concluded; factor

TEXT ANALYSIS
1. author, year
2. a. Seaward (1997)
   b. Seaward (1997)
   c. Bergel (1996)
3. Journal articles: Nerem et. al (1980); Berkman & Syme (1979); Book: Chopra (1989)

Selection 2

COMPREHENSION CHECK

A. First Reading
checks on 2, 3

VOCABULARY

A. Vocabulary Building
1. a, b, d
2. a, c, d
3. a, b, c
4. a, b, d
5. b, c, d
6. a, b, d
7. b, c, d
8. a, c, d

B. Distinguishing Grammatical Function: Nouns, Verbs, Adjectives

1. a. aware
   b. awareness
2. a. tension
   b. tense
3. a. breathing (breath)
   b. breath
   c. breathe
4. a. letting go
   b. let go
5. a. wandering
   b. wander

1. a. V   b. N
2. a. N   b. V
3. a. V   b. N

C. Vocabulary Review
 1. tension; metabolism
 2. aware
 3. let go; breathe
 4. wanders; focus
 5. practice; restore

TEXT ANALYSIS

¶1 *arrange*
¶4 *become* aware; *Take* a second; *Let* it go; *Notice* how; *Notice* your shoulders
¶5 *become* aware; *Let* go; *Go* through
¶6 *let* the breath happen
¶7 *Choose* a word; *choose* a phrase
¶8 *try* labeling; *let* go
¶9 *Don't try*; *practice* bringing it back
¶10 *Remember* that

Selection 3

COMPREHENSION CHECK

A. First Reading
 1. F
 2. F
 3. T
 4. T
 5. F

B. Second Reading
 1. b
 2. b
 3. a
 4. gaining weight; disease in lungs and liver receded; fever disappeared
 5. last sentence of ¶ 24

VOCABULARY

A. Vocabulary Building
1. d		8. m
2. f		9. k
3. b		10. o
4. g		11. l
5. c		12. n
6. a		13. i
7. e		14. h
		15. j

B. Paraphrasing and Skipping Non-essential Vocabulary
 1. b
 2. a
 3. b
 4. b
 5. a
 6. b
 7. a
 8. b

C. Vocabulary Review
 1. diagnosis
 2. reassuring
 3. nourishment
 4. tough
 5. avoid; insist
 6. vital; approach

TEXT ANALYSIS

¶ 1	f
¶ 2–3	c
¶ 4–5	g
¶ 6–17	a
¶ 18–22	b
¶ 23	e
¶ 24	d

Selection 4

COMPREHENSION CHECK

A. First Reading
suggested answers

 1. negative (pessimistic)
 2. die
 3. counting
 4. silly (foolish)
 5. cheerful (happy, positive, optimistic)

 1. F
 2. T
 3. T

VOCABULARY

A. Vocabulary Building
Part 1
 1. b
 2. a
 3. b
 4. b
 5. b
 6. a
 7. b
 8. a
 9. a
 10. b

Part 2
 11. b
 12. a
 13. b
 14. a

B. Vocabulary Review
 1. pneumonia
 2. chance
 3. worth
 4. bare; ridiculous
 5. slight
 6. sin
 7. masterpiece

TEXT ANALYSIS

¶ 14 Cold wind had blown leaves off the vine.
¶ 20 The vine is almost bare already; only four leaves left.
¶ 36 rain and strong wind
¶ 39 only one leaf left; another windy night

Selection 5

COMPREHENSION CHECK

A. First Reading
1. F
2. F
3. T
4. T

B. Second Reading
Stanza 1 g
Stanza 3 f
Stanza 6 e
Stanza 8 b
Stanza 9 h
Stanza 11 a
Stanza 15 c
Stanza 16 d

UNIT 6

Selection 1

COMPREHENSION CHECK

A. First Reading
suggested answers
1. engineer
2. New York
3. Massachusetts
4. far
5. preschool

B. Second Reading

1. T
2. T
3. F
4. F
5. T

Checks on 1, 2, 3, 5, 6

VOCABULARY

A. Vocabulary Building
1. enable
2. ultra-accessible
3. allow
4. were aware of
5. arrangement
6. approved
7. dealing with

8. clients
9. mix
10. manage
11. keys to
12. remotely
13. current
14. out of touch
15. issue

B. Distinguishing Grammatical Function: Nouns and Verbs
1. a. N   b. V
2. a. V   b. N
3. a. V   b. V
4. a. N   b. V
5. a. V   b. N
6. a. V   b. N
7. a. V   b. N
8. a. N   b. V
9. a. N   b. V

C. Vocabulary Review
1. arrangement
2. approved; dealing with
3. manage; mix
4. progress; remotely
5. allows; current

TEXT ANALYSIS

A. Extended Example
¶ 2 b
¶ 3 d
¶ 4 c
¶ 5 e
¶ 6 a

B. New Words in a Language
the Net—Internet
copier—photocopier
e-mail—electronic mail
phone—telephone

Selection 2

COMPREHENSION CHECK

A. First Reading
1. F
2. T
3. F

A. Vocabulary Building
1. b
2. a
3. a
4. a
5. b
6. a
7. b
8. a
9. b
10. a
11. b
12. b

B. Multi-word Expressions
1. f
2. a
3. g
4. e
5. c
6. d
7. b

C. Vocabulary Review
1. remote
2. kiosk
3. hooked
4. inserted; slot
5. disturbing; record
6. available
7. ruled out; asthma
8. vital

TEXT ANALYSIS

2. The hostel
3. The man
4. The clerk
5. the settlement's emergency medical technician
6. The man's primary care physician
7. Kane
8. The technician

Selection 3

COMPREHENSION CHECK

A. First Reading
suggested answers
Part 1
1. preschool
2. enjoy (like)
3. tool
4. quickly (fast)

Part 2
5. best
6. elementary
7. trained
8. read

B. Second Reading
Part 1

1. T
2. T
3. F
4. F

2

1. I (¶ 1–2); S (¶ 8)
2. I
3. I
4. S (¶ 7)
5. S (¶12)

Part 2
Checks on 1, 2, 3, 5, 6, 7

A. Vocabulary Building
Part 1
1. enthusiasm
2. approval
3. typical
4. happening, taking place
5. constantly
6. equal access
7. point out
8. mode
9. tool
10. urban

Part 2
11. may
12. tools
13. appropriate
14. motivating
15. scarce
16. terrified
17. qualify for
18. ought to
19. smarten up
20. folks

B. Word Analysis
Part 1
1. preschooler
2. righthand
3. day-care
4. human-guided
5. parent-volunteer
6. teacher-student
7. child-care

Part 2
8. mind-numbing
9. attention-span
10. non-profit
11. one-purchase
12. years-long

C. Vocabulary Review
1. tool
2. enthusiasm
3. access
4. scarce
5. motivating; state-of-the-art
6. points out; qualify

TEXT ANALYSIS

A. Newspaper Writing
1–2; 3–4; 5–6; 7–8
B. Grammar-Meaning Connection:
Using *may*, *might*, and *will*
sure: *will*; less sure: *may* and *might*

Selection 4

COMPREHENSION CHECK

A. First Reading
suggested answers
1. home
2. computer
3. book

4. hates (doesn't like)
5. fun

VOCABULARY

A. Vocabulary Building
1. funny
2. waste
3. through
4. mark
5. hurt
6. adjusted
7. insert
8. proper slot

B. Multi-word Expressions
1. c
2. i
3. h
4. b
5. g
6. a
7. e
8. f
9. d

C. Vocabulary Review
1. stood still
2. threw away; through

3. funny
4. adjusted
5. take it away
6. one another

TEXT ANALYSIS

suggested answers for "Computers as Asimov saw them in 2157"
1. relatively small compared to the earlier ones; quite fast since papers were marked immediately
2. punch code (no mention of a keyboard)
3. screen
4. in homes
5. every student had one at home
6. possibly networked to inspector's office; repairs not done long-distance

Selection 5

COMPREHENSION CHECK

A. First Reading
1. knows
2. beginner
3. humorous